The Story Within Us

The Story Within Us

Women Prisoners
Reflect on Reading

Edited by Megan Sweeney

UNIVERSITY OF ILLINOIS PRESS
URBANA, CHICAGO, AND SPRINGFIELD

The Office of the Vice President for Research at the University of Michigan
offered generous financial support for publishing this book.

Library of Congress Cataloging-in-Publication Data
The story within us : women prisoners reflect on reading /
edited by Megan Sweeney.
p. cm.
Includes bibliographical references and index.
ISBN 978-0-252-03714-6 (hardcover : alk. paper)—
ISBN 978-0-252-07867-5 (pbk. : alk. paper)—
ISBN 978-0-252-09425-5 (e-book)
1. Women prisoners—United States—Books and reading.
2. Books and reading.
3. African American women—Books and reading.
I. Sweeney, Megan
HV9471.S844   2012
365.43092273—dc23   2012009671

For the ninety-four women prisoners
who generously shared
their stories and insights

[A]s a single leaf turns not yellow
but with the silent knowledge of the whole tree,
So the wrong-doer cannot do wrong
without the hidden will of you all.

 —*Kahlil Gibran,* The Prophet

[Books were] a glorious host, to keep me company.
They kept alive my fancy, and my hope of something
      beyond that place and time. . . .
This was my only and my constant comfort.
When I think of it, the picture always rises in my mind,
of . . . sitting on my bed, reading as if for life.

 —*Charles Dickens,* David Copperfield

Contents

Acknowledgments   ix

Introduction: "All us women have a story within us"   1

1 Mildred
Life Narrative: "Society is coming to prison"   11
Reading Narrative: "I have discovered a love
    for the law"   16

2 Sissy
Life Narrative: "There's a time to be silent,
    and there's a time not to"   23
Reading Narrative: "If you can't relate to it,
    then read about it"   33

3 Olivia
Life Narrative: "It was a bad road that I was on"   45
Reading Narrative: "If I'm going through a struggle,
    I know that's the book to go find"   50

4 Denise
Life Narrative: "I can't even imagine my day
    without a mall"   59
Reading Narrative: "Who *is* this writing books that
    knows the things I know?!"   73

5 Bobbie
Life Narrative: "I've been overcoming all my life"   92
Reading Narrative: "Everybody don't end up with
    a prince"   97

6 Melissa
Life Narrative: "They're trying to brainwash me
and rebuild me" 105
Reading Narrative: "From her life story to mine is not that
much difference" 118

7 Valhalla
Life Narrative: "I've been like a ball that someone threw
and I've been bouncing around ever since" 129
Reading Narrative: "The books I've read are like
my friends" 139

8 Jacqueline
Life Narrative: "I refuse to be another statistic" 147
Reading Narrative: "I wanted his strength to jump
out of the pages into my life!" 154

9 Audrey
Life Narrative: "That's a chapter that's closed" 161
Reading Narrative: "What fueled this fire for the fire
to come all the way over to here?" 176

10 Deven
Life Narrative: "Society, it's a boys' club still" 180
Reading Narrative: "I need to know what's gonna
happen next!" 184

11 Solo
Life Narrative: "That's a soul that you're stepping on" 197
Reading Narrative: "Freedom for me was an evolution,
not a revolution" 211

Afterword: True Stories about Prison 227

Appendix: Study-Related Materials 241

Notes 249

Bibliography 259

Index 263

Acknowledgments

IN 2008, I was in the midst of writing a book about the reading practices of women in prison. Ninety-four women—from the North Carolina Correctional Institution for Women, in Raleigh; the Northeast Pre-Release Center, in Cleveland; and the State Correctional Institution at Muncy, Pennsylvania—had shared with me their stories and reflections, and I was feeling overwhelmed by my efforts to include all of the women's powerful narratives in my book. Avery Gordon therefore suggested that I write two books instead of one, including a volume composed solely of interviews with women prisoners. *The Story Within Us* is the culmination of my two-book journey, and I am deeply grateful to Avery for her wise suggestion. Both Sian Hunter and the organizers of the 2011 Black Women's Intellectual History Conference offered helpful suggestions for pursuing publication. My editor, Larin McLaughlin, and the anonymous reviewers at the University of Illinois Press helped to make this book a reality, and I am thankful for their vision and their understanding of the project's importance.

I offer my deepest thanks to the ninety-four women who generously shared with me their time, words, and wisdom. Although *The Story Within Us* includes only eleven of these women's narratives, I hope that it conveys how much I learned from each of them. Their ability to find meaning, humor, and beauty in the midst of pain continually moved and amazed me. Thanks are also due to the penal employees who supervised my research, including Ann Mullin, Valerie Aden, Richard Shuler, and Sandy Weisner.

The Radcliffe Institute for Advanced Study at Harvard University generously supported this work by offering me a year-long research fellowship. I have also received crucial financial support as a faculty member at the University of Michigan, from the Office of the Vice President for Research, the Institute for Research on Women and Gender, and the Horace H. Rackham School of Graduate Studies. My graduate research assistant, Kathryne Bevilacqua, offered insightful feedback on drafts of the material, as did the members of my writing group: Anne Curzan, Anne Gere, and Mary Schleppegrell. Linda Meakes also deserves thanks for her careful transcriptions of the interviews.

Finally, I am profoundly grateful to Mary Anderson and to my husband, Michael Carlin, both of whom have shown me what it means to honor and cultivate one's own and others' stories.

The Story Within Us

INTRODUCTION

"All us women have a story within us"

DURING THE LATE 1960s, *The Communist Manifesto* was one of the most popular books at San Quentin prison. Incarcerated men copied pages of the book by hand and shared them with each other by way of a clothesline strung from cell to cell. This image of male prisoners reading radical literature stands in sharp contrast to the picture of reading that emerges in contemporary women's prisons. Currently incarcerated women tend to circulate popular reading materials such as evangelical Christian self-help books, narratives of victimization, and African American urban fiction with titles such as *Forever a Hustler's Wife* and *Thugs and the Women Who Love Them*. Yet as I have discovered through more than twenty years of involvement with women prisoners—first as a social worker, then as a volunteer GED tutor and book club facilitator, and finally as a scholar researching women's reading practices in three different prisons—this contrast indicates far more about the climate for prisoners' reading in the two time periods than about the readers themselves.

Prisoners' opportunities for reading and education have sharply declined over the past thirty years. As the prisoners' rights movement of the 1960s and '70s gave way to the retributive justice framework of the 1980s, prisons radically reduced their library budgets, converted library space into prison cells, and installed televisions as a pacification tool. In the prisons where I have conducted research, the libraries are now funded entirely by revenue from the vending machines, and that funding is shared among several programs in the prison. Furthermore, owing to security concerns, prisoners can only receive brand-new books sent directly from publishers, which means that buying books is far too expensive for most women. Even women's access to prison libraries is limited; because some penal officials fear that libraries serve as a "gay bar," women must sign up one week in advance to visit the library, and their visits are limited to thirty minutes.

Many books are also banned, from Harry Potter (because it depicts witchcraft) to medical texts (because they include images of women's breasts). Racialized restrictions on reading, which have been in place since the birth of the penitentiary, likewise delimit prisoners' access to books. As one example among many, while allowing Ku Klux Klan publications such as *Negro Watch* and *Jew Watch*, the Texas penal system has banned Toni Morrison's novel, *Paradise*, on the grounds that it contains "information of a racial nature" that seems "designed to achieve a breakdown of prisons through inmate . . . strikes or riots" (Morrison letter 154). Penal officials fear that Morrison's references to the KKK and the civil rights and Black Power movements will lead to a "breakdown of prisons," yet they argue that Klan publications do not threaten their ability to "maintain . . . order and security" (Vogel 17).

Prisoners' opportunities for reading have been further curtailed by recent legal precedents. In its 2006 decision *Beard v. Banks*, the U.S. Supreme Court deemed it constitutional for a Pennsylvania prison to deny secular newspapers and magazines to prisoners in its long-term segregation unit, on the grounds that this denial of reading materials serves as an "incentive[e] for inmate growth" (qtd. in Breyer 2). Because these prisoners have no access to television, radio, telephone, or visitors, they receive no current news. The two dissenting justices insist that access to the full range of ideas is crucial for preserving one's sense of humanity and citizenship, but the majority opinion deems such claims moot when "dealing with especially difficult prisoners" (Breyer 11). The fact that African Americans and Latino/as are overrepresented in supermaximum prisons makes this denial of citizenship even more troubling. Exacerbating these trends, Congress eliminated Pell Grants for prisoners in 1994, which sparked dramatic cuts in all levels of educational programming and contributed to an increase in the presence of evangelical Christian educational programs and reading materials in prisons.[1]

At a time when the Supreme Court has authorized the *denial* of reading materials as an "incentiv[e] for inmate growth," it seems more important than ever to recognize incarcerated people's humanity and to illuminate the roles that reading plays in their vital and varied efforts to think, understand, grow, and remain connected to the world beyond the prison gates. In this spirit, *The Story Within Us: Women Prisoners Reflect on Reading* features extended interviews with eleven women prisoners. I was privileged to hear these women's reflections while conducting research for my recently published book, *Reading is My Window: Books and the Art of Reading in Women's Prisons*. Over the course of several years, I conducted extensive individual interviews and group discussions with ninety-four women imprisoned in North Carolina, Ohio, and Pennsylvania. Each woman participated in one life narrative interview, one to two interviews about reading, and four to seven group discussions of books; in total, I conducted 245 individual interviews and fifty-one group conversations.[2] As women generously shared their stories and insights, often delving into painful memories and emotionally taxing issues, they taught me that many women prisoners—like the male prisoners who were reading Marx in the 1960s—turn to reading as a means of empowerment and as a tool for understanding the racial, economic, and gender inequalities that often pave the road to prison. Extending the tradition of prisoners' self-education, these readers use popular, female-gendered genres to situate their experiences within broader contexts, experiment with new ways of being, and maintain a sense of dignity, hope, and human community.

The Story Within Us includes eleven chapters, each of which features one woman's life narrative and reading narrative. In their life narratives, women discuss family dynamics, schooling, and relationships, and they describe some of their joyful experiences as well as experiences with violence, substance abuse, and/or crime. The interviewees also reflect on the subject of crime and punishment and share their thoughts about the future. In their reading narratives, women focus on their reading habits and preferences, their favorite books and authors, and the roles that reading has played in their lives. These narratives are followed by an afterword and an appendix of study-related materials. In the afterword, I reflect on the featured readers' insights and offer recommendations about reading and education in penal contexts that I hope will inform penal policy. The appendix includes a chart that lists each woman's pseudonym, self-selected racial or ethnic identification, age, and education level. It also includes a description of the settings in which I conducted research, the advertisement that I posted to recruit participants for the study, the Guiding Questions that I used for the individual interviews, and a list of organizations that gather books for prisoners.

Choosing which interviews to include in *The Story Within Us* was extremely difficult, and I am keenly aware of the many stories and reflections that will remain unheard. I selected the featured narratives, in part, because they represent a spectrum of women's experiences. Seven of the featured readers self-identify as African American or black, three self-identify as white, and one self-identifies as American Indian.[3] Ranging in age from twenty-seven to fifty-six, the interviewees have been convicted of a variety of crimes—including drug possession, drug selling, larceny, armed robbery, embezzlement, assault, arson, infanticide, and first and second degree murder—and their sentences range from three years to life imprisonment.[4] Eight of the women completed high school or earned their GED, and two of those eight have taken some college courses. The remaining three women dropped out of school in junior high, tenth grade, and eleventh grade.[5] The women featured in *The Story Within Us* also discuss a broad array of books, including popular genres such as urban fiction, legal thrillers, true crime, romance, science fiction, and Christian self-help books, as well as biographies and autobiographies, books about world religions, African American history, legal texts, and novels by Toni Morrison. Moreover, the selected interviews offer particularly compelling and detailed descriptions of women's ideas and experiences. Yielding layers of meaning and generating insights about women's complex interior lives, both the life narratives and reading narratives—and the women who offer them—continue to move, surprise, and inspire me. They illustrate the creativity, strength and tenacity, intelligence, and deep humanity that I witnessed in my many conversations with women prisoners.

Read together, the narratives featured in *The Story Within Us* draw much-needed attention to the experiences of women prisoners. As a reader involved in my research observed, "Women in prison are pushed aside because there are less of us than men, but our stories are just as important even if men outnumber us." Moreover, women's presence in U.S. prisons continues to increase. Although women make up only 7.2 percent of people incarcerated in state and federal institutions, the number of women in prison rose 757 percent between 1977 and 2004, largely owing to draconian and racialized policies for prosecuting drug crimes (Sabol, Couture, and Harrison 3).[6] During 2006 alone, the number of women in state and federal prisons increased by 4.5 percent, which is almost twice the rate of increase for male prisoners (Frost, Greene, and Pranis 7).

The Story Within Us draws particular attention to the experiences of African American women. In recent years, some scholars and activists have produced groundbreaking work about women of color's experiences in the criminal justice system.[7] Nonetheless, explicit discussions of black women remain relatively scarce in scholarship about crime. Michelle Alexander's important bestseller, *The New Jim Crow: Mass Incarceration in the Age of Colorblindness* (2010), serves as a case in point. Alexander offers a lucid and compelling account of the historical and ongoing ways in which the U.S. penal system creates a racialized caste system. However, while illuminating "the criminalization and demonization of black men" (17), including racialized disparities in rates of incarceration for drug-related charges, Alexander refers to women only as supporters of criminalized men, as those who "love their sons, husbands, and partners and understand their plight as current and future members of the racial undercaste" (204). This erasure of African American women's own experiences in the criminal justice system is especially troubling given the dramatic increase in incarceration rates for women in general, and for African American women in particular. Although African Americans represent only 12.8 percent of the U.S. population, black women represent 28 percent of all incarcerated women, and they are 3.1 times more likely to be incarcerated than white women (Sabol, Couture, and Harrison 6, 8).[8] According to a 2007 study from the Pew Center on the States, one in one hundred black women between the ages of thirty-five and thirty-nine is behind bars, as opposed to one in 355 white women within that age group (Liptak). As the narratives featured in *The Story Within Us* illuminate, mass incarceration is fundamentally a matter of "racial justice" (Alexander 9) for women, too.

In foregrounding women prisoners' own accounts of their experiences, this collection contributes to a growing body of scholarship that features life-writing and autobiographical narratives by incarcerated women. Recent examples of such scholarship include Paula C. Johnson's *Inner Lives: Voices of African American Women in Prison* (2003); Wally Lamb's *Couldn't Keep it to Myself: Wally Lamb and the Women of York Correctional Institution* (2003); Karlene Faith and Anne Near's *13 Women: Parables from Prison* (2006); Rickie Solinger, Paula C. Johnson, Martha Raimon, Tina Reynolds, and Ruby Tapia's *Interrupted Life: Experiences of Incarcerated Women in the United States* (2009); Jodie Lawston and Ashley Lucas's *Razor Wire Women: Prisoners, Activists, Scholars, and Artists* (2011); and Robin Levi and Ayelet Waldman's *Inside this Place, Not of It: Narratives from Women's Prisons* (2011). Scholar-activists such as Tobi Jacobi and Michele Tarter also facilitate writing workshops in jails and prisons that result in the local publication of women's life narratives.[9]

In contrast to most published life narratives, which are often deliberately crafted and heavily edited by their authors and/or editors, the narratives featured in *The Story Within Us* are composed entirely from spoken, audiotaped interviews. The oral framework enabled a wider spectrum of women to participate in my study, including women with poor writing skills, and it lends a sense of immediacy and spontaneity to women's testimonies. I am nonetheless aware that interviewees may tailor their responses to the presumed desires of the interviewer, and that both interviewers and interviewees engage in "role-playing and impression management."[10] Women inevitably filtered and shaped their stories for me, telling me only what they chose to tell and how they chose to tell it, and our interactions were inevitably inflected by my position as a white, middle-class literature professor. Furthermore, I recognize women's descriptions of their reading practices as constructed accounts rather than literal reports of what takes place when they read.[11] I gave participants an additional opportunity to shape their narratives by asking them to review and redact a complete transcript of their interviews. Some women merely deleted repetitive phrases such as "you know," but others deleted substantive statements that they did not wish to have published. In editing the interviews for this collection, I removed my own questions, omitted some portions to reduce length and repetition, and excised details that would compromise confidentiality. I also rearranged some paragraphs to enhance the narrative flow and make women's contributions as clear as possible; doing so was particularly important in editing women's reading narratives, which stem from two separate interviews. I include ellipses to indicate places where I removed words, and I have taken care not to erase contradictions or alter the meaning of women's statements.

Giving shape to their life experiences is no small matter for incarcerated women. Indeed, women in prison often suffer from the dual condition of hypervisibility and invisibility. On the one hand, prisoners are "routinely denied access to the right to privacy or sovereignty" (Sharma 340), and this lack of privacy often begins prior to incarceration because poor women and women of color are subject to heightened scrutiny by state agencies. Furthermore, prisoners' life stories often assume hypervisible, erroneous, and damaging forms as they become part of the legal and cultural record. On the other hand, many incarcerated women note that formative aspects of their lives—such as their experiences with mental illness or with emotional, physical, or sexual abuse—remain shrouded in invisibility and silence both prior to and during their incarceration. Sexual abuse, domestic violence, and/or rape have played especially prominent roles in the lives of ten of the eleven women featured in *The Story Within Us*.[12] According to the most recent statistics published in the 1999 Bureau of Justice Statistics Report, "Nearly 6 in 10 women in state prisons had experienced physical or sexual abuse in the past; just over a third of imprisoned women had been abused by an intimate in the past; and just under a quarter reported prior abuse by a family member" (Greenfeld and Snell). Yet as women explained in countless interviews, their experiences of victimization have been disavowed in familial, cultural, legal, and penal arenas. Because they have lacked knowledge of broader patterns and dynamics of abuse, many women have felt intensely isolated in their victimization and have blamed themselves for their experiences.

Articulating such experiences—and seeing them validated in written form—enables some women to begin recognizing wider structural patterns and facilitates their efforts to live in the present rather than being held in the grip of a painful past. Moreover, by offering complex portraits of their experiences as both victims and perpetrators of violence, the interviewees generate crucial insights about the potential relationship between sustaining and perpetrating violence, and they elucidate how women's race and class positions contribute to the recognition or disavowal of their victimization. Through their shared emphases on abuse, poverty, addiction, and mental illness, women's life narratives also illuminate the pathways that lead many women to prison and suggest possibilities for addressing the profound social problems that fuel crime. At the same time, the featured narratives draw attention to prisoners' unique and diverse efforts—both before and during incarceration—to exercise agency in restrictive circumstances, to find meaning and beauty in the midst of pain, to cultivate and maintain relationships, and to sustain a sense of hope or at least a "stance of undefeated despair" (Berger). As Brenton Faber says of autobiographical stories, prisoners' life narratives thus "act as protective counterweights to a daily barrage of messages, constructions and images" (qtd. in Jacobi, "Slipping" 80). Or as Suniti Sharma suggests in discussing the life narratives of young women in detention, the featured interviewees "offer counter-stories to the official, institutional stories of their lives" (327), thereby destabilizing reductive definitions of "woman prisoner." In these ways, the interviewees contribute to the important efforts of organizations such as the International Conference on Penal Abolition, Critical Resistance, and the Institute on Women and Criminal Justice.[13]

The narratives featured in *The Story Within Us* also help to tell a rarely told story about the crucial intellectual work that prisoners perform in settings that are far from conducive to reading and contemplation. As I discovered during my research, the unrelenting noise in prisons can seem almost unbearable. Most spaces are open and crowded, sound echoes off the metal and concrete surfaces, and officers regularly shout instructions from their central stations. Being in their two- to four-person cells hardly increases women's sense of tranquility; at least one cell mate is usually watching television, and many penal authorities show no respect for prisoners' privacy. The library can serve as a respite from such a loud environment, but women have very little time for reading during their brief library visits. Yet despite such impediments, many prisoners maintain vibrant intellectual lives. In fact, according to the National Assessment of Adult Literacy conducted in 2003, among those whose highest educational achievement is passing the GED, incarcerated women and men "read more and watch less TV" than their nonincarcerated counterparts (91). Within this pool, 50 percent of incarcerated people versus 22 percent of nonincarcerated people report reading books on a daily basis, and 47 percent of incarcerated people versus 39 percent of nonincarcerated people report reading newspapers and magazines on a daily basis (81–82). Furthermore, whereas only one-tenth of nonincarcerated GED-earners visit their library on a weekly basis, almost half of incarcerated GED-earners do so (80).[14]

Nonetheless, dominant depictions of prisoners rarely emphasize their status as readers, let alone as thinkers; reading tends to be associated only with political prisoners or self-identified intellectuals. Piper Kerman's recent bestseller, *Orange Is the New Black: My Year in a Women's Prison*, reflects this trend. As a privileged white woman who recently graduated from Smith College, Kerman has garnered considerable media attention for publishing an account of her incarceration.[15] On one hand, Kerman draws crucial attention to the important roles that reading plays in the lives of many prisoners. "I tore through every book I received" (84), she writes, and she says of the early days of her incarceration, "With no job, no money, no possessions, no phone privileges, I was verging on a nonperson. Thank God for books" (57). I have heard countless prisoners articulate a similar reliance on books; in the words of an older black woman named Caesar, "Books are a lifeline to people in here." On the other hand, Kerman attempts to distance herself from other prisoners by foregrounding the scope and quality of her engagement with books. Whereas other women love reading "James Patterson, V. C. Andrews, and romance novels" (51), as well as "trashy novels" and "gangsta books" such as Sister Souljah's *The Coldest Winter Ever* (80, 148), Kerman emphasizes the "overwhelming number of good books" that she receives from family members and friends (62), including novels by authors such as Jane Austen, Virginia Woolf, and Pablo Neruda; a subscription to *The New Yorker*; and a rare tome called *Japanese Street Songs*. According to Kerman, this "literary avalanche" serves as "proof" that she is "different, a freak: 'She's the one with the books'" (62). Underscoring her difference, Kerman notes that Austen's *Pride and Prejudice* enables her to escape the prison setting and dwell in "the much more familiar world of Hanoverian England" (51). In dismissing other prisoners' "trashy" reading materials—with no attempt to understand the worlds they evoke or the reasons why women value reading them—Kerman seems to dismiss the women themselves. Moreover, she suggests that few prisoners are "real" readers; those whose reading tastes do not correspond with her own do not merit distinction as "the one[s] with the books."

As *The Story Within Us* illustrates, incarcerated women disprove the common assumption that thoughtful reflection can only ensue from reading classically literary texts.[16] Through their engagements with devalued popular genres, women in prison perform crucial forms of self-reflection and self-creation. Indeed, just as writing workshops in prisons enable women to reflect on their experiences, seek validation in the company of others, and take steps toward shaping their futures (Jacobi, "Writing"), reading enables many prisoners to engage in active processes of reinterpreting and rescripting their lives. As Sidonie Smith and Julia Watson argue in discussing autobiography, we all adopt culturally available narratives and models in crafting our identities. We can exercise some control over the meaning of our lives, however, by "tak[ing] up bits and pieces of the identities and narrative forms available" and fashioning them into our own stories (14). The key, Smith and Watson suggest, is "owning the stories that shape us as subjects" (16).

Many women in prison literalize this process of self-fashioning through their engagements with books. Because prisons offer few resources for helping women to come to terms with their pasts and reshape their futures, prisoners often approach the act of reading with a greater sense of urgency than nonincarcerated readers. Women who are reckoning with the weight of particularly difficult experiences can feel a pressing need to find something useful—a bit of advice, a sense of companionship, a glimmer of insight—in reading a book. Encountering a character who inspires them, serves as a model to emulate, or demonstrates a capacity for change can seem vitally important to women who feel an urgent desire to change but a deep uncertainty about their ability to do so. Furthermore, identifying with a book character enables some women to validate their emotions and experiences by situating them within a broader context; doing so—and perhaps feeling like part of "a community of secret knowers"—allows women, in turn, to tell "formerly unspeakable stories" and/or "voic[e] the speakable differently" (Smith and Watson 15). Women also learn to own the stories that shape them as subjects by engaging with the stories they encounter in books; reading enables them to view their pasts within a new frame and to imagine different trajectories for their futures (14). In the words of Deven, a thirty-six-year-old white woman, "We've just read five different books of women telling us about themselves in like seven hundred different ways. And each of them . . . has been a wonderful learning journey for me of getting more in touch with my inner self and my inner power source, and having some different ways to look at some situations instead of starting with that tunnel vision that I've known for so long." Although Deven speaks of getting in touch with her "inner self," she goes on to suggest that engaging with others' narratives does not lead to the discovery of one's fully-formed story; rather, doing so introduces an array of possibilities from which women can choose as they undertake the ongoing work of crafting their life stories. "All these [authors] had stories inside of them," Deven explains. "All us women have a story within us, and it's just which way do we choose to write it?"

One woman featured in this collection offers a particularly moving illustration of how prisoners use others' stories to mediate their own experiences.[17] This reader told me at the start of her individual interview that she had never had "more than twenty minutes" to recount her life story, and she then spoke very emotionally for almost two hours. Yet in reviewing her interview transcript, she carefully redacted almost all references to pain, including her extensive experiences of sexual and physical abuse. This woman seemed to find it overwhelming to encounter her painful history on paper. She nonetheless loves books about women whose lives mirror her own. "Texts introduce a distance between the immediacy of experience and the self," Eva Illouz argues, and that distance can enable readers to come to terms with their experiences (18). Reading others' stories seemed to provide the necessary distance for this woman to encounter herself.

While enabling women to dwell in the company of others' stories, reading also serves as a concrete means for prisoners to counter the institutional forces that thwart human interaction and communication. Women frequently strive to develop and maintain connections with family members, friends, and each other by sharing and discussing their favorite books. As with writing workshops in prisons, reading and discussing books open up what Anita Wilson calls a "third space," a "space between inside and outside worlds where [prisoners] can 'occupy their minds'" (74); in such a space, women encounter unfamiliar ideas, learn from others' perspectives, develop empathy across lines of difference, and in the words of one reader, "feel a part of society as a whole." Given the importance of human touch, which is largely forbidden in penal contexts, even the simple act of holding a paperback offers some women a surrogate sense of comfort in an environment where gentle human contact is sorely lacking.[18]

Prisoners are, indeed, "part of society as a whole," and I believe that it is our collective responsibility to listen to, and learn from, imprisoned members of our community. My hope is that *The Story Within Us* will illuminate women prisoners' roles as family members, friends, creative thinkers, and complex human beings whose efforts to cultivate rich lives and meaningful relationships continue even when they remain permanently out of public sight. I hope, moreover, that the collection will foster dialogue among readers and thinkers on both sides of the prison fence, catalyzing possibilities for challenging the hegemony of the prison and creating a more just world.

1 Mildred

—ᗰ—

Life Narrative

"Society is coming to prison"

I WAS BORN in Ohio. I was raised by both parents, even though . . . my father and mother divorced when I was like six or seven. It was six of us kids. My father had four of us and he raised me until I was about twelve. . . . And then my mother raised me 'til I graduated from high school. Then right after high school, I had a baby.

Family life was complicated. It was some abuse, not with my father but with my father's brother and my own brother. And it was some abuse in school with a teacher. It was kind of complicated, the abuse, and then it was so many people living in the one house with my father that we didn't get all the things we should have got like the love, and it was so much running in and out of the house with the kids and no adult supervision. It was a lot of things going on in the home that as a child we didn't see, or we weren't supposed to see, and we seen or heard it. Back then I felt it was just normal, but as I'm grown now, I realize that it was a complicated life for a child; it was an unstable home.

The abuse that I experienced was sexual abuse. I didn't expose it to nobody 'cause my brother was the first one who did it. I was seven years old or eight years old, and he was like eighteen; he was the oldest child. And when he did it, I was going to tell, but he told me if I tell, we're both going to jail. So he kind of put fear in me about if I would tell, what would happen. So then it happened with my father's brother. And since being with my brother put the fear in me of going to jail, I didn't even tell about my uncle. . . . I was acting out so much in high school, my father saw my behavior. He told my mother she got to come get me 'cause I was wrecking things at the house; you know, I was acting out 'cause I didn't tell about the abuse. And my father didn't know what was going on. So my mother got me when I was like eleven or twelve, and she didn't know about it, either. I never exposed it to anybody.

And once my mother got me, my brother moved in with her. And it happened a few times in junior high, but I wouldn't let it go on no more. Then my stepfather, my mother's husband, he started doing it when I was in middle school. The teacher at middle school did it, too. So I had no safe place. Not at home, not at school, I didn't have a safe place. Then I graduated from high school, [which] was really shocking when I tell counselors that. Even though I experienced all the abuse, I graduated from high school with my class. I was determined to do that even though I had experienced what I had experienced as a child and as a young teenager.

School was an adventure. I mean, it was an adventure. But then it was something I knew I had to do or my mother was going to yell at me, or if I don't go to school, I knew I would get in trouble for it from my parents. I didn't really apply myself to school 'cause I graduated by the skin of my teeth [laughing]. I didn't get A, B, C. I got C and D is how I graduated. . . . So I wouldn't be at home with all that was going on at home, I went to school just to get away from home and to learn, too. My high school years was better because in high school, it was more to do. You weren't always in the books. I was in a vocational class. I was in graphic arts, and I was working with a press and working with a camera, and it was just a big adventure for me.

. . . I graduated in 1982 from high school, and I had a child in 1983, and my child was a joy to me, but then after I had a child, I got more involved in criminal activity, doing things to support myself. . . . When I was a child, being that it was so many people living in the home, I would steal things. And I was acting out from the abuse. I would steal things like popsicles from the store, candy from the store. And then it got to the point where it wasn't enough food in the home so I would steal, like, a steak from the store, go home and cook it. But then, it led me as an adult to steal more. . . . I was always in the stores stealing clothes, selling clothes to make money. I would sell clothes to people I knew to make money for my pleasures or the things I wanted in life, like the clothes I wanted to buy for myself or material things I wanted to buy that I couldn't steal, like a car. It takes a lot of heart to go into a store and steal a bunch of stuff off the rack and walk out the store. And, like I said, I'm adventurous. . . . But after I had my child, I got caught stealing. And then I kept getting caught, and then I got caught with a theft that escalated into a robbery, and I went to prison when I was twenty-one. I did three and a half years for my first felony.

I've been to prison four times. . . . I violated my parole in '89 . . . by catching a new theft case that escalated into a robbery. [Two other times] I went to prison for drug trafficking. . . . But it's been ten years since I've been in prison. This time I'm here for something to do with my uncle. It's two counts of criminal damaging, felonious assault, assault on a police officer, and a burglary. It's been an ongoing feud with me and my uncle. He just got out of prison last year, but this is why the feud went on because I took care of him every time he went to prison. He put me in here, and I feel like I'm in here for somebody that I always looked after while he was in prison.

[Before I returned to prison this time,] I was living back at my mother's house, and it was like I didn't want to be there. It was always pressure at home because we don't have a close relationship. I mean, she's always been there, but it's no love. It's always judging me and always judging her other children. There was never no love in the home. It could never be, 'cause all this abuse was going on and all this neglect was going on. Yes, she kept a roof over our head and clothes on our back and food in our mouth, but it was never no love. So why women come to prison has to do with a lot of things. No love, no family life. If you got a loving family and the support of family with everything you want to do in life, going to school and going to college, if both parents were there, you wouldn't be in prison. But when it's an actual parent in the home, and there's no love in the home, that's when you have a void in your life. And when you got that void, you're gonna find something else to fill it.

. . . I've been to mental hospitals, and I'm on a medication now, but when I was here before, I had a few episodes where I tried to hurt myself. But I'm not going to do that now. It had to do with a relationship. I was in a homosexual relationship. I've been in a few of them. And when she moved to break up, I felt like she was leaving me like my mother left me. . . . I was always being left, and I didn't want to be left. . . . When I got paroled in '96, the parole board stipulated that I get my psychological counseling. And I did that ever since I was home from '96 up to 2006. But I did have some episodes at home where I hurt myself. . . . I went out getting high at night, and the next morning I walked out in front of a car, trying to kill myself. And I stayed in the hospital like three months. Then after that, I was going to my appointments every week.

. . . My brother abusing me, my uncle abusing me, the school teacher abusing me—I never exposed it until I was thirty-nine. [What led to the exposure] was a trigger from my sister. . . . She was borrowing [my money] all the time, and I could never borrow from her. And I just exploded. . . . I reached my limit where I got fed up with my family using and taking advantage of me. . . . I exposed everything to my counselor. And that was my first time ever talking about my abuse as a child. I held on to that for thirty years, and that probably had a lot to do with me trying to hurt myself.

. . . My plan now is to go home and start over again, 'cause I got to start over again and get my life back where it was when I stayed out of prison for ten years. I'm forty-two years old. I'm a grandmother. So what's next for me is to watch my grandchildren grow up. And to find employment because I never stayed in a job long. . . . This time I want to do something different. I want to get an education. I want to learn about computers. I want to do something with myself this time. I want to do something other than sit around and wait on a check once a month.

. . . I feel a big change now in the ten years I've been gone. The generation that's in prison now is this younger generation who don't value anything. They don't value life 'cause they're so quick to pick up a gun. They show no respect. It's no respect for themselves, their parents. I'm pretty sure I wasn't this disrespectful that I'm seeing now in the prison. It's a constant wanting to outdo each other. The three times before I was here, it wasn't like that. We was more together. I mean, we was more sisters. Now we're so divided, and that's what I see now. . . . This younger generation is so materialistic, and everybody's trying to outdo each other.

. . . I think so many women end up in prison 'cause there's no father figures in the homes to raise the children, and it's a lot of abuse that women don't talk about. They don't get the counseling they need. . . . And there's no jobs. It's got to do with a lot of things involving the economy. I mean, women who worked at Hoover for years, and Hoover shut down, and they lost their retirement. They lost everything. So they got to convert to some type of hustle or something to stop them from losing their homes. So they go to sell methamphetamine. I mean, women that you would never think would come to prison are starting to come to prison so they won't lose their homes or their cars or whatever they worked all their life for. They resort to selling drugs, to stealing, to everything. . . . People coming to prison for murder has to do with drugs. I mean, these young kids are killing each other over money and drugs. . . . No money, no jobs, nobody wants to work in a fast-food restaurant because there's no money in it. Nobody wants to work for minimum wage. You know how long it would take for somebody to work at McDonalds to buy furniture for their homes or to buy school clothes for the kids for the school year? . . . I've been here four times, and in the ten years I've been in the street and seeing what's going on in the street, I'm seeing how hard it is. How easy it is to come to prison, and how hard it is out there to come by thirty or forty dollars.

[To keep so many women from coming to prison], start giving them more health coverage and also more programs. It's a lot of people that's out there that's not educated, and they don't know how to go about passing the GED so they can further on to college. I mean, offer something more free or not so costly for people to get an education. Education costs a lot of money, and people don't know where to get it. Show them where to go get a grant. Let the government and let the state offer more government programs for them to get these grants or more programs that you don't have to pay for. Like an accounting program that you don't have to pay so much money for, or a program that teaches you more about computers.

. . . We all need to get into the Word because everybody's greedy for money. I mean, everybody's jealous of one another. When I say jealousy, that escalates to murder, and greed escalates to thievery or stealing money from other people's funds. I mean, society has to want to change ourselves to prevent us from coming to these prisons, and to change ourselves we have to get into the Word of the Lord. Get into the Bible. We got to change our habits. We got to change a lot of things. . . . People like the Enron people or people off the street, they need to get into the Bible or something to change their ways somehow. Get into a self-help group to want to change their criminal habits. Both [people from Enron and from the streets] are thinking of crime. They're thinking how to get over. I mean, they're thinking of themselves when it's not about yourself all the time. That's what they have in common. When you commit a crime, you're thinking of self. You're not thinking about who you're stealing from. You're not thinking about who you are going to hurt, the children or the family members of the person you're going to kill. You're not thinking about anybody but self.

[One week later]: You know, I thought about [what we could do as a society to keep so many women from coming to prison], and I thought about it for days. I said, "What could somebody do to prevent us from coming to prison?" Well, we are society. The people that's coming to prison, we are society. The Enron people are society. I mean, the people who's in the corporate field, they're coming to prison. And the people who work every day are coming to prison. So society is coming into the prison. I'm society. Everybody that's sitting in this prison was society at one time or another, and it's coming to prison. . . . Even people who got money is coming to prison, so that question is a question we all want the answer to.

People on the outside don't think of us as society at all. They think of us as these low-down humans. But I see on the news, like yesterday, how a cop got pulled over for a DUI because he almost hit another cop giving a citation. That's society. The police are committing crimes. . . . The officers here in the institution, they have committed crimes. They just haven't gotten caught. And the officers out there who are arresting, they have done crimes; they just haven't got caught. . . . [How to keep people from coming to prison is] a question we all want to answer.

Reading Narrative

"I have discovered a love for the law"

I READ ALL the time I'm in prison. . . . I started sitting down reading books when I came to prison back in 1985. That was my first time in prison, and that's when I really started reading. When I was on the street, I wouldn't read. . . . I was too busy in the streets, running the streets, getting in trouble. . . . But once I came to prison, it's like, you got to do something to stay out of trouble, and if you don't have the luxury of a TV or the luxury of a CD player, you got to find something other than that which you can get into and not get in trouble, so you read. . . . Here in prison, it's like, after you get off work, you want to get back to where you left off at that book. I mean, you're thinking about that book all day because you're in a controlled environment . . . so you only have certain things you can do, and reading is one of them. And here there's not a gym you can go to, so you're limited to what you can do. So when you sit the book down and have to go to work, you want to get back to that book later on because that's part of your activity in prison. You can't wait to get back to that book!

. . . I read like four hours a day, every single day. My favorite place to read is they got a desk in my cottage; I be by myself in the desk area. I get most of my books from the library. . . . I go to the library every other day.[1] I go there to read the magazines or the newspapers or if I'm looking up something. . . . They give us a lot of projects in the groups we're in, so we have to use the library for those projects 'cause the library is the place where the encyclopedias or the almanacs or all that stuff is held.[2]

. . . I love John Grisham, *The Pelican Brief, The Summons, Bleachers, The Runaway Jury.* Right now I'm reading *The King of Torts,* about all the lawyers.[3] I just love John Grisham. . . . If it's John Grisham and [another prisoner] has it, I will borrow it from them. If they order books from home or out of the book catalogues, and they get a John Grisham, they'll come tell me, "Ms. [Mildred], I got a John Grisham." Every day I'm reading newspapers, magazines, John Grisham, and I pick up my Bible every morning. I read my Bible and my Daily Breads[4] and all that before I start my day. Then after I do my cleaning here at the institution, I go and read my John Grisham.

. . . I love everything he writes about. Anything that has to do with the law. All he writes about is laws and crime and I find him very interesting that he knows so much about it, 'cause some of his books do come out to be what's really true with the law. . . . His books help me understand if I can compare it with something I've learnt in my experience going in front of the judge . . . or seen in my life or somebody else's life. . . . When I see the judges leave the courthouse in Canton, they're incognito, they put their hats down. They don't want to be seen. I'm like, they was doing that in John Grisham!

. . . I'm not educated enough to understand the law books. If I understood it, I would be in the [law library] every day! . . . [When I read a John Grisham book,] like *The Runaway Jury,* I put myself right with the people that's watching the court proceedings, like I'm one of the spectators. I'm just trying to understand the law and understand how they operate. I'm trying to understand it more on the opposite side of the fence, you know, being a spectator instead of being one of the defendants. 'Cause when you're a defendant, you think the judge and the prosecutors are the bad guys and your attorney is not doing a good enough job. But when you sit back as a spectator, you're getting a feel of everybody because you're not seeing the judge and the prosecutors as the enemy. . . . You're trying to understand the prosecutor's point and the judge's point.

. . . And when I read, it's like it helps me to learn to write more structural letters. Like if I have to write a letter to a judge, I reflect back on what I've read. How can I reword this to make it sound more businesslike and less slang? And I use that reading knowledge that I learned in those books, how to prepare a letter that's more presentable for somebody as important as a judge or somebody more important to the world.

You know, I only have one child, and he's doing the same thing I was doing in the streets when I was his age. And if he gets in trouble, I want to go in the courtroom and know how to talk to the judge and the prosecutor for his defense. I don't want to see my child in prison. And in the men's prison at that, 'cause men do some really ugly things to each other. . . . I can use all my knowledge from what I've learned from my book reading, from John Grisham books, from sitting in the courtroom being a spectator, or from my own personal experience as a defendant. How can I put all that together in one to help with the defense for my child or my grandchild in the future?

. . . I find John Grisham's books very interesting because he talks more about not just crimes but also the white collar crime. I find it more interesting that they're getting caught. Like Enron, they're getting time for twenty-five years, thirty, ninety-nine, and it should have been going like that years ago because no crime is better than [another]. If you shoplift and you steal people's money that works in retirement funds, theirs is no different than mine. They just got more money than I do. It's no difference.

. . . I like [Grisham's] topics because he writes more about corporate law. . . . Like all the lawyers who's in the *King of Torts* group have got caught in the insurance companies, and the insurance companies don't want to carry them because they are taking on the corporate medicine thing . . . and they're stealing from the clients by keeping more of the money than they should. And you know, that holds my interest right there. That they're finally getting caught. It's telling society that not only does black people, but the white corporate American commits crimes, too. It shows that white and black people think alike as far as trying to get money or trying to get a little extra something in life. . . . It's like the turn of the card. It's not me as a black person all the time. I'm seeing now that white people do the things I do too, and the things my fellow black inmates do. . . . I've been in prison four times, and every time I came, the majority would be black. Well, this time, in our county jail, . . . every time when I would go to rec[reation], I would count the whites, and I would count the blacks, and it would be like eight blacks and twenty-five whites. . . . We are outnumbered any more.

So it's like, okay, they finally got caught, and they're finally seeing their own kind. 'Cause when you go to jail, to the courthouses, the judge that sits on the bench is a white man. When you see the prosecutor, he's usually a white man. . . . Where I come from, there's no black judge on our bench. There was one, but he died years ago. And they gave him such a problem that he wanted to step down. . . . And I think it's one black attorney now, or maybe two, but we don't have black attorneys. We don't have black prosecutors. We don't have black judges. In the John Grishams, I look at that as the white people finally getting caught, and I think about how our criminal courthouses are filled with white judges, and they're finally getting caught, too.

After I read a John Grisham book, I look around in here and I'm like, I wonder what she's in here for? I wonder what she's in here for? It would be a white woman that I would look at. Black people, I can probably look at and tell what they're in for. But the white people that look like they wouldn't break a egg, let alone the law, I would look at them, and I say, what did she do? Did she do something involving something I read in a John Grisham book, like the corporate thing, or stealing from a business, or stealing money from an account? When I look at the white women that look like they never would commit a crime in their life, that's where I think they did the John Grisham crimes.

. . . And like the methamphetamine, that's a white man's drug. Crack is the black man's drug, but methamphetamine was thought up by a white man. And that's why most of the white people come to jail now, methamphetamine and committing crimes to get the meth. It's like I said, society is coming to prison. We are the ones that's filling these jails. . . . It's a woman that's from Starr County where I'm from. . . . She looks like she works in a downtown office or at one of the courthouses. . . . But you know what she told me she was here for? She had a methamphetamine lab in her home, and her home was located in the rich part of Canton. . . . [But] if it's a big drug bust on the news, it's black people. Like for instance last night, when we was watching the news, they put a big drug bust in Starr County, forty pounds of cocaine. . . . I knew it had to be a black man, and you know what, I get mad because the law always think it's the black man doing this with the drugs.

. . . John Grisham writes a few books about African Americans. When I first began *The King of Torts,* it talked about how Clay Carter, he's a public defender, he was appointed to represent a black young man. And attorney Clay Carter said he always gets the African Americans' crimes, that's what the public defender's office really represents is African Americans. So John Grisham tries to implement black people in some of his novels, but it's hard, I guess, because he's a white man and he doesn't really know how to approach black people to write about black people.

. . . That's what I like: crime. I watch crime movies. I like *Law and Order.* I like all that kind of stuff. And as a child, I always wanted to be a lawyer or a judge. . . . But my son said, "You ended up needing a lawyer or you ended up going in front of a judge." My son, he graduated from criminal justice class in high school. . . . I told him, "You're going to take this criminal justice class." I kind of forced it on him. This is stuff I wanted to do so I made him do it to live my dream. . . . I've always had a taste for the law. This was always my dream to be a judge or lawyer. . . . But I got more involved in crime than preventing it.

Now this may sound strange, but when I'm at home, I go to the courthouses and I sit and watch the proceedings. . . . I've been out of prison ten years, so for the past two years, I would go to the courtroom and just listen to the proceedings in Judge [Smith's] courtroom. I listen to find out who would be the ones that I could determine would come back in front of the judge within the next few months or the next week or so. And I would determine what I saw in them. Who would be the repeaters? Who would come before the judge again? Or I would look and see if I could find myself in the defendants that were going before the judges. . . . I would just look at them and say, "Do I see myself in them?" 'Cause I would see myself as knowing it all, and thinking I could get over on somebody or thinking I can get over on the system, and if I would see that in that person, that's how I would know they would be back. Or the ones that just made a mistake and who would not come back. . . . If you had a misdemeanor, you would just get like community service, or you would get a fine. Now, the one judge, when the Katrina thing happened with the hurricane, instead of doing community service, he would order them to bring in groceries or something like that. And I found that very interesting. That's the kind of thing I like to go and watch. . . . Or if they would have to come back to court, I would go back for that person and see what would happen to that person. If they had another court date set, I would write down that court date to see what the outcome would be.

Judge [Smith], I would go to his courtroom when I would see the younger ones going before him, and they would be like eighteen, nineteen, or twenty. They'd come before him for underage drinking . . . or marijuana and they'd be charged with a misdemeanor. . . . And being that Judge [Smith] knows me now, he would say, "Ms. [Mildred], would you tell them what they would have to do for community service?" I said, "If you do your community service, he won't put you in jail. If you ain't done with the community service by the time he say it's supposed to be done, he's going to throw you in jail. It's not no second chance. You can come on your own, but don't let him have to put a warrant out." Yeah, he would ask me for my opinion. He would do that with a lot of them. . . . Matter of fact, his bailiff and his secretary testified for me at my court hearing. And they testified, "Ms. [Mildred] would help with the young ones that would come before the judge. Ms. [Mildred] would go out in the hallway and talk to the young ones and tell them, 'Judge [Smith] just wants you to do your community services or pay your fine and court cost or just do what he tells you to do and he won't throw you in jail.'"

Matter of fact, I write Judge [Smith] once a week and ask him how he be doing, how his court proceedings is going. I tell him how I miss the courtroom and miss being there and just to hold the fort down until I come back. . . . I said, "Judge [Smith], I know you care what's going on with me. But you know it's not necessary every time I write you a letter to send a guard to ask me how I'm doing. I know you care so it's not necessary. I know you're a judge, and you're in a position where you just can't correspond all the time, but you're also a human being and our relationship is one human being caring for another human being. . . . I know you sit back and read my letters every week that I write, but you don't have to call and check up on me, or write back."

I have discovered, like, a love for the law. Before I didn't care about the law. I didn't respect the law. Now I respect the law; even though I'm here now on these charges, I respect what they gave me because back then, I didn't respect it. I was always, "It's the police's fault that I'm here. It's the judge." . . . I was twenty-one. I didn't know no better. Now I can only respect the law because I did the crime, but I didn't do the [most recent] crime I got charged with, and it's eventually going to be worked out, but right now I'm here. And I'm dealing with it. I mean, they're only doing their job. A crime was committed, and I'm here for a crime that they say I committed, but my attorney is working on everything right now. And I'm not mad at anybody about it. Back in the day if I didn't know no better, yes I would be mad.

[When I watch in the courtroom,] it helps me understand the law. I watch the defendant, and I'll watch the judge, and I'll watch the prosecutor. It helps me understand the prosecutor's stand and the judge's stand and the defendant's stand. Okay, if you get charged with DUI,[5] the prosecutor's job is to convict you on it, but it's also your attorney's job to prevent you from going to jail, and it's also the judge's job to judge it fairly. So the prosecutor, his job is to get a judgment out of it, and I understand his part because this person committed a crime for DUI, and the prosecutor's trying to prevent him from going out and committing another DUI to hurt somebody. So his job is to put this person in jail or take this person's license. But I also understand this person don't want to go to jail, 'cause I done been to jail before. And I understand this person doesn't want to lose his license. And I also understand the judge's part as far as him determining what should be done here. Should I go along with what the prosecutor thinks should happen, or should I go along with what the defense attorney thinks is fair? So I get an understanding of everybody's reasoning.

. . . Terry McMillan, I like her too. . . . The first book I read of Terry McMillan was *Waiting To Exhale*. Then I read *How Stella Got Her Groove Back*.[6] I picked up one the other day, but I put it down 'cause I got four of John Grisham's in the middle; I'm trying to finish reading *A Painted House* and I'm going to start *Street Lawyer*[7] after I finish *The King of Torts*. So, I'm more of John Grisham. If I could find another author who was more the John Grisham type of writer, I would read more of that writer's books.

I also like politics books. I just finished a book about Bob Schieffer, the newscaster Schieffer. And I just read a book about Hillary Clinton. And I read a lot of the magazines with politics in it, like *Vanity Fair*. I read a lot of political stuff; if I see a magazine lying around and spot politics, I'll grab it and read it. . . . Like I picked up an encyclopedia just the other day just to go through it, and I read about Henry Kissinger, about President Kennedy, about President Johnson, about all those. Politics and law, I read that. I don't like love stories, Danielle Steel and Jackie Collins. I picked up one before, then I put it right down after I got through a couple of pages 'cause it was more of a love story.

. . . Sometimes I read self-help books, like self-esteem. Matter of fact, I just grabbed a self-esteem off the rack. We have a variety of books in our units, too, so I saw a self-esteem book and I grabbed that, and I put it in my cubicle so I could read it. I go to counseling for my mental health part, so I read, like, family problem books and books to build my self-esteem, and parenting books. I only have one child, but I have grandchildren, too. If it's something I feel I need some help in, like the self-esteem, and I feel that it would help me, I would grab it.

I would like to read a book with people who've had the same experiences we've had in prison and came out of prison and became a entrepreneur or got a good-paying job. You know, truthful books about what people have accomplished from their release from prison. Because it shows how you can accomplish something even though you have done time. Some kind of self-help book that shows that we as ex-offenders can accomplish things upon our release or accomplish things in society with our criminal backgrounds.

I think we also need to read some books about parenting skills. Because one day our toddlers and our teenagers will be adults, and you don't want to see your children come to prison. We need some parenting skills to prevent our children from coming in these walls. . . . The majority [of prisoners] is young adults, like eighteen, nineteen, twenty, twenty-one. And I first came to prison when I was twenty-one, but I had more knowledge. I was educated. I had a high school diploma. These young kids, they dropped out of school at middle school and first year of junior high. They didn't have any parenting skills from their parents to show them how not to come in here, and now they're mothers and they're nineteen, twenty. How are they going to teach their children not to come in here? . . . The young people who are committing the crimes would be our future doctors, our future lawyers, our future everything. But the future is coming in here. How are they going to be our future if they're coming in here?

What can we do as parents to prevent our fourteen-year-old from committing a murder? What can we learn as prisoners to help our fourteen-year-old at home when we are in prison? What can we do as prisoners when we go out there to instill in our child not to do this? We need some parenting skills to teach our kids and our grandkids. My son, he's running the streets, and he thinks he can't be touched. Evidently, seeing me coming to prison wasn't enough experience for him. So what can I teach my grandkids to prevent them from coming in here?

2 Sissy

—ɯ—

Life Narrative

"There's a time to be silent, and there's a time not to"

I WAS BORN in Ohio, I think. I have a birth certificate saying that. I was raised in Mississippi by my grandmother, my mother's mother. My one older sister and one younger sister, both are the two that my grandmother raised besides me, but my mother, she had other children also. I learned family values. You know, you stick together with your family. We had a lot of family values. No matter what's going on, your family's always supposed to stick together. I was a middle child. And I basically raised myself because my oldest sister, she was over the younger ones. And then my younger sister, she had all the attention, so I wasn't even there. Basically, that's how it was with me.

School was all right. I never had help with school from home. Because well, my older sister, she was the brain of the family and she got all A's, and I was a B/C student. And I don't know, I felt in her shadows. Because it was always, "Why can't you be like your older sister?" and that kind of cut my self-esteem down a little bit. I didn't understand that then, but I understand it now. . . . But I loved just learning things. It didn't matter what it was.

. . . I loved Mississippi. Oh, I loved it! The free space. It's so open. . . . I used to always just go in the fields after we finished our work and everything, just go in the fields and read my books. I'm a bookworm. That's why I have these glasses because I'll always get up in the middle of the night and turn on the TV or read a book. That's how much I love reading and everything, and that was one of my best subjects in school. Reading class, English, social studies, you know, anything that could just get you to read. . . . And I'm an artist. I love colors. And down south was just colorful. The trees, the birds, the ground, the fields, everything was so colorful. I guess that's where I got my understanding of how I loved art.

. . . One of my biggest joys was when I was eleven going on twelve and I came up here to Ohio to finally meet my mother and my father, because they were just these pictures in my life and telephone calls. They were never physical forms. . . . And when I finally met them, I was so happy to finally see the others who made me, you know. Where did I come from. . . . [But] I didn't like it up here. My mother was getting married and she wanted to know if we wanted to come up here and live with her. So I said yes. . . . [But later] I went to stay with my dad for a year. And then I went and stayed with my grandmother for some time. And then I went back to my mom's.

. . . I walked to school when I was in Mississippi, and . . . you're not supposed to really do that because it was a lot of racial tension down there. And we were going to our own school, and then we had to be bused and everything. And that was a scary experience, you know, to go to a school that you're not wanted at. That was a scary experience. And then to come up here and everybody's in the school. That's a different thing. Because down there, you lived on this side of the railroad track and the Caucasians lived on the other side of the railroad track. You did not cross that railroad track at a certain time unless you were escorted or if you're a young kid, you got to be with an adult. In the morning times, it was all right, but at night, no, no, no, no, no. Do not go over the side of the railroad track, you know, 'cause you'll be responsible for whatever happens to you.

It was a big experience when we were bused. I was in like the second or third grade, and I would say there was about ten of us and about twenty Caucasian kids. . . . Me and my sister was talking about when we got bused and about how they didn't want us, and how they'd throw things at us and call us names. And we'd get in the school, and we'd have to sit in a certain area of the classroom, and then we couldn't drink out of their water fountain. It was something. And sometimes we'd come home with gum all in our hair and my grandmother had to cut our hair to get stuff out. Or our clothes would be messed up where somebody threw something at us. . . . We'd come home, and we'd look like we'd been dumped on and just dirty all the time. And we were scared to go outside and play. We would come back looking worse than when we went because of what we had to go through just to be there. And so a lot of the parents didn't let their kids go to that school anymore. Some of them pulled them out and said, "I'll teach them at home." And that was when my grandmother said, "Suck your gut in. Hold your head up high. You get back on that bus." She said, "And whatever they say to you, do not say anything. You say 'yes ma'am.' You say 'no ma'am.' You give them respect at all times." And so she taught us to not talk back, not argue back or anything like that. She said, "Because it could be worse on you." She said, "And I don't want you to come home dead." So that's what she told us to do, and that's what we did.

... It was emotional. It was scary. You wonder what's going to happen the next day. I'm so glad it's over, you know. If I had to give somebody advice going through that, I would give them the advice my grandmother told me because nothing's ever guaranteed, and there's some things you have to get past. And it's no different than like today. There's some things that you have to suck up and hold your head up and get through it because you have no other choice. You really have no other choice. I could have ignored my grandmother and started arguing back 'cause I wasn't around her anymore. But I didn't. And that stuck with me, you know, you keep your mouth shut because anything can happen. And so today, I learned that certain things you have to be quiet about, and let it pass because it could be worse for you. There are some things that's best left unsaid.

It got better because people get used to you. They have to get used to you whether they liked it or not. And the thing about it is the teachers are the ones that have to set the example because once you're away from your parents, then you have that leadership figure right there in front of you. And if the teachers didn't open up their mouth and say anything, then the torture and torment would go on in our recess and going to the cafeteria and things like that. . . . It got better with some people, but with some people who still didn't care and still did what they did to us, it would never get better. And some people grow up that way. That's just how they are, you know, and I can't fault them for how they were raised because a lot of our attitudes and things that we do, it comes from home. And that's something my grandmother taught me also: how you act when you're out in public is how I allow you to act at home.

I was the type of person that stayed to myself. I stayed to myself and they couldn't figure me out. They picked on me and picked on me and picked on me, and I'm like, whatever. Whatever. I don't see you. I don't hear you. You can do anything you want to me. I am not getting ready to let you make me feel that I am less than. Even though I didn't get the love that I wanted at home, what I felt that I was denied, I did get the understanding of how to take care of me when I needed it. I was able to show them and the rest of us because we all hung around each other. And there was some of the Caucasian children that would come and talk to us. Or ask us our name. Some of them were nice. They didn't act like the others, ignorant and everything. You know, they were nice. And they got used to us. And they would tell [others], "Don't pick on her. Leave her alone." And then *they* would get picked on. They would be called "nigger lovers" and ugly stuff like that. And it was like, okay, I don't want to cause you no problems because you live in their neighborhood and I don't. I live way over here across the railroad tracks and you live in the neighborhood where these other ones live at, and I don't want to cause you any problems. So I just stayed to myself. My sister, she was a little bit bolder than me, and she argued with them and everything to where they gave her a little bit more respect than they gave me. 'Cause she wouldn't back down, and once again, I was in her shadow. I wasn't scared, but I wasn't going to put myself out there. I fought because I was pushed to the limit, and that was the only reason I fought back.

[In the Ohio school, it was] strange because there was no racial barrier. Everybody was equal and everything. And I didn't have to wait for somebody to call me out my name or say something derogatory towards me. And it didn't happen. And I was like, "What's going on here?" It was so strange because, you know, we all sat together and sang together, and we did recess together. We played together. We ate together. There was no fights. You didn't have to worry about coming home with gum in your hair, dirt in your underwear, or anything like that. You didn't have to worry about none of that. If you got dirty, you did it [laughing]. And it was a relief. It was a relief, and I didn't know how tense and wound up I was until I [realized] I was scared to play with anybody because I didn't know what was going on, and why is everybody just playing together. I was just waiting for something to happen, you know, and it never did. . . . We were all equal. We sat next to each other. We laughed. We hugged and we shared our food together and everything. . . . It took me a while to get used to it. Because I was on defensive mode, and I always had this wall of waiting for something to happen. And it took me a long time to get adjusted to that.

. . . My mother, she's so light-skinned everybody thinks she's Caucasian, and none of us is light like her. And she's redheaded, freckled and everything. . . . It was just one of those things that I had to grow up with, you know, my mother being different from me. When I first met my mother, I'm like, "She's not my mama." It's like, "Where's my mommy at?" And my grandmother said, "There's your mother!" I would not go to her because when I seen the pictures of my mother, she had on darker makeup. She would always put darker makeup on. And I never understood that, but I guess that was a self-conscious thing for her that she had a problem growing up being passed off as not a African American child. And when I seen her without that dark makeup, I didn't know who she was. . . . I was scared of my own mother. . . . And I'm like, well, why wasn't she there when I went to school? She could have helped me back then. They wouldn't have treated me that way. I don't know if that's true or not, but that was where my mind was at.

. . . I didn't know how to act with my mother because she wasn't like me. . . . It was just the strangest thing, you know, being around her and learning from her ways and how she was, compared to how my grandmother raised me in the South. . . . It was just, you know, getting to know my mom, getting to know my dad, getting to know the other half of my family. And I didn't like them! They were all stuck-up! They made me *sick* they were so stuck-up! Because my family up here, they were well-to-do. My dad, he had his own home and his own property. . . . Down there it's just my grandmother. I didn't have to make a choice of who to live with. Or who to be around. Or if I was giving enough time with this one. Or if I visited this one. I never had to make a choice down there. But up here . . . I was traveling between all these three people, and I was just trying to please them, you know. They wanted to get to know us, me and my sister. But it felt like I never had the time for none of them. And I just felt so torn. . . . I didn't know how to love my family back. I care about them. I will fight tooth and nail for them. But I wasn't able to bond with them the way that I should have. I just know I was supposed to be there. Through thick and thin, we were family, and nobody is supposed to come between family. I don't care what problems the family has, what arguments or whatever. Family was family. . . . But I never was able to have anybody to talk to, you know, sit down and talk about my problems. . . . I would ask a stranger a question quicker than I would ask my dad or my mom or my grandmother. . . . I had so many down times that, I don't know, I had bad experiences. . . . I started talking back to my mom and running away from home.

. . . When I was about nine until right before I left to come up here, I think about eleven, I was subjected to being molested. And that was an experience that just drew me back into myself again. And it got to the point where I felt less than. "Look, you're ugly. You're not as pretty as your sisters. So it doesn't matter. Nobody wants you anyway so you might as well do what I tell you anyway." You know, stuff like that. . . . So my grandmother would send me over to [my abuser's] house to drop things off or get things. . . . Sometimes I would sit out in the rain just to keep from going in the house, and then my grandmother would punish me because I was soaking wet and caught cold because I wouldn't go in the house. . . . It was always my fault, so I never said anything. So it got to where when I went in the house, he would always rape me, and there would be nothing I could do. Nothing I could do, you know.

I just always tried to figure out what it was about me that these men would want to just hurt me, you know, and like, they never bothered my sister. I was like, "Do I have a sign on my forehead saying 'damaged goods, do whatever you want with it'?" I just had the worst experience. And I always considered myself less than. . . . Whoever wanted me could have me because I wasn't worth anything anyway, you know. So I grew up like that. Until I got pregnant and had my own kid and everything, and I only got pregnant to have somebody to love me [crying]. You know, somebody that I didn't feel that I had to give myself to anybody. Somebody that could love me for me. That was the only reason why I got pregnant. You know, and my sister had a baby, and to me, she was grown, and I had, I had [crying], I'm all right. I didn't think I would get this emotional. I didn't think I would go there. I just, I don't know, within the last couple of years I had to reflect back on all those things, and every time I talk about it, I get emotional 'cause I kept it buried for years. I kept all of that buried before, and I would never tell anybody about it. It was hard having to talk about it and admit all the abuses that I had to suffer. And then to be abused by somebody that you love. That was the worst thing. To have that done and to keep it buried for so long. And I think it shaped a lot of choices that I made, the people that I dealt with, the men that I allowed to have control over me whatever way. And I think it had a lot to do with why I'm in prison. . . . All the times that I did speak about it nobody believed me, so who cared anymore? I'm a grown woman. So what? It happened. Whatever. But it shaped a lot of things that happened to me and the choices that I made in my life. And instead of speaking out or trying to get help, I just wouldn't speak at all. . . .

I [already] had my daughter, so I went on ahead and got my own place. . . . Then I met this other guy. And oh man, oh man, that was the worst mistake of my life. . . . He got me drunk, and I had sex with him and I got pregnant. I didn't want to be pregnant. . . . I didn't know what a drug addict was back then, so I didn't know he had a habit and he was using me for his habit. And one day I came home, I was six months pregnant and my son and my daughter was sitting on the floor, and they had these needles and I was like, "What's going on here?" And he was in the kitchen with his friend, and they had all this stuff on the table. . . . We got into this big fight, and he went and he busted everything up in the house. He busted a hole in the TV. He turned a refrigerator over, and he busted the furniture up with a hammer and everything. He took my son and threw him up against the wall and pushed my daughter and everything, and then he just beat on me. And I'm like, "Oh my God. What did I do? What did I do?" And I just took me and my kids, and I went over to my sister's house and I was scared to go home to my own place. . . . My cousin and my uncle went back to the house with me and everything, and my uncle took all his stuff and put it outside.

. . . So I asked my grandmother, I said, "Would you watch my daughter for me? 'Cause I don't know what to do." . . . And I didn't tell her what happened 'cause I was scared she might not want to watch my daughter. And I went down to the Children Services and asked them to take my baby. I said, "I can't do anything with my son. I don't know what to do. I need help." So they said, "Well, when you get yourself together, you can come get your son." So my grandmother said, "Where's your baby at?" And I was like, "Oh, he's over my cousin's house." I never told anybody I gave my son away. She said, "Well go get him. I want to see him." So he was about six months old when I finally went and got him. I told them, "I'm ready for my son back" even though I wasn't ready for him. My family wanted to know where was my son at, and so I went and got my son.

. . . I was on a rollercoaster, and I didn't know, I was just, I was going down, you know. I was, I was just, I don't know what it was. I just, it was too much for me. . . . I just started drinking more and drinking more. I think I weighed about ninety pounds, you know, and drinking was my breakfast, lunch, and dinner. . . . So my grandmother, she owns these two houses on the eastside, and she told me to go move in one of them. And I did. And me and my kids was living there.

. . . [My ex-boyfriend] would stalk me. . . . He would come in the middle of the night and leave in the morning. . . . And then crazy things started happening. . . . Me and my sister, we went shopping. And I came back, and my furniture was all smashed up. . . . Then one night my [current] boyfriend came over, and he woke me up, and my house was full of smoke. Somebody set fire to the chair that was in the basement. And if he hadn't came, we'd all been dead. So I went and stayed with my grandmother then. I stayed with her for about a week 'cause I thought I was going crazy. . . . I used to get all these crazy threatening phone calls. . . . And I woke up once again to smoke in the house. And it was the craziest thing because I was just, oh me. I was so disoriented because I had been drinking all night and when I went to bed that night, my son was in the bed with me. And I reached over to get my son and he wasn't there anymore. He wasn't there anymore [crying]. And so the house was full of smoke and I was just crawling around on the floor trying to find my kids, and I couldn't find my baby [crying]. And I was just looking and hollering and screaming. . . . I went over to my cousin's house and I was banging on the door and asking her if she seen my kids [crying]. . . . Me and her boyfriend went back over there and we tried to get in the house and couldn't get in. . . . And my son died in that fire. And that's why I'm in prison because I was accused of starting the fire. And I know I didn't start any fire. But I don't know how it got started. And they never really proved that I started the fire.

. . . I had the craziest trial. The craziest trial. It was so hurtful of being accused of killing your own children. That was the worst crime a mother could be accused of. It's the worst thing [crying]. . . . My family was going to pay for a lawyer, but I'm like, "No, no, no. I don't want you wasting your money on me." And so I got a public defender. And my public defender knew nothing about criminal law. So I received the death sentence and was on death row. And then Governor [X] commuted my sentence and I got off death row. . . . They could not show that I had any animosity against my children. But my kid's father, he testified at the grand jury against me saying that I hated my kids and I killed my kids because of him. . . . [He] started a process that almost took my life for something [he] knew wasn't true. . . . The reason why the governor commuted my sentence, he said . . . that my frame of mind was so distorted, and that I couldn't handle taking care of my children, and I was not mentally, emotionally capable of taking care of myself. And the governor's wife, I stayed in contact with her my whole bit on death row. And she would call my family for me and everything. She came and visited me. . . . And it's because of her that I got off death row. Because she listened to my story, and she believed in me, and she believed that I wasn't guilty of deliberately doing anything to my children. And I received life without possibility of parole. And so I'm very grateful for that. Very, very grateful. I was blessed. Very blessed.

I feel that what happened to me, it went on to my child. She made the same choice that I did. She got with some guy, and she thought this is gonna be a perfect marriage and home and all that. I mean it, it was so, so, so uncanny how everything is the same. . . . It's just that she was not on drugs, and she doesn't do alcohol. And she was able to leave. I wish somebody would have told me, but back then you didn't speak out. But I told my child, "Leave. Leave and get as far away from him as you can." She went to a homeless shelter to get away from him. I told her to do that because I reminisced so much that it hurt my head so bad. I'm like, oh my god. This is a repeat of the past, and it scared me so bad because I was so afraid for my daughter. . . . I said, my baby will not go through what I went through. She will not be fighting, have no man beating on her. Nothing. That is not what's going on these days and ages. You just don't have to live there anymore, and I don't care how much he say I love you. This hurts. Those scars don't go away very fast. And you emotionally affect your children, and they're also in the middle of it. . . . And all I could think about was when he threw my son up against the wall because he was berserk or he was in a drug-induced state of mind, and he didn't care, not even about his own child.

. . . Within the midst of the families, there's always something that goes wrong, you know. It's what they call the black sheep of the family. But they're not the black sheep. Something happened to impact their life that brought them to where they're at, and then they labeled them because they didn't understand what's going on in their life. And nobody wanted to know. Nobody asked questions. And it was just basically a cry for help. . . . One of the things that happened when I came to prison is that my family said, "Don't tell them your business. Don't tell them nothing about you. Don't tell them this or that." And I didn't. . . . Case workers come and ask you your history about yourself and all of that, and I was like, "It's none of your business. I'm not telling you anything." . . . And I kept all that in for years and years and years.

. . . I think it changed for me after my mom died. My mom died in '96. . . . And that just hurt me so because I had just lost my uncle. Then I had lost my grandmother that raised me. . . . I was just like, "What am I gonna do?" And that's when I had my friend, her name is [X]. Oh, and she's wonderful. She's been my best friend for ten years now. And she helped me get through all of it, because she's had those things happen in her life. . . . She, like, took me under her wings as my bigger sister. . . . She knew more about family influence and breaking away from it, and she started talking to me about it. And gradually—it took awhile, years passed by; many years passed by—I just started opening up and everything. And she just became my big sister. Then we had, like, family days up there and her family would come, and my daughter would come, and my sister would come, and her family just made me a part of them. And then my daughter and her daughter were talking on the telephone and things like that.

And it made a difference. It made a difference to me to have somebody there. Because all these years, I've just been by myself. And they'd visit, but then they left, and that was over until the next month, so I had all those empty days until I seen them again. And she filled those days as my big sister, and that made a difference because I learned so much from her. I learned about life. I learned about everything. She told me the things about sex I didn't know. I said, "Well tell me." You know, things I had read in the book. Is that true? Do they really do that? I could talk to somebody, and once I was able to talk to her, she really gave me honest answers and was really interested and like, "What? You don't know about this?" No, I didn't know about a lot of things because I never had a chance to experience. . . . My family were, you know, "You do this. You do that. This is how you do it," and that's how it was. That's what I felt would make me part of the family, if I didn't rock the boat. And when I did, it scared me because I didn't know how to say I'm sorry because it was a big thing when you rocked the boat in the family. It was a big thing. And then when all this happened . . . it was like they just all surrounded me, and "Don't touch her. Leave her alone." And it just really, really surprised me, how they just embraced me and wanted to protect me. But that's not when I needed you, you know, and that's what I kept saying: "I needed you when I was going through all this and didn't know up from down or left from right."

And all during my trials . . . I would just sit there with my lawyer right there, and I was just all mellow. And what caused that? Because my family told me to be quiet and not say anything. Even in the trial when I had spoken up to say something, my dad said, "Shut up and sit down." And I'm like, "Okay." That's what I did. I shut up and I sat down, and I shouldn't have. I shouldn't have. . . . I don't put the blame on anybody for me being in prison. I don't blame myself. I blame not speaking out and everything, but I can't blame myself because I wasn't in my right mind all the time. So I just blame my choices, and my lack of understanding as to there's just a time when you need to open up your mouth and stand up for yourself.

I've been in prison, this is my twenty-third year. . . . And my daughter, she kind of went through a lot of things that I went through because I left her with my aunt to raise, but she wanted her mommy. My baby, she wanted me. And that's what kept me going. That was what kept me going. My baby wanted me. She wanted me. And she didn't want anybody else around her. She wanted her mommy [crying]. And I felt so good after being accused of that, and my baby still wanted me, and she didn't want to be around nobody but me. And when she came to visit me [crying], she would just cling to me. Oh, she would just cling to me, and she would just cry. And they would just have to peel her off of me. It was just so hurting, but I felt so good because she still loved me. And she still loves me today regardless of what I was accused of. She still loves her mommy today [crying]. And nothing, nobody, can't nobody tell her anything about me. That is the best thing I could ever have is her love and her support and her being there for me. And not letting anybody tell her about her mommy [crying]. And the times that she would come and see me, we just bonded. We just had such a strong bond. And that's the best thing that helped me a whole lot. It helped me do this time and helped me through the depression time. It helped me times when I felt like I couldn't make it, and just knowing that she was there [crying]. She's all I have left in this world, you know, she's a part of me. And I love her so much.

One of the reasons why I wanted to come [to this prison] was to see my grandmother—she passed away in November—and to see my dad because I wanted to let him know I forgave him. I wanted to let him know that I had to find myself and to come to terms and come to reality and accept what happened and move on and not let any of that hold me back from being who I really am. You know, I deserve to be somebody. And I wanted to let him know I forgave him. And I wanted to see him face to face to do all this. I didn't want to do it on the telephone or do a letter because he had been sick, and he had heart problems. I came here to make peace and make amends, but my dad passed away and I never got a chance to tell him; he died of a sudden heart attack. But that's all right, you know, because I made my peace with everything, and I made my peace with myself.

... [It's important to] live in the reality of what today can bring you 'cause tomorrow's not promised. Just look at the world as it is today. Tomorrow's not promised. So we have to live our life today to the best of our ability. And I want each day to be where I did something good to somebody. I don't want anybody to remember my name. I just want to know that I made a positive impact in some way for somebody. . . . I just want to be one of the ones to make a difference today because we, as human beings, we're affected by everything each other does.

—ᴔ—

Reading Narrative

"If you can't relate to it, then read about it"

READING IS SOMETHING that I love to do. You know, 'cause there's always something in it that you can get out of it. I'm a fast reader, okay. Sometimes I have to slow myself down; if it's a good book, then I'll pace myself. . . . Sometimes I don't get through a whole book because if it starts off boring, then I'm not going to read it. But if it's something that I know somebody tells me it's good, you just have to get past all of that. Sometimes you have a book that's 500 pages long and it don't get to the good part 'til the middle of the book. So you have to read if you really want to get something out of it.

Because these different new authors come out, I've been getting into a lot of African American books, and I've been getting into just everything. I really don't have a particular type of book that I read. I like to read if it catches my eye. . . . I like art books. And I read comic books. I like funny books. I like mystery, drama, murder, science fiction, everything. There's nothing that I won't read. 'Cause to me that's just another world, you know, that's how it is. I love news and everything. I love to learn about other countries and what they do, how they do it. I read magazines, newspapers.

. . . I've grown up basically in prison. And it has impacted my life a lot because there's things that I don't know about society. I don't know them 'cause I haven't lived out there in twenty-three years. . . . Even though I'm in prison, the different things that's happening out there still affects me. And I keep up on a lot of the politics, radios, papers, all that's in the news because that affects me.

I read for enjoyment 'cause reading, it stimulates my mind. If I read and there's a word I've never seen before, it takes me to the dictionary. And if I can't find it in the dictionary, I'll go to the thesaurus. If I can't find it, then I have to ask people. And you learn things out of books. It helps you ask questions. It helps you just find out about the world that you live in. It tells you about people. It tells you about places. I like Victorian books, you know, way back then. I mean, it's a wonder. I love to read books back in time. . . . I read about this king and queen . . . and it showed you about the church and politics. Some of it was fiction, and some of it wasn't, but it taught you. The places that they wrote about, they were real. The cities, the islands that they were on, all of those were real. And it taught you about their culture and how they did things. And you learned about how they taxed, how they lived, the food they ate, how they liked it. How the rich, the poor, the middle class, it's all over the world. It doesn't matter where you're at. So it's just education in all books. . . . The details of the places, the descriptions of the buildings, the castles, and way in the mountains, all that is real. So I don't have to get on a boat or a plane to go over there. I can pick up a book and learn about that, and if I ever meet anybody that's from that type of place, I understand where they're coming from. It teaches me about people, their culture, the way of thinking, their way of doing things. And that keeps you from being preju-diced. Like, "Oh I can't understand her talk." Or "Look at how she dresses." Or "Her hair is weird." You know, when you see somebody that you've never seen before, they look out of place. Then you ask them, "Where are you from? Oh, I read about that." And I can understand why they're dressed like that, why they talk like that, why they are acting the way they do because I've read about their country. So that's one of the things that I like when I read.

Even religion, I read all religions. I've learned about Muslims, Protestants, Catholics, Jehovah Witnesses, Mormons, Seventh-Day Adventists. I'm learn-ing about Jewish. I just learned about all of them. I learned because they are part of who society is. And when I leave out of prison, these are the people that I have to walk and talk and associate with, regardless of who they are, and that makes a big difference. And if you read and educate yourself about the world that you're surrounded with, it makes it easier for you. To me, it helps people from being prejudiced.

My prime example was this girl, she's Jewish. . . . And she was speaking about how a lot of people are prejudiced against Jews. And I'm like, "Why?" She went through this whole thing about the Holocaust and how her family was part of that. And I was like, "Oh, okay. We have something in common." She's like, "What do we have in common? We went through the Holocaust." I said, "I'm African American. My ancestors went through slavery." "What does that have to do with it?" I said, "It has to do with a culture that had to conform to a way of somebody dictating their life. And if they didn't, then they died for it." I said, "And even though the way that it happened was different, somebody still suffered behind it." I said, "And it's the suffering that we have in common, that we can say our ancestors suffered for us to be where we're at today." I said, "Anything else, we can't claim because we weren't there. All we can do is make things better. All we can do is not hold a grudge. Not say, 'Oh, because of you, my family . . .' No, no, no, no, no. That's past. You have to grow out of that. That's part of how we build society is with our attitude. Even our children, how do you raise a child in their thinking and their way of doing and their way of treating people? That's what makes a difference. And when you educate yourself and your family to other people's way of life, then your children will not grow up being ignorant to somebody that they don't know anything about. If you teach them one little thing, it makes a difference. It makes a big difference." And she was like, "Wow. I never thought of it that way."

Some families are very strict in how they want their children, but I feel that when you get older, you have a choice. You have a choice, and to me it's your responsibility as a human being—whether you're in jail, whether you're across seas, or whether you're out in the world's society—we still have a responsibility to treat each other as human beings. You know, and to learn and understand you have to put yourself out there. And some people are afraid. They really are. And because they're afraid, they need to read. To me, if you can't relate to it, then read about it. And if you still can't relate to it, at least you'll know. At least you can't say I never tried to understand. To me that makes a big difference. If you don't try to understand, then that's a loss to you. Maybe somewhere you work and somewhere you have to go to—the park—I mean, every part of our life we touch has to do with somebody of a different culture. The supermarket, every store, even the law enforcement. All walks of life is everywhere now. And we have to educate ourselves to them. I think that's why we have the problems we have now. You know, some people don't want to go there.

. . . [I started reading books about religion] because I got into a spiritual debate with an officer, and she was atheist. This was when I was on death row, and I had these different pamphlets. You know, you get your Daily Bread and things like that. And she just happened to have brought my mail and she said, "Why do you read this? Everybody comes to prison and wants to get saved." I said, "Well, I was saved before I came to prison. I was raised in a Baptist church." I said, "And my grandmother did not want to hear 'No, I don't want to go to church.' You went to church, and you went to Sunday school. So it wasn't something that I just found since I came to prison." She said, "Oh, okay, then if it's all that, then why are you in prison? How come the Lord didn't help you get out of prison?" I was like, "Sometimes the Lord allows things to happen in people's lives in order to wake them up to things they may have been doing wrong in their life. You know, sometimes people are on a roller coaster to destruction of themselves. And sometimes the Lord allows things to happen." I said, "It is not about him saving me because he's already did that." I said, "It's the choices that we make when we're on that roller coaster to destruction as to where we end up." I said, "So no, I'm not gonna stop my praying." She said, "I used to be a Protestant." I said, "Well what's a Protestant?" 'Cause I didn't know what a Protestant was. I just knew a Baptist. And she said, "Why, you're supposed to be the religious person. You figure that out." So it got me to thinking. Well, what do I really know about religion? So I said to her, "Well, I'm gonna answer that question for you."

So what I did was, it just so happened that I had wrote for this spiritual book, and in the book it had these different things about the Sabbath day. What do you really know about the Sabbath? What do you really know about the holy days? And I'm like, what is this? I said, well, let me write these people and find out. So they sent me a book about the Sabbath and they sent me a book about the holy days. And it all reverted back to Jewish. And I'm like, what is Jewish? So I sent a kite¹ to the chaplain: "Could you please come over here? I need to ask you some questions." . . . So I'm like, "What is this? What is that? What is Protestant? . . . All I know is the church I went to and them big, beautiful churches that's always quiet and that was the Catholic church." . . . So, that got me to reading the Jerusalem Bible. . . . I was like, "Is there other Bibles?" And the chaplain . . . named the Qur'an and the Jehovah's Witnesses' Bible. And I'm like, "Wow!" I said, "I want to know about this." He's like, "Well, that has nothing to do with you because you're a Baptist." I said, "But I want to know about what this is. Because this book is telling me about the Sabbath, and I thought the Sabbath was Sunday and this book is telling me it's Saturday and why it's Saturday and all the history behind it that brought it to where it is today, and that the calendar that I'm looking at is not the calendar at all!" And it was wonderful because it was teaching me about another culture. I got books on Islam, Jewish, Jehovah's Witnesses, Catholic. The chaplain gave me the information and I wrote these people and they sent me everything free. Then when I got off death row, I started going to these different services. I went to Mass. I did Ramadan with Islamic people. I did the Catholic thing. I went to Jehovah's Witnesses' studies. And I learned. I learned about the Mormons and what they believe 'cause I found somebody who was into Seventh-Day Adventists. I learned about Christian Science. I just went through the whole world!

. . . I've read so many spiritual books it isn't even funny, and that taught me about life in general as to how I want to be talked to and how I want to be treated. . . . Now I'm reading this book called *Prayer and Fasting*.[2] It speaks about the biblical way of why people pray and fast, as to how to pray when you fast. . . . Because fasting is not simple at all. To me—because I've fasted many, many times before—fasting is a time when you are in need, and when you feel that there's something in you that's not going right in your life. Or that you just need time to bounce back. . . . To me, fasting is just to have time with the Lord and just have that mental peace with him. To find peace to be able to just make it through the next day or to be able to deal with people on a certain level. . . . I've done a lot of spiritual fasting when I feel at odds with myself or at odds with something that's happening in my life. . . . Sometimes when I feel attacked, I pray and I fast. I've fasted, and goodness gracious, they don't like you to do that. They really don't.

. . . [When I was on death row,] I learned about law. My attorney that I had, she wanted me to be a part of all of my decisions as far as my appeals and things like that. So she gave me law books to learn what this meant, F2, 3, 4 and all that. And I learned those are the pages, this is the name of the book, this is the page you have to find, this is the cases and everything. I learned how to read the case, why the judges made their decision, and the dissent of the judges. Then she sent me a *Black's Law Dictionary* of my own to learn the legal term for everything. And so that was another world I went into. I went into the legal world to understand what the laws are. I'm still doing things for my case. . . . And if somebody don't understand something, I'll go and research it for them and tell them how to understand what the judge said, what this meant. Because the law has changed now and so you have to keep up with a lot of things.

... I like to read art books. I used to love to go to museums. You know, walk around and just look at the pictures. Goodness gracious, art today is weird [laughing]. Okay, I have no other way to describe it but weird. And the art books show you pictures of way back, fifteenth-, sixteenth-century pictures, and I like to look at them and compare them to like Picasso and Monet ... to see how did they get where they are. The art that they do to me seems very simple, easy. . . . It was something that you can just go in the country and look at beautiful scenery, or beautiful physical human being bodies. Or just people sitting there, looking, writing, fruit and flowers and just those little things, the simple things of life. And I'm like, how come they can't still do that? Because they were beautiful back then. What makes them any less now? You have this art today where they just take a piece of metal and bend it this way, and it's worth $50,000. Excuse me!? What?! There's no work in that. Somebody just piled a bunch of cans together and made a frame and put a picture in it, and they pay $20,000 for things like that. I'm just trying to understand why did art change? So I like to pace the years and centuries and come up into the decade of time today and look how art has changed. And how they judge art today. It's strange, you know, because people died in poverty [from doing] art back then. . . . [But] today you can do anything and be rich! They're rich just like that [snaps fingers]! And the work back then, there's no comparison with the beauty of the work. It's such intense work that you can see.

... I started drawing for my daughter. I started drawing picture after picture. I would look out the window and just draw the cows in the background of the trees. I'd just draw things for her because this made my baby happy. And I had nothing else to give her 'cause I was in prison, so I would draw for her. She has stacks and stacks of folders of all my work that I drew her. And when she got older, she put them in her apartment as pictures. And she's like, "Mommy, when are you going to draw for me again?" She still loves my drawings. I stopped drawing because my hand started hurting. I guess it's arthritis, but I draw every once in a while when I can grip right. I started that because of my daughter. I did it to make her happy, to let her have a part of me because I couldn't be there. So she has something of me that she could be proud of. You know, her mommy's time in prison wasn't wasted of not doing anything. I gave something back to her.

... I'm going to start an art and craft class here through the rec[reation] department to teach people the different techniques and ... help them do things for their children. You know, send home nice little cards to their family. . . . To me, you have to reach out to other people. One of the important things my mother always taught me is there's always somebody less fortunate than you are. And you never, never know who they are. . . . Some people look real nice, and they don't have a cent in their pockets. And their families have nothing. And when they go home, they might have to go to the soup kitchen or be on welfare for the rest of their lives. Or have to have handouts because some people can't take care of theirselves. Some people don't know how. And you don't look down on those. I've been there. I know what it's like to have and then not to have. What it's like to be too proud to ask. To be too proud to hold my hand out and receive. . . . I'll never tell a person "no." You're hungry, if I have something to eat, I'm going to share it with you. . . . So I can teach you how to make certain craft items. You can go on the street and make some money. I can show you how to crochet. You can go out on the street and buy you some yarn cheap and make money. I can teach you how to design things. . . . And I learned these things by reading books. I learned about crocheting by reading. I learned about art by reading a book.

. . . Sometimes, I don't even look to see if a book is a fiction or if it's nonfiction. I'll just pick it up and read it. . . . It's a challenge to me to say yes, I've been able to read this book without being critical of it, regardless of what the title says. . . . Like Dean Koontz and Stephen King, they're gross. They're just totally gross. Their imagination is whew! To me sometimes it's sickening. . . . But even though a lot of these things they write about are sickening, they actually happen, and you can't say, "Oh, that don't happen." You never know. You have so many different places where you've never been. And we have so many people who do things that you would never expect them to do. . . . Always keep your mind open. Always. You never, never say never. Because anything is possible.

I used to love Stephen King's books but they started getting boring. To me they just say the same old thing over and over and over. It was just the weirdness of it, it got boring. So I picked up Dean Koontz because he was in the same line as Stephen King, but then I started thinking about Stephen King because their books are kind of the same. . . . So I stopped reading those because they started getting boring. I used to read Danielle Steel. I loved her books! But then as she started getting popular, her writing changed and she started getting boring to me!

. . . Then I went on a kick with Sidney Sheldon. I loved his books! Oh, I loved his books! I loved *If Tomorrow Comes*![3] That was a crazy book! That woman and her partner, they were thieves. He taught her how to steal, then she learned how to be a international thief. And they were bad! And they went all over the world! . . . You learned about different places. You learned about jewelry, about how you can have beautiful jewelry but it's fake, and how they can make it look fake. And I never knew that. And then *Master of the Game*.[4] Oh, man! That book was the bomb! You had to really, really love to read books to read that one. It was long! Her name was Kate, and it was about diamond fields in Africa. Her father took over diamond fields, and there was murder behind it. . . . And she had to take over the business . . . and she became the master of the game. A shrewd businesswoman! . . . The woman had it going on! She did! It was a wonderful book!

Then Sheldon wrote sex books. Oh, my goodness [shouting]! This one book, *79 Park Ave.*, was a sex book.[5] . . . You know how you walk in a room and see your mother naked or something and you go, ooooh [laughing]. That's what I did! I didn't know they did that kind of stuff. I learned about another side of sex in that book. It showed me that sex is not ugly. Sex can be fun. Sex can be enjoyable. And it gives me a sadness because I've never had that. I've never enjoyed sex. I've never had fun with sex. I just lay there and whatever you do to me, that's what you do. That's all I knew. I knew to shut my mouth and let him do whatever he wanted to do. . . . I felt that I was worthless enough to where I didn't care. . . . I never got any enjoyment out of sex because I was never taught the right way of sex.

And reading about it, that's why to me it's like, wow! You know, I've never had a man give me a orgasm or anything like that. I never knew about masturbating until I came to prison, even though you're not supposed to do it [laughing]. I never knew about those things. I never had a man rub my body or give me massages or anything like that, or just rub my arm. None of those, you know, nice things that you do. I've never had anybody do anything like that to me. And to read about those things? I felt sad, you know. But then, I was like, well that's all right. That's all right because now I know. Now I know that you can be intimate with a person without having the penetration. You can have a man kiss your cheek, or just run their hand through your hair, or just tell you that you're pretty or you're beautiful and not have to feel that you have to give them something in return for it. . . . I've never had a man tell me I was pretty or anything like that. I've always been told I was ugly. "You're ugly. You're ugly. Your eyes are too big, you know, your nose is too big, you're ugly." So I've never cared how I looked or anything like that.

. . . But today, I care about the kind of underwear I wear, you know, whether it's cotton, or whatever fabric I put on, you know, I notice those things because the woman's body is different from the man's. Big difference! I've learned how to take care of myself to where if I want to look nice, I'm going to do what I need to do for me. Not for them or my child, for me. I learned all these things from all the books that I read. Even the spiritual books I read, I learned to love me and not worry about what someone thinks about how I smell . . . or how I speak. I used to worry about if I'm saying the right words. Do I sound educated? Do I sound stupid? Do I sound ignorant? I used to worry about those type things, so I just kept my mouth shut and I wouldn't say anything. I wouldn't talk. A wallflower, that's what I was. I was there but I wasn't there. I always tried to stay invisible.

I also like V. C. Andrews's books. She wrote about incest. You learned about incest and how . . . it was always kept in the closet, behind closed doors. Skeletons in the closet that people sometimes never, never find out. And then when a family finds out, they still keep hushing it up, but they still keep doing it and keep doing it from generation to generation to generation. And it was sad but it's true. It's really, really true. . . . It touched on the things that happened with me when I was younger, about families don't tell things. Whatever business is in the family, it's nobody's business outside of the house. You don't speak about what goes on. . . . It made me see that it still happens. It's not stopped. . . . You know, some men still put the fear of God in women, and some women die behind it, and there's still that fear, but you can't die behind it if you open up your mouth and say something. Some people [will say], "If you say this, I'll hurt your mama, I'll leave your mom," and "He'll break up the family," and "You don't do that to family," you know. And some children still have that, and some have to wait until they get older for that to come out. And that's the sad part that there's still that fear today. . . . My heart goes out to people because I can relate so well to a lot of them. But some women still won't speak out. . . . They're embarrassed, they're ashamed. You know, [some people say to them,] "Wow, you let your brother do that to you? What else did you let him do? . . . I don't know if I want you over my house. You might try to take my father." It puts a stigma on them. It really does.

. . . This year was the first time I've ever put myself into Black History Month.[6] I would always be a participant in it, but I never was a person that researched or studied it. So I worked at the rec department in Marysville. And my job was a program aide. I was to create programs. . . . So I did a booth of black history. And I drew this big gigantic tree out of paper. I made a tree of branches and roots. And I researched, I had to go to the library and read all about the blacks, from the inventors to the people that were in politics. People back in slavery time, I went in and researched all that. And I learned things that I never knew. It was amazing. I had to read about my history a little bit more than I've ever read before. I was reading a book about black authors. A book about where did the roots of African American music come from. I read about the '6os. Okay, how did African Americans come into television? How did they come into radio? I read about singers, about opera singers. About how the president, you know, used different black leaders. I read about Frederick Douglass. I read about poets. I just, my mind was just boggled down with all of this stuff! And I read about civil rights and everything, and I'm like, wow!

. . . I had to do a trivia about black history where people come in and had to research. Well, what do you know about black history? How well do we understand our roots? They said, "Well, we saw the movie *Roots*. We don't need to know no more" [laughing]. And I was like, "I do. I need to learn more." So I learned about a lot of the roots of black history. And I read in magazines about sports. Okay, I went everywhere, and from this side of the wall all the way around was nothing but, and the gym was yeah yeah big. BIG, okay, and oh my goodness, I had so much information. And I still had information after it was over with. I still had a big folder of information that I had nowhere to put it. So what I did was I built a tree in the admission unit, where people have to stay when they first come in prison, and I put all the information on it.

. . . And the next month was women's month, March, and I researched that, and I went through all walks of life. There was no barriers. I went everywhere, to all the cultures, and I didn't limit it to anything. Japan, I went to Spain, I went just everywhere, Hawaii, every place. About women and all the things—astronauts and everything—a woman does. Also from back in the western days. Even homemakers, the women who made women's suffrage, all the women. Nothing was untouched. I even went biblical and from the time women began until today. It was like, "Well black women didn't . . ." Yes they did. They were back then, too. . . . It just blew my mind all the things about women, how they made a pathway for women today.

. . . I like little journals. They're nice to keep up with different things that happen in your life, like somebody's born, I got a telephone call, or you know, something different, special things. The only thing about it is that . . . you have to write them and tear them up because accumulating them, you can't keep them all. So you have to pick and choose what you really write inside. . . . I keep it for the end of the year, and then I'll throw it away. . . . It's not something I write every, every day. It has to be if something happened, like I got a chance to talk to my daughter. See, that's important. That's a special thing. Or if an accident happened, I would write that down, and just a little note to myself of this happened this day or we had Bill Glad's ministry come in. . . . Or if they had a guest speaker and if it was somebody that was real popular, I would write their names. I don't take up a whole page of writing a whole bunch of stuff. 'Cause all I would have to do is look at what it says and then remember why I wrote it. I just keep little different notes about certain things in life.

'Cause when I get out of here, I want to write a book 'cause I've had so much in my life that's been going on. . . . Since I've been in prison, so many things have changed within me in my life. My attitudes, just me period, how I think, act, and do things. . . . I want to write [a book] because of the drug and alcohol situation in my life. Because of the cries of help that I tried to give my family, and they wouldn't [listen], because they felt that I was grown. I wasn't a grown woman. To me grown is you really, really got your head together and your life together and you know which way you're going and what steps you're taking to get there. To me, that's when you're grown up. You know, you're taking that responsibility to move forward. I had alcohol problems, and that alcohol problem was really, really taking me down. And then I had a relationship that was not healthy. It wasn't healthy for me, him, or my children. And I had a family that was, "You do not tell your business outside." I don't care what it is. Family do not tell their business. So it was like my mouth was shut. But that hurt me more than it helped me.

. . . And that's one of the reasons why I wanted to write that because of the events that led up to me coming to prison. Because there were very, very, very serious things going on, and not speaking up about it . . . I should have pushed more because look at what happened. Look where I ended up. I lost my children, and I basically lost my life. . . . I had to go back and find the things that impacted me more to change me for today. Because if I couldn't go back and face my past and all the things that happened, then I couldn't help me today. I couldn't help myself or my child.

. . . Everyone from teenagers on up [could read my book]. Basically, it's a book about coming to terms with life. And life choices. Learning to know who you are. To know what's a healthy choice and an unhealthy choice. And not, oh my goodness, not let anyone deter you from doing what's right, not only for yourself, because whatever I did, it affected everybody. It affected my whole family. It affected my child. It affected the judges. It affected the attorney. It affected everybody. It affects the community, because they were told certain things, and half of it wasn't even true. But because I was told to shut up, none of the things that should have been said were said. So I'm just looking at that as there's a time to be silent. And there's a time not to.

. . . . I don't want [my book] to be long, but I want it to be real. I want it to be very informative. And I want it to be where they will understand life goes on regardless of where you're at, whether you're locked up, you know. Anything that happens in prison, the same thing happens in society except that we're a closed community. That's the only difference. [People say that] just because you come to prison, you always think like a criminal. That's not true either. Some people want to go out and make a life and be productive, honest citizens. Regardless of the things that have happened to me since I've been here, regardless of all the letdowns or the troubles I've gotten into or any of that stuff, I still have that desire and I know without a doubt, I can be a productive citizen. You know, I can live a law-abiding life. Why? Because I know my past, and I have no reason to live it again. And I know me today. And I know which way I'm going, and I know how to get there.

3 Olivia

—ᴍ—

Life Narrative

"It was a bad road that I was on"

I WAS BORN in Ohio. I was raised by my mother, mostly my mother. She was single. It was a single home. I have two brothers, one older and one younger. Family life was real hard. Tight with money. Mom wasn't home a lot, so we basically kind of fended for ourselves and had to make it to school, you know. And we was on welfare. You know, wasn't money for lunches, so we had special lunch tickets and school clothes and all that. It was tight with money, so growing up like that makes a lot of pressures in the home. Not really pressures. It was more like, it wasn't really no definite rules, so we just did what we wanted to do, you know. So that's pretty much how I grew up.

School was really bad for me because of the money situation. I didn't have what the other girls had so, you know, I slacked. I skipped out. I didn't feel like I belonged anywhere in a certain place. Where I did belong was with people like me. On the same poverty level, you know. So we all ended up skipping out just to start smoking cigarettes and hanging out in the alleys and stuff. So I didn't really care for school.

The joys in my life are my family. My mother and my brothers. They're a joy, you know, because we're tight. We're close, and I trust them, and there's always unconditional love, so it's a joy now that I look back on it, even though we had our hardships. . . . I've had an important relationship with my children's father. My two girls. We met in high school, dropped out together. Moved in together. Lived together for four years. So that was an important relationship. Then when we split up, I got into another relationship with another man. Didn't have no children with him. I started drinking when I was with him, so we split up. He split up with me 'cause of my drinking. And then I met another man, which is my third child's father. That was a very important relationship; yeah, it's probably the reason I'm here.

In 2004, I gave temporary custody of my kids to my mother. I gave her the custody because I was using. So I said, you know, something's got to happen. So mom said, "I'm going to take them for you." So she got the two girls at that time. I hadn't yet had my son. So I raised them until they were about two or three, yeah, well, one and two. Then I gave them to my mom. So, they're still young. Because they live [far away], my mom can't make it up here with them. And she's got a block on her phone; it's a money issue. You know, they're writing me letters and stuff and coloring me pictures, and you know, it's contact, but it's not communication with them. There's a difference.

[Violence has been part of my life,] very much so. From the time I was a baby until I entered the [prison] gates. The violence on the end of it wasn't my relationships. It was my mother's relationship with her boyfriend at the time. I was between four and five when it started. She was with this man. He physically violenced my mother, physically violenced me and my brothers, and was sexually abusive to me until I was in second grade. So that would be about five to eight, in between there somewhere. He was physically abusive to all of us and then sexually molested me and things. And then my relationships with the children's fathers were all violent. They was all violent relationships. You know, we had domestic abuse.

. . . I want to [participate in a group about domestic violence], but I don't trust a lot of the people in here with my information. Like the women I live with, I don't trust them because I've had roommates that I've lived with, you know, and I would talk about it to them. And they would use it later for ammunition against me 'cause I still have contact with this person. . . . There have been things that have been said to hurt me, not trying to help me. I understand the difference. There's a line. There's a very fine line with the women that go through domestic abuse, there's a very fine line of who you can—especially inside here—who you can tell about your situation. There's a fine line, so even if you know it's confidentiality in a group, that's all good and well, but it don't always stand like that. You know, they tell the next person. The next thing I know, if I'm having communication with this man, they're over here telling, "Well, she's still talking to him." You know what? That's a personal decision that I choose to make for whatever healing process I'm going through. We all got our own laws. So some people look down upon it if you tell them you're going through that situation, and then you turn around and be talking to the same person. So I don't trust a lot of people in group settings. I've talked about it just to a couple of friends and things, but not to the extent that I really want to. I think I'll know when it's the right time and the right person.

. . . I've talked to a lady before. I kind of, you know, briefed her on my situation and things. And the first thing they ask you is, "Do you want to take some meds?" . . . So I said okay, let me start these meds. She put me on a psychotropical drug. I did it for a couple of days, and it made me feel worse. It put me out of my character. So I stopped taking it, and I went to see her. When I told her I wanted to stop the medicine, she said, "Do you want to take anything else?" I said no. . . . But every time you went there, that's what they asked you. They figured you need some medication. I'm like, "No, I don't need any medication."

[Then] she said, "We're going to put you on a treatment team to share. You're going to see a doctor." . . . I see him once a month, but he don't ask me anything; he just surfaces. He just says, "How are you doing?" You know, the basic surface things. So I've never gotten into it with any of them over there other than the intake lady. . . . I got a long sentence. I got a big number, so they always ask me, "Well, how do you feel about your time?" I'm okay with it. That's what they're maybe seeking is if I'm doing okay about my sentence. "What do you plan on doing? How are you gonna get through this sentence?" You know, they just surface. It's a hard situation . . . 'cause sometimes I feel like really, what can they do to help me? I realize it's a self-process because, I know this because of my childhood sexual abuse and then with domestic violence. I tried when I was younger with child sexual abuse to go to counseling, and it just never brought anything out then. . . . If I want to talk about [my abuse], I'm sure she'd find me a liaison, but I've never wanted to do that yet. I'm trying to work it out on my own.

[Drugs and alcohol have] definitely been part of my life. Alcohol started when I was eighteen. Well, actually, it started when I was fourteen. We used to steal it, me and my brother and our little friends. We used to steal bottles from the grocery, and we'd skip school and get drunk. So then it was more of a play thing situation. But then I guess really now when I think about it, it was already an addiction then. . . . When I turned eighteen, I was living with my girls' father. We didn't have children then, but I dropped out of school and stuff, just 'cause I was using cocaine and drinking beer heavily. And I was able to get in the bars at eighteen 'cause I knew some people that would let me get into some of the clubs that I wasn't supposed to be in. . . . So I was drinking heavily, heavily when I was eighteen. That went on from eighteen until right after I turned twenty-one when I first got pregnant with my first child. That went on for five years. Just going to the bars, getting so drunk, driving home. I lived thirty miles from the bar. I don't even remember me driving home. I'd wake up and I'm like, how did I get here?

I had [my first] baby. She was only a week old and I said, "Mom, will you babysit so I can go out?" And I didn't come home for three days, on a binge. 'Cause I didn't drink the whole time I was pregnant with her. You know, I did good. I didn't drink for the whole time I was pregnant. And she was only a week old and I went on a binge. So then I started drinking for about a couple months, got pregnant again with the same father. . . . And then with her I experimented a little bit with crack when I first was pregnant with my second. I experimented with it for a couple of weeks. I knew that was dead wrong, so I stopped. I drank until I was five months pregnant with her. And then I had her. I stayed sober for a little while. Then I got a job in the bar, and it started all over again for another few months.

I got pregnant again with my third. That's when I had the abortion. So that's why I say I have one deceased because I still count him now that I think about him. I took his life. I had the girls back to back already. I think [my second daughter] was only three months old when I found out I was pregnant again with the same man. And I just decided at that point, you know, I love these two little girls that I had. I was raising them at that time. I was drinking, but I was raising them. I would get off work, go get drunk, pay the babysitter, go pick them up and all that. I realized I didn't want another baby at that point, and so I decided not to have him.

What happened after that, I came home from the clinic. My friends, they'd already been into the dope scene, smoking crack. I always watched them do it, and you know, it didn't bother me 'cause I liked to drink. They liked to smoke. Well, I picked up the pipe that night, and I hadn't put it down until I walked in this gate.

When I started smoking crack at that point, I had just had the abortion. And I met a man. He supplied my habit. Of course, that comes at a price. So I had to start selling dope. So the whole time I was selling dope, I was smoking dope. I'm doing this from 2003 'til 2006. Selling dope, smoking dope. Well, in between there in 2004, I got pregnant with my son. I smoked my whole pregnancy with him. He was born crack cocaine addicted. And the state took him. Gave him to my mother 'cause she already had my other two, 'cause I had to sign them over in 2004. Before I found out I was pregnant, I had signed them over. I smoked the whole pregnancy with [my son]. Then the night that he went home with my mom, I had a choice. I was at the hospital. I could have went home with my babies or I could have went home with my dope man. I chose to go home with the man. So my mom went home with the babies. And that's where it stands now. All three of my kids are with my mom. And my ex, he's in trouble like me.

... The lack of the father-daughter relationship [was important in my life]. My dad was in my life, but he wasn't in my life until I was fourteen, so at that point I was already wilding out a little bit. My mom tried to send me to him for punishment. He was so soft because of his lack of duties throughout the years that he let me get away with more. And so when I needed something, I would run to my dad. "Here's $20 and get some of this, that, and all the other." Of course, I'm going to get my dope or my drugs and my alcohol, weed, cigarettes, whatever it was. And so I was a daddy's girl. And then we became really, really, really, really, really close. And it was a unhealthy relationship because we enabled each other, 'cause he smoked weed. I smoked weed. I started my dad smoking crack.

My father, he was an encouraging man. He was an alcoholic. So he was still trying to get his life, he was still trying to get his life together 'cause he came off the alcohol for a couple of years. But he relapsed. So his sisters were his only family living. They blamed me for his relapse, of course, because of my little addictions 'cause I was living with him, between him and the street. So they blame me a lot for his relapse, and it took them awhile to forgive me, which I don't really think I needed forgiveness for that. . . . It was a good relationship with him, but he passed away last year, so it was a loss. He's in a better place than I am. And I know he's happy that I'm not in the same situation that I was in because during my abuse, a lot of my abuse, I used to run to his house, you know, beat up, broken toes, fingers, legs, arms. And I would go to his house to hide from the perpetrator. And it killed him every time to see me walk in like that. But he would always open the door and take me in, and if I brought my old man over, he'd let him in. He couldn't stand him for nothing, but he would deal with it. And he supported me in that way. So I thank him a lot for that. He showed me a lot what it's like to get an education. He graduated, and he always was reading material. He was a smart man. So he was good in that aspect. He was a good teacher.

. . . I've got a little bit of time to serve so I know that I will work on my past issues to find out where it led up to that. Being in prison has been a blessing. I ain't got beat up. I don't have to chase dope. I don't have to worry about the bills. I've got to read a lot. I've got to find myself a little bit again after all these drugs this past ten years. Got to find myself a little bit. It's been a little lonely at times. 'Cause my family can't come to see me 'cause it's five hours away. You know, they're tight on money. But other than that, I mean, it's been a little nerve-wracking actually, because with my case, they took me back in September and gave me some more charges. So they added five more years onto my sentence. But I was expecting it, so it wasn't like any big surprise or anything. . . . So other than that, it's been really a blessing that I came here 'cause I know it was a bad road that I was on.

[Women come to prison] mostly for drugs and stemming from domestic violence issues. There's quite a few women here for killing their husbands, killing their lovers, or hurting their lovers. Quite a few women here for that, and there's quite a few people here for dope cases. I think in my own case, the men only had what you needed so we fought, and you stuck with him, you know, getting beat up or having to steal drugs to stay high. And I think women stay on drugs 'cause that's our outlet where there ain't no out.

. . . [What we need is] outreach, I mean on a personal level, if you know a sister and you know that she's in the same situation that I was in, try and let her know. . . . But if I knew somebody that was in my situation and I could reach out to her and say, "Look," you know, if she is on drugs, she's not going to want to hear it. She's not going to understand it. A lot of women are going to have to come here. They're gonna have to come here to save their own souls, to save their own life.

. . . What's next for me? School. See, that's what I stopped. That's where I went wrong. You know, if I would have got my stuff right then, I don't think that I would have been in the unhealthy relationships I was in. It all started in school. I found that one latch. He took me out and gave me money and drugs, and the relationships that I've had since then, it was just like that. . . . So what's next for me is to go back and get that education. The piece of paper, you know what I mean. That way I can go do whatever it is that I want to do. What it is that I want to do, I don't quite know yet.

—⟋⟍⟋—

Reading Narrative

*"If I'm going through a struggle,
I know that's the book to go find"*

I'M HAVING A lot of fun reading. . . . It's something to relax, you know. People can be talking in the room, listening to their TVs and music. I'm reading my books. I'm minding my business. So it just keeps me away from everybody else's drama. . . . I read every day. . . . I usually read two books a week. . . . I like new, contemporary books, like fresh stories. I just read one. It was about out in Beverly Hills. They're talking real fresh, you know, about the cell phones and the LCD screens and stilettos and Prada and all that. That was a good book. It was fresh, new, stylish, up-to-date. . . . [But] I don't want to read them type of [urban] books. What makes you want to read that when half that stuff in them books is what brought us here? . . . Why would you want to read a book called *Crackhead*? I mean, that's what brought 90 percent of us here, crack.

I go to the library about three times a week. . . . The first place I go is to the shelves from Cleveland Public Library. I prefer to read new books. I like it to where I can open a page, and it smell fresh. . . . I look for a brand new book that ain't even going to have a bend in the bind. I don't read hardbacks. I haven't read one since I've been locked up. It's more comfortable to read paperbacks. I lay in my bed all day long with a paperback. I can't get past the first chapter in a hard book.

. . . I read to keep my mind busy and I'm trying to get smart and trying to educate myself, and I think that's the only way I can do it right now. 'Cause I can't get into the process with GED here.[1] So I'm going to keep my mind busy by reading books. Even if it is just a love story, well at least I'm reading something, and it's sharpening my mind up a little bit, you know—how you think, how you talk, how you speak. . . . It's making your mind sharper, and with the all the drugs and things I've done over the years, I think I lost a lot of that sharpness.

. . . I'm a book freak, but I guess that's okay. So I joined the "Reading the Classics" here. It's a group they started. . . . They posted it up in a bulletin, and it said, "We will be starting 'Reading the Classics' if you would like to participate and join." . . . The employees that's here are donating the books. . . . They're all classics, and we go every Thursday night for an hour. [Martha] assigns us three or four chapters to read. She's an inmate. She says she's crazy over the classics. Six women are in it. We're gonna take about four weeks per book. We're going to read *Moby Dick*.[2] *Pavilion of Women*.[3] We read *Scarlet Letter*[4] and a couple of other ones. . . . She gives us little printouts. We each get a question. We all put our input in on it. . . . We had to write an essay because the institution wants to know what we're getting out of the books and what value does this book have on society. And how has this book changed your outlook or perceptions? . . . We have fun. We laugh. Some of them cry. Some of them cuss, you know, 'cause some of the characters in *Scarlet Letter* was kind of evil, so you got one girl in there, she's in there cussing.

. . . In county [jail] there's absolutely nothing to do. So we had a little library, and there's a lot of books, and I had a friend that read. She'd been down in county for a while, and she said, "Hey, look. It's a good book. Why don't you read it?" . . . We'd pass along books, and we'd talk about them and come in there and smile and say, "I know what's going to happen," you know, and mess with each other about, "Tell me what's going to happen." . . . So I got crazy addicted over books, right? I read nonstop twenty-four hours a day. I'd read until 4:00 in the morning, sleep 'til 5:00, and I was just reading a novel in two nights, you know. And sometimes in one day I'd read the whole book. And I was reading four and five books a week. I was reading a lot of Danielle Steel and John Grishams, them little books you find in county libraries. Not no self-help. Novels, stories, and I liked them because they took me out.

. . . I did like to read John Grisham. I like that whole attorney scene and, you know, murder for hire, ransoms, and flying overseas, $200,000,000 at stake. I like that kind of stuff. I read quite a few of his. But they're all about the same after a while. . . . [I don't read them much anymore] because they have all hardbacks here. . . . I really enjoy his books, but they just don't have them in paperback here. I cannot force myself to pick up a hardback. It's not comfortable. But you know what? If they had a paperback, and it was fresh, I'd read them.

. . . If it's a good crime novel, say like a John Grisham book, a lawyer book . . . I kind of look at the aspects of their case and how they work, to compare to my situation, how my lawyer did. . . . I can see where my lawyer would have made a certain move or said a certain thing for his benefit instead of mine. . . . I don't read the law library books, so I read it in there. . . . I'm not trying to figure out an appeal or nothing like that. Because it's past that time, and I just wouldn't even want to go there anyways. But I could look and see how the world really is. How the back scene is. You know, something I didn't see then, because then I was just coming off of drugs. I was in the corner. They had me backed in a corner, you know, but I can see when I read some of these books why my lawyer would say, "Just take this deal, and let's just get on with this." 'Cause he was court-appointed, and he was an appellate lawyer. . . . And so I kind of see what it is now. You know, which is okay 'cause I'm already sentenced and done, but I guess maybe the next person down the line when I get out, if they was ever in trouble, I could offer them advice, what to do in that type of situation.

. . . And Danielle Steel, I liked her because she had this setting, it was a romance. I guess it was a lot like what I had been looking for in my life. She would take the romance, and she moved it to Paris. And she talked a lot about Paris, and the whole falling in love phase or falling out of love phase. So I liked that. It was a different life. It was like a dream, you know. Like some kind of dream like that was me. . . . She opened me up to a new horizon a little bit about this handsome dark-haired man in Paris, and it really made me feel good. It kind of opened me up a little bit to another country. It opened me up even to that aspect of you really could fall in love. . . . Romance—I don't think anybody has a romance like mine [laughing], so I read those just to smile.

. . . And here's another thing, another factor. I dated black men most of my life. Well, in her books, they're really only the white man thing, you know what I mean? You just don't read a Danielle Steel novel and think there's a black man. So it made me wonder, you know, what would it be like to really have an honest relationship with an honest man? Black or white, but it kind of took me out of that mind frame, that "I had to have a black man" box. It kind of opened me up a little bit. . . . I was molested and raped as a child. . . . I think that him being a white man did it. I think that kind of prejudiced me. So when I was thirteen, I had a black boyfriend. Well, I gave him my virginity. And ever since then, I have just been attracted to black men. I hang around black men. I like black men. . . . I don't know if it was defiance or a rebel thing or because where I'm from there weren't a lot of black men there. . . . I continued to read [Danielle Steel] for a while. Then it got monotonous after about, you know, the seventh novel.

. . . I like southern tales. Like out in the country, little farm girls that fall in love with the quarterback. Karen Kingsbury, I've read a couple of her books. . . . She's good. A Christian writer. . . . I discovered her in county [jail]. *Oceans Apart*,[5] I didn't read the whole book, but what I did read was really good. It was emotional, so I stopped. But then I read another one from her. I read *A Time to Dance* when I got up here. She's got one, *A Time to Embrace*.[6] I just like the stories. To see if it compares to mine or if I can add some of their truth to mine. I like to read stuff where kids grow up, marry, and you know, they have a good life. I like to read that. It makes you smile. It makes you cry. Brings out joy, tears of joy, and it kind of replaces a little bit of the hurt I've felt, you know. It kind of gives me something back a little bit.

. . . 'Cause in her books, they reconcile. In *A Time to Dance,* the subtitle is *A Story of Reconciliation.* They made it through this situation of infidelities and kids going off to college. It kind of reconciles yourself at the end of the book. You can look and see where these people have been even though they lived a little bit higher class of life. In the book, the parents are both school-teachers and coaches. They have money and stuff. The situation wasn't a lot of difference from mine. So it kind of just gives me a joy to see if they reconcile in the end, and the family didn't get tore apart, which gives me something back, 'cause a lot of families do get tore apart. And it lets me know there's hope for me later 'cause I might meet a man that's gonna take care of me like this man's taking care of her. But at the same time, I don't never get off that reality line neither to where I might fall into that trap again in another abusive relationship or something like that.

. . . I don't like to read smut. You know, like sex scenes. . . . If I read them type of books where sexual relations are going on, it makes me uncomfortable. . . . And I can't read a real sad childhood book and then another one. If I'm reading a real sad childhood book, sometimes I might stop. But if I read one like that, the next one's going to be a good one. You know, a love novel, something different. Not too much negative. But not too good to be true, either.

. . . I got one book that I really liked. It was by Jude Deveraux. It's called *[An] Angel for Emily*.[7] It was a romance, and I just thought it was the sweetest thing. . . . She accidentally hits [a man] with her car one night. And he tells her, "You can't hurt me. I'm an angel." . . . It goes through the whole story, you know, he's following her. She's like, "Get away from me," 'cause she had a boyfriend and he was bad to her. And this guy knew everything about her. He called himself Michael. He told her things from her past, so she wouldn't let him go. Plus, they made him real sexy in the book, you know what I mean? It was like a dream. It was a real good book to me. It was a dream come true. She married him in the end. They both died. They ended up getting in a car wreck or something. But they ended up dying together. . . . He didn't have a very good vocabulary because he was an angel. . . . And so he would say little funny things, like he would call this a pew or a table or something different than what it was. So it was humor. It was romantic. It was dreamy. It was sexy. And it ended up happily ever after. So it was just a good book. When I took that one back, I said, "I'm going to read this one again." It just touched my heart.

. . . On the outside, I would go to the library with my dad. And I would pick up something that looked good, and I'd get a lot of material. And then I would get so confused with it I would say let me take all this back. . . . I went through a spell, I think eight weeks, where I was reading self-help books. You know, about the domestic relationships that I had, and I was trying to find out about my childhood. I was getting these books that I didn't understand. And I wanted some way to understand them. So I would get them and read parts of them and then get frustrated 'cause it would start pulling these emotions out of me that I didn't want to feel, that I wanted to feel but I didn't know how to handle. So I would get frustrated with it, and I would take the books back and go to the bar instead. . . . I'm trying to do this thing all on my own, and I'm trying to read this material and really I don't even know what it is I'm looking for. So I feel just cluttered, and then I just have to throw it all back, you know, and then I'd feel like I can't accomplish anything.

. . . And I still feel that way today a lot. I'll be reading something that I need to be educated on, and it will pull these feelings up, and they'll get right to here [hand gesture]. I feel real ambitious about it, and I want to read it and write on it. But then I just sit down mentally, you know, and I have to take everything I got and throw it back in the bin. . . . I prefer a story. But I also know that if I want to help myself, it's necessary that I have a self-help book, too. . . . [But] a lot of times it's feelings that I don't want to handle at that time. Sometimes I'll read, and it'll bring up, oh, I remember when this happened to me, and then I get burned out. Then I'll have to go back to my regular story.

. . . They've got a very good spiritual library, I can say that. I like to read spiritually uplifting material. . . . I go [to the spiritual library] and pick up little poetry books. And right now I've got a book that somebody lent to me that's called *I Never Told Anyone*.[8] I call it a self-help book, but it's written by women who are survivors of childhood abuse, sexual abuse. And I like to get books like that from there. I like Joyce Meyer. Max Lucado. . . . A couple of titles are *In My Father's House*[9] and *Come Thirsty*.[10] . . . In *Come Thirsty*, he uses scripture, like "I'll give you everlasting water." He writes a whole book about that little passage. . . . Max Lucado, he's not really talking about his life. He's talking about his point of view. You know, it's pretty straightforward. It's not saying, "I think" or "You should think." He's just saying it from somebody's point of view. Now Joyce Meyer, she speaks it from her biography, you know what I mean. She speaks from her experiences. That's the difference between them, I think.

When I first started reading Joyce Meyer, I did not appreciate her work. And I went into the spiritual library one day and three of the old-timers, they were sitting in there. And I turned in Joyce Meyer's books. . . . I went in, and I'm like, "Here, I'm returning this Joyce book." She's like, "You read it?" 'Cause she's a real nice librarian. I said, "No, 'cause I got frustrated with it. And you know, I don't like the way she writes." That's what I said. "I don't like the way she writes." I don't even know what I was talking about. She's like, "Well," and then all three ladies that were sitting there, the older ladies, they all put down their books and they were all looking like, "You don't like Joyce Meyer?" I'm like, "No, I don't like her." They was like, "What? Did something hit home with you?" And I was like, "Okay. All right. I'll see you later." I walked out and then it crossed my mind: there was a reason they was all sitting in there, and then when I said it, everybody looked at me. . . . I walked out and walked right back in and picked the book back up and checked it back out. Went back, you know, started to read the book, and then I really enjoyed it. . . . I kind of related with her sexual abuse. *Beauty for Ashes*[11] is what it was. I still haven't read it all the way through. It's like it touched home with me. . . . It was the reality that I was trying to deny, you know, trying to hide behind. [But the second time] I paced myself. I took my time with the book.

And then I ended up reading that book *Battlefield of the Mind*.[12] I've read that book probably five times in the past year. Every time I start to get frustrated about something, I'll go to one of those verses, and I'll read in-depth into it. . . . You can ask my roommates. They probably get so annoyed with my books sometimes. 'Cause sometimes I'll have eight books on my table. You know, I'll have five in my lockbox. If it's at my disposal, if it's right there and I'm feeling down spiritually, I'll grab the book and I'll read a little bit until I feel better about my situation. If I'm going through a struggle, I know that's the book to go find.

Then I read Anne Graham Lotz's book. That's Billy Graham's daughter. And I read one of her books, and I've read it probably six times. It's called *My Heart's Cry*.[13] It's a really, really, really, good book. It studies John 13 through the 20s somewhere. And it's really good. She's good with words. She knows how to speak, and you can hear it and understand it and relate to it, and quote it later and remember. I really wish they'd get another down here. I'm sure she's got one. But that whole Billy Graham library selection, I'll always look 'cause I see on the binder "Billy Graham Selections," 'cause it's got a gold band on it so you can recognize it about anywhere. If I see it, I'll always pull it and look and see who the writer is, 'cause there are six different writers, and they all write spiritual.

I go to Women's Spirituality here on Monday nights. . . . It's really good. We're reading a book right now called *Blessed Is She*[14] about the Virgin Mary and the conception. . . . [But] lately, I've been kind of shying away from [spiritual books] a little bit because I think sometimes this has been an issue with me. If I read too much of something, it isn't good for you. I'll get frustrated with the whole spirituality thing. And then I'll stop reading them totally. So now I've kind of backed away from spiritual books a little bit. Well lately, I haven't read any, but I'll say maybe three hours a month I read spiritual material. I guess it's too many points of views. I'm getting too many different authors, reading their point of view. Too many points of view is confusing me, making me question myself, and then giving me convictions that probably aren't even realistic.

. . . I'm going to take part in a program they got going on here, an essay contest. It's called the National Women's Month Essay Contest. It's outlining one or two serious problems that [affect] women in your house, neighborhood, or city and what we as women can do to help them. So it's a five hundred–word essay. I'm trying to get quite a bit of factual information. If I can't find it, I'm just going to come up with something. I've never even done a legit essay in my life as far as I can remember. In school I blew them off. So I'm using my GED study book to try and outline a rough draft, which my rough draft is on domestic violence of myself. And then I'm going to decide if I'm going to do domestic violence or childhood sexual abuse. . . . I'm just trying to find what I got more facts on in these books right now. So it's a little confusing. It's a little much. But I'm going to work through it somehow. I want to get this essay done, and I'm going to get me a prize.

[In a later interview]: I chose childhood sexual abuse, and I had this book. I forget who the author is. I didn't pay attention. It told some statistics in there, and then it got to some stories. Some girls gave firsthand experiences of what was happening in their homes. I read a few into it, and I stopped reading it. I got what I needed out of it and closed it. So I did this essay about recovery, first about childhood sexual abuse, the statistics, the results, and then the end, but the recovery part was real short in mine 'cause I guess I haven't totally recovered myself. But I think it kind of helped me a little bit, you know, to connect to others. You need to organize other survivors. To find a voice and to grow in our own sexuality.

Reading that book, I didn't go too far into it 'cause it brings back memories for me, and then I have two young ones at home. Same age I was when I was molested. . . . They're out there, and they're vulnerable just because of their age; they're vulnerable just because of their gender. So when I start reading that material, I just think, in the back of my mind, it's just something chewing at me saying, "What if this is happening with my kids?" . . . I know the story. I've lived it. I've survived it. There's nothing I can do really inside this wall. . . . I'm kind of stuck between a rock and a hard place at this point in my life because my daughters are at home that I can't protect, that I don't know what's going on because I don't have a lot of contact with my family members. I don't know who babysits them. I don't know who's in that house around them. . . . I could talk to my mom about it to help me out, but I don't think she fully understands it herself about what happened to me. So she don't like to talk about it. She just want to cover it. . . . I think if I reached out to her like that, she would assume I was assuming. . . . She's like, "Well, how could you ever accuse anybody?" I said, "Well, you never thought about that when it was happening to me. That's why what happened to me happened to me because you didn't assume that it would happen. But it happened. Quit ignoring that fact."

And for me to just jump out, I'm in the penitentiary. I'm a criminal. I'm a crackhead. Not now, not anymore. I'm recovered now. But you know, that's the thing they still see me as. They don't see me as a serious mother. When I'm trying to be serious with [my mom], she says I'm just assuming things. . . . She don't know it, and I would never tell her that, but she makes my life difficult. And I know she don't have to make it peachy keen 'cause I put myself here. She's raising my daughters, and I'm going to come home in five more years. But I would just pray that she wouldn't turn her head like she did when I was young.

. . . It's hard for me to move forward when I got this thing, you know, that issue just holding me back right here. I don't think, honestly, until I walk out the gate and I got my kids in my arms or until I see them in this visiting hall with the people they live with, . . . until I see them with my eyes, and I can look in my kids' eyes and know that everything's okay, I can probably then go ahead and move forward a little bit. But until then, there's nothing I, I mean, for myself personally, my recovery's I think pretty much done. I think I'm recovered from my childhood sexual abuse. I think I did recover from that. But there's a whole 'nother story coming up. It's real hard. I'm sure people are stuck in my situation too that feel the same way that probably want to talk about it. . . . [But] I don't like to tell people that I'm worried about my kids at home. They would say, "Well, why?" Then I have to go into that. And then I know they're going to say all we can do is hope and pray for the best. That's all I can do. So other than that, I don't know what there really is. With counseling and all that, it's not like they can call their angels and say, "What's going on?" . . . As far as me, I think I'm kind of recovered. I'm just scared for [my kids].

4 Denise

—ᴍ—

Life Narrative

"I can't even imagine my day without a mall"

I WAS BORN in a little town called [X], North Carolina, and we was raised in a farm atmosphere. As a young girl, like from nine to fifteen, I worked in tobacco. I picked tobacco, picked cotton, picked peaches, cucumbers. We did that type of job. Those were the only jobs actually that were available to black children in this little town. Still kind of racist a little bit. . . . Actually, it's the town, some years ago, back in I think it was '96, an Imperial chicken factory exploded there and killed a lot of people in there. Yeah, I lost four cousins in that fire 'cause it's a little small town. It's the only factory in our town, and it only employed maybe ninety people, and out of those ninety, like seventy-five were injured. Yeah, so I grew up there.

There's eight boys and four girls in my family. And I'm number twelve. So by the time I came along, most of my brothers and sisters were like in their twenties. My mother worked very hard. She cleaned houses, and then she went back to school and became like a nurse's assistant. My father, I never knew him to work. He owned like what we call a juke joint and sold bootleg liquor and had card games and things like that. And I was the only little girl that was allowed to go in this place because it was my daddy's place, so I could go in there. And my daddy was an alcoholic, and I used to take care of him when he got drunk.

. . . I had a simple childhood. I wouldn't change it for nothing in the world. We was poor and didn't know it. We grew everything we ate. We raised hogs. We raised chickens. We had a blackberry patch, strawberry patch, you know, all around the house. . . . We didn't have running water. We didn't have heat. We had a outhouse, but eventually when I was about maybe ten, thirteen, we started getting those things 'cause my brothers and sisters were working now, and they were sending money back home. And they were having a bathroom put in the house for mama, and we got running water and things like that.

And a lot of people don't believe somebody in their forties lived like that. But it was like a place left in time, you know, and I loved it. I cherish those memories 'cause I don't think too many people will ever experience that kind of life again.

And I didn't get toys. I used to get like animals or things somebody made for me, you know. And when I went outside to play, we played catching snakes or catching praying mantis, who could catch the biggest frog. And I got a pony one time when I was about twelve. And you know, I used to ride him through the cornfields. I had a pet goat. I had a pet duck. I had things like that, not store-bought stuff. The only thing we got from the store was moon pies. My mother went to town once a month to buy flour, sugar, and lard, and she would buy a box of moon pies. And it would be twelve in the box, and we used to all get one. Moon pies always were special things to me 'cause we always got those moon pies.

Four of my brothers were in the service in Fort Bragg. Everybody went to Fort Bragg. And I used to love when they'd come home on the weekends 'cause I would get a quarter to shine these buckles on their boots, and all their friends would come home with them, and I would get so many quarters. And my oldest brother worked at Perdue, and he used to pay me to wash his apron and his boots. And I used to make little change like that to run back and forth to the corner store.

And my daddy was a gambler, and because I would be allowed in the club, I used to go down to his little joint, and he would be gambling and I would get all his money. Every time he went, he'd let me get all the money, and I'd get on my bike and ride it back up to the hill and bury it out in the backyard. My mama used to be, "Give me that money so I can get you all something to eat." And I'd say, "Nu-uh. I'm saving this money 'til my daddy sober up." And then the next morning when he would sober up, I'd be like, "Daddy, I saved all your money," you know.

. . . First we had our own school, like the black kids had our own school. And when we went to school, we didn't have to wear shoes to school, you know. Everybody knew everybody, and then when [de]segregation came in, they tore down our school, and we had to go to school with the white people, and that was my first experience with white people. I was in the sixth grade the first time we had to go to school with white people. And it was kind of, it was new. Everybody was excited. . . . We in our little town had to catch the bus to these schools.

And then when I got about fifteen, I was acting up in school because we had this boy named Johnny. He lived with his grandmother, and his grandmother died, so somebody in town was supposed to take care of him. So my mother took him in, so Johnny kind of grew up with us like a brother. Then when I got fifteen, he started trying to mess with me. And my sister lived here in Cleveland. So I called her and I kept telling her, "Johnny keep messing with me." And she say, "Well, you want to come up here to live?" And I had been working in tobacco so I had that money, and I caught the Greyhound bus to Cleveland and came up here to live up here with her.

So I did my twelfth grade here in Cleveland. I came here on Valentine's Day in 1978, and I did the rest of my school year out, and I became a straight-A student up here, and I did good in everything. . . . And then I got into my first boyfriend. I was still a virgin. I'd never even kissed a boy. I was straight out of the tobacco fields, you know. And I met this guy here when I was in the twelfth grade. He was nine years older than me. I was with him for fifteen years. And he beat me every day. My sister decided to move back to North Carolina after I graduated, but I felt like I was grown. Plus I got a boyfriend, so there's no way I'm going back to North Carolina. And when she left me up here, he became real abusive. He beat me for fifteen years.

And he used to make me go shoplifting. I'm a shoplifter. I've been to prison five times for it. And the way it started, when I had my first daughter in 1980, a friend of mine bought her this cutest little dress, and it was too little for her. And she got it from the May Company, and I went to take it back, and they gave me the money for it. It was $63.00, and he was with me. And he said, "Oh, you can get one of those in your purse and we can take it to the next May Company and get that money." So he unzipped my purse and put it in my purse. So as it escalated and time went on, he became demanding, making me go to the store and get stuff and take it to the next store.

And then he started sending me by myself to where the malls actually became a safe haven for me. I would take my daughter and go stay at the mall from the moment it opened 'til the moment it closed because I knew if I didn't come home with some money, he was going to beat me up. So I might as well prolong it as long as I could. While at the malls, I would steal stuff and return it and get this due bill, this merchandise voucher and shop with it so I would have something to do while I'm at the mall all day. And I would catch the bus in the winter from mall to mall to mall, scared to come without enough money, you know. And it became a habit for me. And I did that 'til 1989, and my mother passed in '89, and I finally got away from him in '89.

My day to day life, we didn't live together. I had my own place. I had no family in Ohio. In the morning, he would come over my apartment and be like, "You're going to the mall today. Get up. Get up. You gotta go to the mall today. I need $400. Can you be back here by 4:00?" And all I would say is, "Yeah, I'll get it. I'll get it." . . . At 4:00, I'm sitting on the couch. I'm scared 'cause I hadn't made but $150, so I know he going to be mad. . . . He'd snatch the money. "I told you what I needed. You can't do shit right. You can't do shit right. See, you wonder why I knock you upside your head." . . . So I'm back out on the bus going somewhere else before 9:00, before the malls close. . . . When I'm leaving out the door, I don't have a clue where I'm going. All I know is . . . if I can come up with another $100, it might be easier on me when I get home. . . . So I come home. I give him the money. . . . And he leave and I'm happy. I'm happy 'cause he happy now. He ain't mad with me no more. He might kiss me when he leave or something.

And that's how I went through my life. I called my mother and them, but I didn't want them to know he was treating me like that. I didn't want nobody to know I was stealing. When I went to prison for the first time in '85, my mother had never even knew I'd been in no trouble. . . . The social worker told me to call my mother. She kept asking me where was my family 'cause I was nine months pregnant, and she had gotten in touch with [my abusive partner], and he told her that that wasn't his baby. And she kept saying, "You gotta make arrangements for this baby." And I said, "I can't let my mother know I'm in jail. I don't want my mother to know I'm in jail." So she called me in her office and called my mother for me, and I told my mother I was in jail. . . . And my mama, she just said, "Don't cry, baby." She say, "It's gonna be all right. . . . We're gonna take care of the baby." But [my abusive partner] came to visit me [in county jail] and he told me he was going to come get the baby. . . . Well, when I had the baby, he told them that he didn't even know me. So my baby went to foster care until I called my mother again . . . and my mother came and got her.

. . . I did my time, and I came home. My mama wanted me to come to North Carolina, but I came to Cleveland. [My abusive partner] and his girlfriend kept my oldest daughter. And when I came home, he was living with his girlfriend, and I had to stay with his aunt. And then by about a week, it went right back to the same thing. "You need to get you some money so you can get you a place. You can't stay with my aunt forever." And he started sending me back out to the malls and fighting me within a week. . . . He had told me nobody would ever want me. Now I got two babies. Nobody else is going to ever want me. I done been to jail. Nobody's ever gonna want me. And then I had slept with him without marrying him, so I'm stuck with him for life. That's actually how I thought, that this is who I got to be with for life.

Just like I didn't let my family know, nobody could know that you're being treated like that. Basically at that time it was because he told me, "You don't tell what go on in the house. You don't talk to nobody." He used to tell me, "Don't talk to other women about what you do with your man or what's going on between you and your man." He used to come in the house and he would tell the girls, "You all go in the bedroom. Daddy needs to talk to mommy for a minute." I knew I was going to get beat then. And he would have me sit in the chair across from him like this, and he would teach me these life lessons or whatever. He would slap me, and he'd say, "You don't listen. I'm trying to teach you how to be a woman so you won't be stupid. Don't never tell nobody what's going on in your house. Don't never tell nobody nothing about what your man tell you!" You know, and he would slap me, and I would be like, "Well, why you gotta hit me?" He [was] like, "'Cause you don't listen. That's the only way you listen."

. . . He had gotten a girl pregnant. I believe he was in love with this girl. And she happened to call my house. . . . She said, "He told me you was gay and he hasn't been with you since his daughter was three months old." . . . And he came in my door with his key, and she heard him, and she said, "Well, I'll be damned" like that and hung up. So he left that night, and the next morning I was getting my girls ready for school, and he came in the door, and he said, "You took something from me I love. Now I'm going to take something from you." And he turned around and pointed a gun at my kids. And I beat him all over the living room. I saw my oldest daughter grab her sister and they balled up in a knot together with their daddy standing there pointing a gun at them. And I beat him all over my house. And I came up with the gun, some kind of way. I got the gun from him, and he was on the floor, and I pointed the gun at him, and he balled up like in a fetal position, and I knew he was scared of me. I saw the fear in the man. And I told him, "If you stand up, I'm gonna shoot you." So I opened my front door, and I told him to go out my door just like that. And I made him crawl out my front door. And ever since then, everywhere I see him, I beat him to this day. He's terrified of me now.

For all those years, I took all those beatings and all that humiliation for nothing. He would dump me over if I be sitting at the dining room table eating; he'd just grab a chair and dump me off the chair. Or I could be trying to run the kids' bath water, and he'd come in and just push me in the water and all my clothes. You know, just do stuff to humiliate me. I didn't have any friends, but I finally befriended a lady across the street, and I was over at her house one day, and he blew the horn, and I'm trying to get down the steps, but he came up the steps and grabbed me and dragged me all the way down the steps by my hair. . . . I learned not to even cry. My mother came to visit me one time, and he was in the bedroom beating me up, you know, and she was sitting in the living room. And I gotta take these blows without making a sound. And one night I was in the bed with my kids, and he came in, and he just punched me maybe twenty times in my head. And my little girl was laying there just squeezing my hand, you know. I could feel her little hand just squeezing my hand every time he hit me, and I had to not cry for her.

And I went through that for years, and I don't understand why he treated me like that [crying], you know, and I keep asking him when I see him, I ask him, "Why did you have to treat me like that? It's like you had a retarded child. You could have made me be anything in the world." I believe if he had told me to be the president, that's what I'd have been 'cause I'd have been whatever he told me to be. And he cannot answer me as to why he treated me like that. . . . He made me into a shoplifter instead of letting me be what my mother raised me to be, which was a strong, smart young woman. I believe I could have been anything in the world. . . . I feel like he should do every day I did [in prison]. If I could ever really tell a judge my story, he should be the one in prison. He beat this into me, and now I got to figure out a way to get it out of me.

. . . I've been in jail for shoplifting six times. My first time was in 1985. I was shoplifting at this place called [X] and I fought off store security. And I ran outside and got hit by a car. I was pregnant with my second daughter at that time. And they gave me a robbery charge, which was a two to ten [year sentence], and I came to prison for that. I only did like eleven months, and I came home.

. . . Then in '89 I came back to prison for violating probation. And while I was in prison this time, my mother died. And this is one time I can truly say I know there is a God, and he did a miracle. . . . My mother died, and I prayed to God one night. It was like it was more than I could bear. And I was like, "Lord, I got to find a way to get out of here." They said I couldn't go [to the funeral] because she lived out of state, so they had told me, "There's no way you're going to be able to go." And I just knew I couldn't live with my mother dying and me never seeing her. So that very morning they knocked on my door and told me to pack my things, that I was going back to my county. I get to my county that morning, and the judge released me on probation again. And I got out that evening, caught the Greyhound bus, and made it to my mother's funeral. When I got to the house, my family was lined up to go to the church. But I made it to my mother's funeral. And I always look back at that time like it was truly a miracle because there's no way I was supposed to have got out. I don't know who this attorney was in the courtroom. Never seen him before. And the same judge that had sent me to prison for violating this probation released me again on probation. It just don't fit. So I know that was a miracle from God.

But I went back to using drugs again, and I ended up going back to prison again. This time in 1990, pregnant again. And I had a son there this time. And my sister came to Ohio and got the baby. She had all three of my kids now. So she came and got this baby, and I did my three years and I went home to North Carolina and got my kids, brought them back to Cleveland. When my mother died, when I got out and went to North Carolina, I met this guy. My sister convinced me, "Oh, go ahead and give him a chance. It's time that somebody be nice to you," 'cause I hadn't been with nobody but this guy that had beat me for fifteen years. So I went ahead, and I slept with this guy one time, and I get pregnant. And he's crazy! He tried to stab me about something he imagined. And I found out from his mother that [he fought in] Vietnam and he's killed four people before. . . . So I hightail it back to Cleveland 'cause he said he's going to kill me and all this.

. . . My life has just been one big old mess. One big mess. Now this is my sixth time here, and I'm trying to do something different. I'm tired of the shoplifting. I've got to stop. I don't know how, but I've got to. I don't want to come back to prison. . . . The only tools they offer is in the NA and AA programs. They tell you to apply those same steps to your life, which could possibly be true, but it doesn't work for me. . . . To me, it's all a matter of mind. I realize that when I was pregnant with my last daughter in '98, I was using drugs, and the instant that doctor told me I was pregnant, I stopped that day. I didn't use another day until she was four years old. . . . That's why I know you can stop. But the shoplifting is stronger than the drugs for me. . . . When I try to talk to people about my shoplifting issues, theirs is not as deep as mine seem like.

'Cause I can't imagine what it's going to be like to go out there and not go in the mall. I can't even imagine my day without a mall. It's almost like it's a part of my arm or something, a mall. I love them. I love them. I love the smell of them. I love the lighting. I love the floors, like going from the cushion to the cement. I love that feeling, walking from the floor and then going to the cement. And I love the way the dome lights are shaped, and the way they shed the light on certain items. I like the lighting. And I like the music that play softly over the air. I like the whole atmosphere, and stealing the clothes is just like icing on the cake. Just being in the store, I don't know. It's a beautiful place to me. It's just a beautiful place to me.

It became a safe haven for me. And I don't know if that's why I have such an attachment; it almost became like my home. That's where I would live, you know. I knew if my daughter got tired what area I could go and lay her down in. I knew where I could store our coats. I knew where to go eat. Everything was there. I knew where to go wash her up or whatever. You know, if she got something dirty on her clothes, I could go to J.C. Penney and steal her outfit, and I'd go in the bathroom and change her. It was just like home. . . . The mall and my neighborhood was two different worlds. It was two different worlds. The malls was things I saw in magazines, like a dream world, where home was reality. Home was dark. Home was pain. The mall wasn't. I could be anything I wanted to be in that mall. But at home, I couldn't.

. . . One time I went to Dillard's, and they had this Christmas tree in there, and I stole the Christmas tree . . . and I stole every ornament off of that tree because I wanted that tree in my house. And when I sat on my couch and looked at that tree in my house, I used to love coming home, just opening the door and seeing that tree. I brought that whole tree home, and I loved it. That whole tree, I brought home. And people would come in my house, friends would be like, "I seen that tree in Dillard's. They got a tree like that in Dillard's." And I'd be like, "This is the tree," you know, 'cause I took every ornament off of that tree and hung it on my tree. I made that tree in my house. . . . It was a high success. Like I made it.

But when I get caught, it's like they're telling you you're not who you think you are. You're not successful. You're a thief. So when I get caught, it's like the worst thing in the world. It's like, I don't even know how to explain the feeling inside when you get caught because again, they're telling you you're not who you are. You're not successful. These are not your clothes. This is not your stuff. And when they say, "You can't come in here no more," oh! I won't let them tell me that. I'll do anything to keep them from telling me I can't come back. When you get caught shoplifting, they make you sign this paper saying you're not allowed on their premises. Oh, man! I refused to sign all those papers because that's worse than me going to jail. . . . They don't understand what it means to me. I need the malls. It's like that's where I feel my self-worth. I feel like that's the only place I'm gonna reach what I'm trying to be or what I aspire to be: to live that type of lifestyle, to be around working people that work their job and bring their kids shopping on the weekends, or the businessmen in their suits buying stuff for their wives. This is where I should have been in my life. I should have been successful like that where I would have been able to bring my children to the store and shop. . . . [When they say I can't come in their store anymore] they're telling me I'm a failure. That I don't belong. That I'm less than.

. . . In prison this time, it's been hard on me because I've been more worried about my children. Before I always had my sister here, and I didn't worry about my children. And before I always knew I was going back out to steal. I knew beyond a doubt. I lined up people, my customers and things. They supplied my money here, you know. I never wanted too much 'cause my paying customers took care of me here. If my children needed something, I could call them. . . . But this time, I don't want to steal anymore 'cause I don't want to come back to jail. My children don't have anybody anymore. And I wanna see, can I be better? I'm scared because I don't know if it's too late. I don't know how far I can go now. But I gotta see. I gotta try. I have been living like this for twenty-five years, and it's got to stop somewhere.

Actually, I believe I've had a spiritual awakening about it. Because for all these years, I never thought I was doing nothing wrong, no matter what they said. I wasn't doing anything wrong in my eyes because I was helping people. I always felt like everybody would love to wear something nice. Everybody want their kid to have on some decent shoes and decent shirt, or a cute outfit every now and then, you know. It doesn't hurt to help these people have a little bit of something of this life. It shows everybody what you can have if you work hard for it. This is what you can get if you work for it. . . . I don't want to teach nobody to steal it, but if they don't know it's out there, they'll never know to strive for that. So when I go steal a pretty dress for somebody, and they say, "Well, where did you get this?" I say, "From Dillard's. Learn how to go in Dillard's to buy your clothes. You get nice clothes in there and they got them cheap. You can get cheap clothes in there." But I may steal them a $500 dress for some teenager that's going to the prom so she can look like Cinderella, where her mother was going to buy one from Fashion Sense for maybe $20, but everybody would have had one just like it. So I want her to feel special this day. She deserve this. You know, she ain't did nothing wrong. It's not her fault she can't afford this dress. It's not this child's fault, and she should look just as beautiful as those girls whose mother can afford it. So I go steal this dress and sell it to her mother for the same $20 that she was going to pay on that one. And this girl looks beautiful. See, and maybe she'll grow up and remember this dress and want her daughter to wear something like that, and she'll know how much it cost, and she'll get a job or she'll go to school where she can earn this kind of money to buy this dress. . . . I just felt like if they could just see what's really out there in the world, what's really out there just through clothes. And clothes is just a small glimpse of what's out there. And that may be a wrong way to look at it, but that's how I looked at it for all these years is that I was just helping. I was just helping, that's all, just a little bit of help.

Like I used to steal Liz Claiborne socks, and Ralph Lauren socks, and I would pass them out to the homeless people downtown. Not that I couldn't go to Kmart and steal a bunch of socks, but these socks, they keep their feet warmer. You get what you pay for, actually, and I learned that in boosting.[1] That it's all about the stitching, the knitting, the material, the yarn that keeps the foot warmer in these socks than these Kmart socks. And so that's why I did that, you know. I thought, if you're gonna give it to them, give what they need. And so I thought I was doing something helpful. . . . So long as I was stealing and taking care of my kids and everybody in my family and neighbors and everybody, I thought I was doing good. That there was nothing wrong with what I was doing. You know, I'm not stealing from nobody. I would never take nothing out of nobody's purse, nobody's house, nobody's car. I'm not that type. I only deal with Nordstrom's, Dillard's, Neiman Marcus. They gotta be stores like that because it's all about that lighting. Every store don't have that lighting and those chandeliers and that perfume smell in them. Only those stores do. It's like a certain aura too, just pulls me. I love those stores. I do. And I don't know what I'm going to do when I get out of here, how I'm going to stay away from them.

. . . But you know what? When I got here this time, it was like one day I was thinking about it, and I had a revelation that this is not right, that stealing comes from the devil. It's not from God. So what you've been doing all these years was not something God wanted you to be doing. It's wrong. It was a lie from the devil. It was a trick from hell, to trick you into staying in sinful bondage like that for all these years. And if you want to live right, you gotta stop stealing. You gotta stop stealing. . . . I started reading my Bible and really listening to God because I feel like God is the only thing that can help me. I got to follow somebody. Somebody's got to lead me, and I choose to follow God. I choose to listen to God this time. But God has always been in my life. My mother was a deacon. I've known God all my life. So I asked myself, how could you get it so twisted to think that you was doing something good when stealing is wrong? They tells you don't steal. How could you think you was doing something good? Because I thought God was blessing me by not letting me get caught the kazillions of times I didn't get caught because I thought I was helping people. I was doing what God wanted.

So maybe I can go further with my life. See, 'cause every time I start to progress a little bit, I catch a case, and I'm back, all the way back. I restarted homes so many times just to lose everything, all over, every time I go to jail. I probably could have bought a home if I could have stayed out long enough, but I wouldn't have kept it because things you get with ill-gotten gains is not going to profit you. That's something I learned, too, that it's never going to profit me anything. Wrongdoing would never profit you anything. And I can look back and I can see that. Because all the stealing I have done for twenty-five years, all the money I have had, has profited me nothing. . . . I have nothing and nobody in my life. I have no friends, for real. I sat back and I looked back at all the people I know, and none of them are really my friend. I wouldn't know not one of them if I didn't steal. And would they be my friends if I didn't steal?

You know, I got invited to this basketball player's birthday party because I sell clothes to his sister, you know. And I'm in this place and I got on this fabulous $2,000 suit, and I'm with all these people that's dressed just like me, and I'm dressed just like them. And I don't even have a job, you know. I'm nobody. And it's like I'm in here pretending. And when I lay on my bed, I think about these things how I was pretending. But to everybody else I was somebody because I was at that birthday party, you know. And I got this judge that buys these suits from me every week . . . and by selling to people like that, they pass you onto their friends who got money just like them, so you become a part of this elite group. . . . When I moved to Atlanta, everybody wanted to send me a plane ticket to fly me back to Cleveland for special events to get their clothes.

This made me feel like I was somebody, and it made my family feel like I was somebody. 'Cause then they can call me, my nieces and them can call me, "Auntie, I need to pay my light bill. I need $300," and I'd be like, "Okay, I'll have it to you through Western Union" because I could get it. If I didn't have it right here, I could call one of those friends and say, "Look, I need $300. What you want for that $300? Just tell me what you want and give me the $300, and I'll bring the outfits to you later." I always had excess money, which made everybody look up to me or think that I was somebody. But when I'm in here now, I look back at all these people I used to talk to daily on the phone. . . . They're not really my friends because they have no purpose for me if I'm not stealing. . . . There's no reason for me to even call them. . . . There's no reason for them to ask me to the party. There's no reason for them to ask me, "Let's go out to dinner." . . . The end result is me here, by myself. All of them got blocks on their phone, 'cause see, once you hit jail, they don't want to be associated with you 'cause then you're a blemish.

My kids are struggling. So what was it all for? All the years I done missed out on their lives in prison, what was it all for? . . . When I came home [from prison the second time], my son was four and it was like I didn't feel him. I couldn't feel him. I brought him to Cleveland to live with me, and I would catch him peeking around the corners to look at me. . . . He just was scared of me. And one day I was trying to tickle him, and it felt fake. It felt phony. . . . So I let my sister go ahead and keep him. . . . [Now] he's fifteen. He's so messed up. . . . When [my sister] died, I went and got him. He was thirteen then, and he refused to accept me. We fight all the time, you know, and I don't know if he got problems from his father, you know, his mental illness or if he just don't like me, or because of the death of my sister, if all this is messing him up. He's real messed up. My daughter, who's twenty-six, put him into a group therapy home, and I talked to him about a week ago, and he's so angry. He said, "She don't know. She's destroying our relationship. I hate her. I hate her." I said, "Well, maybe this is where you need to be" 'cause he tried to rob a little chicken place to get into a gang.

My seven-year-old is with another sister of mine. My twenty-one-year-old, the one that I had in '85, the first child I had in prison, she lives in Atlanta. And my twenty-six-year-old who went through everything with me, that girl is a trooper. She just graduated from college. She just works at Target here and goes to school, but she is such a hero. She is. She has taken care of me all her life. And I really wish her the best in this world because she has been through it all, all my drug uses, all the abuses I went through, and she still loves me. And now I see where I put so much on her. All her relationships are abusive and she has low self-esteem. She done graduated from college, and she's working two jobs, and she'll get these guys that won't work. . . . She got this no-good boyfriend who's there all the time, and I know he's no good.

And I will fight her boyfriends if I have to. You know, she had one boy-friend, a neighbor called me, and told me he was fighting her one day and I was over there like this [snaps fingers]. And I was like, "I will kill you if you put your hands on her." And that's something that scares me because I believe that I could [kill him] if I saw some boy hit my daughter or something, 'cause I'm not going to let them go through that. They don't need to experience that. And I tell them, "I took all the abuse that we're gonna take. I'm not going to let it happen." And I'm like that with my nieces and them, too. You know, I can spot a man in a minute that's abusive, and I tell them that. And I'm scared my son is gonna be abusive because my son will fight me. I know he's going to be a woman beater, see, because he got mother issues because I was never there for him. . . . He swings at me and fights me back whenever I'm trying to chastise him. "You ain't my mama! You ain't my mama!" And if I push him or something, he'll swing at me, and we be tussling, and that's not right. That's why I know he's gonna fight women.

So I got to stay out of prison to get my kids together. I got to. I can't let them go on and be messed up. And it'll be my fault if I don't help them. This is why I can't steal no more. They may hit me with a habitual criminal and never let me out. I can't afford to take that chance, but I'm scared because I don't know how to live without the malls. The malls was, is everything to me. They're the biggest part of my life. I don't have a memory of my life without a mall involved in it. How am I supposed to live without that? What do I do? I can't afford to go in there and shop, so I ain't got no business in there. If I go in there, I'm liable to steal. But I don't know how to cut it out of my life.

You got shoplifters all the time in and out of here. And I don't want to make mine seem more special than theirs, but it feels different than theirs. . . . I don't believe nobody's been where I've been. They may have been in abusive relationships that took them down other roads, but mine led me into a hole, into a hole that I don't know how to come out of. . . . When I talk to other boosters, they talk about, "Yeah man, we cleaned up at this store. We cleaned up at that store." It ain't like that with me. It's not about cleaning up. It's not about outrunning the police. I don't want the police after me at all. I want to walk out of there like Elizabeth Taylor or somebody. You know, I wanna be able to be back tomorrow, and this lady greet me with respect because she think I'm a shopper. I'm a part of that. [Other shoplifters] go as the enemy. I'm a part of the scene, you know. . . . But see, that's my illusion.

I came up with a thought that maybe I could go into theft prevention. You know, maybe if the stores would allow me, that's what I'm trying to look into now. Like to go in and give back all my theft secrets, to consult with their theft department just to kind of deprogram myself. Maybe if I give up every-thing I used to use to steal, disarm myself in sort of a way, maybe that can help me. And that way I'm getting both of the things that I need: I'm still at the mall, but I'm deprogramming myself, too. So that may help me to wean myself off of malls some kind of way. And it's sad to be sitting here talking about a place that I'm addicted to. The shoplifting really just comes with the territory. It became a reason for me to be at the mall. . . . I love being at the mall. I can't go there just to walk around. I got to be in the mix. I got to be doing something, you know; I want to walk around with a bag. So I'm in a messed-up place.

What's next for me is a blank; it's just a blank white wall. It's whatever I paint right now. It's up to me which way I go from this point on. It's like everything's been laid out on the table for me. No excuses no more. Now I know. I know that shoplifting is wrong. I know that I'm not going to profit nothing from it. I know it's going to keep putting me back in jail. I know I'm not rich. I know those people are not my friends. But now do I hold onto that because that was comfortable? It came with its pitfalls, but it was comfortable while I was there. Or do I try something new? I'm ready to try the newness, but I'm scared of what's out there in the newness. I don't know. I ain't never lived without the mall, so I don't know what it's going to be like. I can't even imagine what it's going to be like.

If I live in Cleveland, that's where most of my customers are. But Atlanta has more malls. All I did in Atlanta was went from mall to mall. Atlanta was like my mall heaven [laughing]. North Carolina is so small that I don't think I could live there. And I don't want to go back there as a complete failure. . . . But North Carolina is home. I can't do the things that I do in these other places at home because the people ain't going to be so acceptable of it there. It's people there that if they called me a rogue,[2] it would hurt my feelings to be labeled a rogue where people in the city may not even know what a rogue is. If a old person say, "Oh, that girl's a rogue," it would crush me, 'cause for an old person to call you a rogue, it's like utter banishment, you know, you're banished. You wouldn't be welcome in nobody's house, not being called a rogue.

My little town, they know I been to prison, they know I go to jail, but they have my children to raise so they don't say things about me for my children's sake. . . . So it's a safe place. That's where I go to rest. When I go there, I don't go to no malls. I don't stay long either [laughing] 'cause I have to get back to a mall. . . . It's like before, when I know I'm going home, I'm in those malls from the time they open 'till they close. . . . There's no mall in my town. They have shopping centers, and I don't like shopping centers. They're not the same. And plus nobody there really condones stealing. There's nobody there that want to buy my clothes. You know, everybody's kind of on the same level. They don't care about Ralph Lauren. They don't care about Liz Claiborne or none of that stuff, you know. So it's nobody there wanting that from me. . . . So going back there to live may be the best thing for me to do, but I'm afraid I'm gonna resort back to that cotton pickin', tobacco pickin' person that I was. It's either you be this or you be that, 'cause you can't grow for so much in this town. You know, you're gonna stay stagnant there.

That [tobacco pickin' person that I was] is submissive. She's scared of white people. She don't believe that she can go but so far because the white people won't let you. That was just her, her way of thinking, but when I came to the city, I realized that that's not true. That these people are just people, you know. We were raised that the white people were like a diamond, just for you to look at. But when I came to Cleveland, I worked side by side with them because I had a job at the federal building, and this was a big deal to my little town. They announced it in the church that I had a government job and everything. . . . I worked side by side with white people so I learned that white people were just people, just like me. And I used to write all my friends back there, "You can get a job in an office. You don't have to work in the fields. I work in the job with carpet on the floor, and air conditioner, and there's a telephone on my desk. It's two different worlds."

But if I go back home, it's like I'll lose all this momentum I got. You know, I have to become submissive again, and I don't want to do that. I don't want to do that 'cause I might stay there, 'cause everybody that leaves and come back home stays here, and they settle for a trailer house or they go back and live in their grandmama's old house and they settle. They do nothing but walk around all day, go work at Perdue . . . or Georgia Pacific. Everybody works at these factories, and that's all there is to do. It's nothing to spend your money on 'cause people don't care about clothes. They put on a pair of jeans and driving suit and get out in all the dirt like everybody else. A lot of people still got hogs and chickens, so everybody ain't on the clothes things, you know. So it's nothing to do. And I don't know if I could live like that, but it might be where I need to go to get off the mall thing for a while. It's an option, but I'd like to beat it in Cleveland. This is where I'd like to beat it 'cause this is where it started. It's like I gotta meet that demon head on, right here.

—⚋⚋—

Reading Narrative

"Who is this writing books that knows the things I know?!"

I'M A SERIOUS reader. I don't like to be disturbed when I'm reading because I go into character. In my mind, I already have a tone for that person's voice, a way they say it. If I read a sentence and it comes out not right, I'll go back and change the tone and make it fit right. And I can change accents, the way I think a person should sound. . . . If it's a kid talking or an adult or a preacher, I change how that character should sound.

. . . I read just to find out what's out there. I read to find out how other minds work. I read to go other places. I read to see other things. I love to go places that I've never seen. And I can actually see those places. When I read, I take myself so deep I can smell smells. If I go to the rainforest, I can see bugs crawling on the leaves. I can see water dripping off the leaf. I can hear the snake on the limb crawling. You know, I go there. I jump from reading to just thinking about what it's like to be there. . . . It's sort of like the movie *Jumanji,* where . . . the kids open this book and everything out of the book comes alive. . . . The elephants is running through the house. The monkeys is all over the house. . . . I love that movie because it's like the story just come into their life. And it make you wonder: What if all the stuff you're reading just appeared in your life right there? And that's exactly how it is for me. Everything comes alive. And when I read a book, it stays with me for days. Once I close it, it's not over. I see it in my daily life for maybe two or three weeks until I read something else, and then it's like I jump into that book. But a book stays with me to where I'll be talking to people and use phrases in the book. . . . Or I'll see things in the book, and I'll imagine that person could play a part in that book. I may take books a little too serious, but that's how I do personally because I enjoy reading them, and when I find a good book, it just stays with me, and I be wanting everybody to enjoy it.

I started reading with the Sally, Dick, and Jane books in first grade. *See Spot Run.* I used to *love* that. Then my sister that lived in Cleveland, she sent me this book for Christmas, *Madeline.*[3] And it was a book from the city, so this book I cherished. *Madeline,* about the little girl in the orphanage. I *loved* that book. When I was growing up, reading was my window. It was my window to what the world really was. I used to love to read billboards and I would make up a story to go with that billboard; what this person did after she got off this billboard.

. . . And my father used to tell me a lot of ghost stories and stuff like that. We had a swamp a little ways from our house. To keep us from going to that swamp, him and my aunt, they were great storytellers, and they used to tell us stories about how they'd wrassle these alligators twenty feet long down there in the swamp, to keep us from going near the swamp. Or they would tell us about this monster that had chased their daddy when he was a little boy and how he's still there. And you'd visualize these things in your head. It would be like two hours we'd sit there and listen. And then my brothers had a lot of comic books. *Archie* comic books, and *Casper* comic books. I would read all these comic books all the time. So that's where a lot of the reading came from. . . . And my mother got us a set of *Childcraft Encyclopedias,* and I used to love to read those. I think that's where my love of reading documentaries and things like that come from, because I love factual stuff.

. . . And the Sears catalogue. I think that's where my love of fashion and clothes come from [laughing]. I used to read the Sears catalogue just to know what everything meant. . . . Everything had to have a meaning and a why. Like if it was a picture of a crib made out of cherry wood in this book, then I want to know how did this company, Broyhill in North Carolina, get this cherry wood. And I'd make up a story of how they sent these men into the woods to find cherry trees and they brought them back to this company, and how they trimmed them down. Each man had to make his own crib out of his own tree. . . . And then I would take the pictures and I'd make my own stories to them. That's how I'd fantasize. I'd go out in the cornfields and fantasize. . . . My mother sure didn't have a credit card. Wasn't a Sears nowhere around.

My abusive years, I didn't read. Those years were just spent riding buses from mall to mall. . . . When I get in prison, I love to read. I read the newspaper every day. . . . You don't know what you'll find in the newspaper from day to day, so I read every inch of it. Even when I don't understand, I read it. The NASDAQ and all that, I have no clue what all that is about, but I read it anyway because what I don't know, I create my own story for what it is. I read any paper over there. I don't care what city it's from or anything because it's just stuff that's happening. It doesn't necessarily have to be happening right here to be of interest. It can happen anywhere. And especially anything dealing with women causing any crime. Any women that commit a crime in the state of Ohio I'm liable to run into. So I like to read and know what she went through because when I meet her, then I can form my own opinion and I'll know how to approach her. I'll know how to help her.

There's a lady that came here from Lake County that was in a car wreck. She was drunk driving, went on the wrong side of the road, and she killed a man. And I met her in the county and everybody was mistreating her. . . . But I read her story in the paper, and it's *so sad.* She was upset 'cause her husband had left her for a twenty-three-year-old girl. She had been married twenty-one years, and her mind just wasn't there. . . . I know how a man can mess up your mind to where you don't even realize what you're doing. And that's what happened to her. . . . It was just pain, blind pain that made her go on the wrong side of the road. . . . I talked to her and I tried to tell her, "During these five years, you're going to get something out of this that's gonna make up for all the pain and hurt you done went through. . . . This happened as a plan, a part of a bigger plan than what you can see right now."

I read something every day. My favorite place to read is on my bed. . . . I don't go to the library that often. I usually, like, network around with people. And if they'll tell me, "Oh, such and such is over in the library, you might want to check that out," I'll go check it out, the same way I would do with them. "Oh, I read this good book but I had to return it, but it's over there now. If you go now you can get it." We do that. Because a good book here, it takes forever for it to get around to you 'cause for some reason, a real good book they only have one or two copies. And most people get them and they pass them on to their friends. So you got to get in a certain circle to really get good books. And I hate that because when I want to read a book, I want to read it now. So it's a unwritten list. Like I can go to Susie and say, "Are you through with that book?" She'll be like, "Well, such-and-such has got it next." And it's like, "Well, where she at?" And I've got to go find her to let her know I want it next. She may be like, "Well, somebody already got it next." Then I'll have to find that person and say, "Well, can I get that book after you? Who got it after you?" And then they'll say, "You can get it next." So then I know when my turn is and I try to estimate how long it's gonna take them. I ask each person, "Well, how long is it gonna take you to read it?" And then I'll go to that person [later] and say, "Did you get that book?" So if you want to get a book, you track it like that. Because once it gets to the library, we might not get it again. Somebody else may get it who really don't want to read it and have it in their lockbox or their cubbyhole somewhere and just have it sitting there . . . so we pass it along to people that we really know want to read it.

[When I'm choosing a book to read,] I read the inside of the cover or the back of the cover, a little bit about the author. . . . I love to know where the author came from. I would like to know how many brothers or sisters they had, or if they got kids. It helps me understand where they come from on the inside. . . . And from knowing a little bit about the author's background and things, sometimes you can get a feel for how this book is gonna lay out. Like with this new author, Alice Sebold, *The Lovely Bones* is her first book.[4] And I read that book *because* it was her first book. I feel like any author, on that first book, is gonna be awesome. They're gonna do their best because it's their first book. And it really was a great book. . . . Somebody had told me about it. . . . And now, it's like I've taken it hostage, just to give it to people that I know enjoy reading. Everybody wouldn't enjoy this story. It takes somebody who mentally can go in depth with this little girl in this book, and can feel for her, you know. So I pass it along to people I know are compassionate and believe in the spiritual realm, believe in heaven and things like that.

Oh, *The Lovely Bones* is a great book! It's the story of a fourteen-year-old girl who was murdered by her neighbor. And in this book, she's trying to tell her parents where to find her bones and let them know that this man next door did it. She's in their life as a ghost, as a spirit. . . . And it tells how much she missed her father, and . . . it shows her sister missing her and she can only stand by and watch it. . . . It showed me that people that you love that die really do be there. And I have seen things like that, spirits and things of loved ones. I got a sister that passed and I seen her before. And in this book, she tells how her father was laying in the bed and she was standing at the foot of the bed. But the instant he saw her, she had to disappear. . . . And it made me think, "Well, maybe that's why [my sister's spirit] left." Because I seen her she had to leave, because that's how they do it in heaven. . . . And it would help anyone who got a loved one that's passed understand how they work. You feel a comfort in knowing that they can come back and that they are watching you. . . . It's just so good 'cause it gives you a whole different perspective on dying. And then she tells about her heaven. She's sitting on a swing set looking in *Vogue* magazines, because she was fourteen when he murdered her.

. . . When I'm reading crime stories and somebody's being murdered, I can feel that. . . . I can't feel the person who's doing it, but I can feel the person that's being hurt. Like with *The Lovely Bones,* this little girl was being raped and murdered and she trusted this man 'cause he been living next door to her all her life. . . . And while she was on the ground being raped and stabbed, you could hear her mother calling her. And my heart just dropped for her because I could imagine how you hear your mother so close and this man is hurting you. And he got his hand over her mouth and she can't holler, but she can hear her mother. . . . Oh, it just stayed with me for days.

Another girl had *The Lovely Bones* on her bed. . . . I told her I wanted to read it, but I had already read it. I really wanted to give it to a friend of mine that I knew would enjoy it. So I got the book and took it to this older lady, and I was like, "It's an excellent book. You gotta read it." And I explained to her what it was about. So I gave it to her and checked back with her the next day and she was like, "Man, I could not put that book down." And we talked about the part she had got to. I didn't want to tell her the ending. And I was like, "Oh, it's so much more in there. You're just going to love it." And so actually today I've got to go back to her and see if she has finished it so I can get it, 'cause there's somebody else I want to give it to because I was telling her about it. . . . She asked me this morning, "Do you got that book yet?" I said, "I'm gonna check on it today." And she said, "Well, I think I got one that you'll like to read." So that's how we do with books.

. . . I like family books, love books, struggle books, just everyday struggles. I like struggles from the past. I love stories like where they start off hard-pressed, like from the farm and abused or mistreated, and they come up out of it and they make something of themselves. Or they *don't*, but they just learn how to cope with it. Just stories like that where people just learn how to deal with life. Where they are survivors; where they make it. And everything in them is things that could happen in everyday life. None of it is really fantasy. It's real. . . . Like when you got everyday common people whose mother worked hard at a menial job and this person had to work at a menial job and they was trying to make it, and they make it, not with this big grandiose house and all of this, they just make it. I don't like those stories where you've got a girl who became a movie star and lived all this luxurious life, because that's not everyday, commonplace things. That's a rarity that that happens to people in their lives.

. . . It's not healthy to daydream on that or to think you can achieve that when you are at a certain place in your life, to think, miraculously, this is gonna happen for you. Or, "Next month, I'm going to be rich." That's not healthy because you end up in the malls, like me. Loving the mall; faking it. Like I used to say, "Fake it 'til you make it," you know, but I wasn't doing anything to make it. I was just trying to hang on and hoping it'd just rub off or brush off. . . . I've never liked reading books about people living lavishly when they came from humble beginnings because it's like they pull the cover off of me 'cause they make me face that I'm not really like them. Because all the things they went through to get to where they're at, I didn't. Their friends in those books are really their friends. The people in my life were just my customers.

. . . They've been flooding this place with a lot of what I'll call "ghetto books" and I can't stand that because it's what these girls, especially these younger girls, have lived all their lives. It's what brought them to the penitentiary. And it gives them a hype that this is what they should aspire to be. . . . I read a couple of them just to see what they're reading. . . . And it's like, why would the system allow all this garbage to come in here about all the drug selling? They're just gangsta-life stories. And to me, it's garbage to put this in these kids' heads. And I watch the girls walking around calling themselves the characters out the book, you know? "I'ma get out and do what this ho did," "I'ma stack my chips," "I'ma make some money." . . . And a lot of people die in these books. Their boyfriends get shot by the next dope man. This is what you want to *live*? But they see the glamour in the books. They see the big cars with the big rims and they see them going out to clubs. . . . Some people live that life, but maybe one out of a hundred do. And they flood [urban books] in here. I bet you there is a *thousand* of those kind of books in here. I don't think that should be the only thing these girls are allowed to get in the so-called "black library." These are not good books.

I got the sense that a lot of those that read those urban books wasn't reading before they got here. They weren't readers. So this stuff they're reading, it's just amazing that somebody has put their lives in a book or the lives that they want to be in a book. They're reading these books trying to figure out how to do it. This is the life they aspire to be. It's what they pretend to be. . . . And I listen to them when they're playing volleyball, calling out these characters' names and saying little lines from these characters. In one of these books, there's a guy name Vegas. He was a real big drug dealer. And he bought his girl the best clothes, the nice cars, and the jewels. And I watch girls walk around like, "Yeah, I've gotta call Vegas to send me a money order." Or, "Just call me Ms. Vegas." And it's so many of them that says that because they read these books and he's in a lot of these books. But in the book I read, the girl murders him in the end. She comes home and catch him in the Jacuzzi with three other girls and she kills everybody in the Jacuzzi. And she got away with it.

 . . . And in the next book I read—I just read the cover 'cause I don't want to read the book, and on the cover she's standing there in this little short mini-dress with a .45 automatic pistol in her hand—it tells how she's stripping now, trying to keep up with the lifestyle he had for her and how she can't get out the game. . . . It's another one of those books that just does black life injustice, you know, where Toni Morrison and Alice Walker shows true black life. Just the struggle, the strength, the honor, the history, the respect. It shows that for black life. Maybe I can't relate to those [urban] books 'cause I didn't live that life, or that's what's going on in the world today and I'm not out there like that. Maybe that's the reason I don't relate to those books, where I can relate to the struggle books, the parentage and the heritage and the grandmom who's in your life and all of that type books, where you got whuppings. I can relate to those things better than to this drug scene and the music and the cars and things like that.

The women between [ages] thirty and forty read Eric Jerome Dickey books, like *Milk in My Coffee*,[5] but the girls from eighteen to twenty-five only read those gangster books. I don't prefer [Dickey's] writings. They are just common. You can know how it's gonna end before it begins. . . . That's the same for Carl Weber, [author of] *The Preacher's Son*.[6] . . . The story lines is gonna be the same. Girl meets boy. Girl gets pregnant, finds out boy got another baby by another mother. They fight. They run into each other. And in the end, girl leaves and the other girl stays with him. . . . They're real simplistic to me.

I used to read all of Danielle Steel's books, and then all her books started seeming the same. . . . If I thought of a title, I couldn't tell if it was this story I read or that story I read because they all just became the same. I liked the family atmosphere, the family struggles. I liked how they get through the heartbreaks and things like that. But then you could know in the end that she was gonna be back with the man she left in the very beginning of the book. . . . Sometimes the female character will be old by the time she find her old love, you know. And it's like, why hold onto all of that for all these years and go through this whole book for you to go back and end up back there? It seems fake. It seems unrealistic.

I can't stand a book that just lays there. It's got to make me figure it out. . . . I try to project what the ending is gonna be before I get there, you know. And I try to see if my mind can match this author's mind and see how he's gonna carry this out. So I love a book that outsmarts me, that can outfake me and tell me, "See, you thought I was gonna do this, but I did this." I love a book like that.

. . . Stephen King I will always read because you don't know what to expect from him. I love Stephen King! Now *that* mind is a mind to reckon with! Man, Stephen King is something else! Oh, I've read so many of his books! I like that they're scary but could be true. . . . I've read so much about him. And when I learned that a lot of his stories he wrote when he was *seventeen,* I'm like, wow! He had these thoughts in his head at seventeen! . . . His stories, they stay real until the very end. . . . They're everyday until you get into it, and then he adds a little bit of mystery and a little bit of spookiness. . . . Like with *Pet Sematary,*[7] this book is about . . . a cemetery they could bury their dead in and they would come back. But when they came back, you thought you was getting your loved one back, but you was getting something that was dead. . . . Where *The Lovely Bones,* she never actually came back. Her spirit did. . . . I like those books about people that come back from the dead. I don't like those where they come back from the dead scary and evil. I like them when they come back from the dead good and try to show something or teach something or let somebody know something.

. . . I love reading about Native Americans 'cause their struggle was a lot like mine. You know, they knew hard work and everything. . . . I started reading those kind of books because they were the only thing available throughout the county jails. . . . And I like those books where they were moving from the reservations to civilization, where one Native American went to American college and went back and tried to educate more of his people. They always let a Native American man marry this white woman, but she decides to stay with the tribe. I read one book, *Tame the Wild Wind*,[8] where they lived in a home on a ranch and all that. She took him out of the reservation and took him home and turned him into a suburban husband. But when it was problems on the reservation, her and him packed up and went back as Indians to help them fight. I love that book. . . . And it was realistic. . . . This is what would happen if he went to college, and he got a suburban wife, and he married her, and she was accepted and understood his lifestyle. Then she could go back with him, and she stood behind him for what he believed, and he stood behind her for what she believed. Their children got to know both cultures, you know, and got to understand both struggles, even though she had opposition from some people in her family.

But one thing I didn't like is that it's never two Indian people go to civilization and live and fit in. You know, make yourself a part of this society. You're a human being just like everybody else. Stop believing that you need [a white person] in order to fit in, somebody to validate you're a person. When you're a human being, you and your Indian wife should be able to go get that suburban house and go to college and raise your kids right here just like everybody else. . . . [But] you don't never see an Indian woman going with a white man. It's always the Indian man with the white woman.

. . . And they always end the same way either with him getting killed, and she having to go on back to her family with her mixed kids and then try to hold on to his side of the family, or he's dead and she rides off into the sunset with the Indian tribe. It's like, if he's gone, she don't feel like she'll be accepted back in the white culture. She has to choose the Indian side. And I hate books with prejudices. I hate stories that end like that. It's like it makes the fact that she can't go back acceptable. . . . Eventually the reservations are gonna be wiped out, so then what becomes of her? She's eventually gonna have to come back, but now she's coming back with the stigma that she's put on her children. If she had [chosen to remain in white culture] from the beginning, then it would have proven to her children we can live like this. But now it's we *got* to. See, and that's a whole world of difference, when you can choose and when you just got to.

. . . Sometimes they'll have the articles in *Reader's Digest* or *Time Magazine* about different people. Like Dana Buchman is a designer, and I like a lot of her clothes. I used to steal a lot of her clothes. And there was a article in *Time Magazine* about her daughter, who's autistic. And I never knew that. And I felt bad for stealing from her, and it's like reality hit me: this is the lady that you have been stealing from for so long. You know, she's a person. . . . She didn't have diamonds on every finger. She didn't have a jewel crown on. She was just a simple mother with two little girls! . . . So I'd never steal none of Dana Buchman's stuff. I have a whole new appreciation for Dana Buchman clothes.

. . . I'm gonna have to branch out on my reading 'cause I get stuck to a certain type of book, and I won't look for anything else. Biographies, documentaries, things like that, I'm stuck on that now. I want to find something on World War II. I want to know exactly what World War II was all about . . . I love reading about the Holocaust. I just want to know why it all happened and what all happened. I watched the movie *Schindler's List* and that's what gave me a interest in the Holocaust. . . . When I saw that movie, I was like, "This couldn't have really happened in the world. This could not have *never* happened!" And it just boggles my mind; how could somebody let one man do this to so many people? So I want to read to understand why this happened and how did it come to be? . . . I got a seven-year-old and a fifteen-year-old son, and I can tell them these things so they'll know. . . . I want to know who Hitler's parents was, in the time he grew up, how he grew up. How did he grow up to be so hateful? . . . Once I read one book like *The Diary of Anne Frank,*[9] then I try to read stuff all the way around *The Diary of Anne Frank,* other people's stories from that time. And when I'm reading other people's stories, I think they was going through this while she was over here probably across town going through this.

. . . My favorite book is *Song of Solomon.*[10] That's my *favorite* book. I could read that book over and over. I've read it three times already. And every time I read it, I find something that I didn't see before. I love the way the father kept coming back, telling her to sing, the way she incorporated that in the story. . . . I go back to the author's mind. Like how could she see all of this before it happened, you know? How could she envision, "This is how I want this book to go"? How could she know to make this man say "sing" and then turn out that Sing was really her mother's name. That all these years, she'd been walking around singing, thinking that's what her father wanted her to do, when actually he was telling her her mother's name because she never knew her mother's name. . . . And then when [her dead father] kept saying, "You can't just go off and leave a body," she thought he meant, "Go back and get these bones of this man y'all killed in this cave." But that's not what he meant. He meant, "How could Solomon just fly away and leave this baby?" You know, and I just love the way all that just came together like that. It was awesome to me! That right there is just the epitome of everything!

. . . I started reading Toni Morrison in prison maybe about five years ago. I was looking for *I Know Why the Caged Bird Sings*[11] and I ran across Toni Morrison. And I think the first book I read was *The Bluest Eye*.[12] And when I read that book, I was like, "Wow!" and I realized how this girl felt that she was ugly, and I related to her because she wanted blue eyes like this white girl. And I remember when I went to school with the white people how I wanted their hair. I wanted to be them, you know, 'cause they had hair that was *always* straight. They didn't have to get their hair pressed. So I could relate to this girl. And I was like, "Well, who *is* this writing books that knows the things I know, that done been through the things I know?!" And I just started reading her books. *Sula, Tar Baby, Beloved*.[13] I read all of those.

Song of Solomon kind of reminds me of me in a certain way, even though it's a brother and sister, 'cause I see me in both of those people. Because Pilate's brother became this doctor who wanted to be a rich doctor, but he really wasn't. He was just the owner of shacks. He was just probably one of the wealthiest blacks in the neighborhood, which made them think that he was somebody, but he really wasn't. And then there was Pilate, who still stuck to her old ways and lived in the house with no electricity and used the pee pot and all of that. And I relate to both of them. . . . And the part about where these people could fly, it's like, that's my fantasy life. Like I got this side of me that lives in a fantasy world, and it had to come from my childhood as theirs did, you know, when their father flew up in the air off the fence. . . . I love that book 'cause it reminds me so much of me. I can see so many things that I can relate to in the *Song of Solomon*. And I try to tell girls, "Read *Song of Solomon*. Man, that's a great book." But their mind won't go that far for them to sit down and read that. I believe they *can* comprehend if they take the time and read it. There's no gangster stuff in it, but if they take the time and read it, they'll love that book.

Song of Solomon, I see so many people in that book. So many parts of life, even though it was written a long time ago in the '40s, you can see it today in 2006 in people's lives. How brothers and sisters, some can make it, and the other one don't, and this one don't want their children mingling with this one. I have cousins that are well-to-do . . . and they act like they're scared to talk to us because we're not well-to-do, or because we don't have corporate jobs, or you know, like they're afraid we're gonna want them to give us a job or something. And it's the same way it was in that book. It was all because [Macon Dead] thought he was the rich doctor in the town, and his sister was this bum or whatever he considered her, and he didn't want his kids mixing with her kids. And he stagnated his children by the way he raised them. And that's how I look at my cousins, like if they would really get to know me, they'd get to know they got a cousin that might could teach them something. No matter how far they done went in colleges, it's little things I might could teach them. Yeah, I done been to jail, but I can teach them some things about hey, don't hang with that person. I know her, you know, where they might not. Or I know that guy. He sell drugs. Don't date him, where they wouldn't know because they won't talk to me. They think they're better than me because of the way they've been raised, and I see that whole scenario in *Song of Solomon*.

Song of Solomon addressed abuse because Macon Dead was mean to his daughters and his wife. . . . [His wife] was afraid. . . . He did hit her because Pilate came to her rescue one time. And he used to didn't let her be a mother to her baby because he was mean like that, and that was abuse. . . . It made me feel like I understood why I stayed there, just like she did. Don't cause no trouble. Don't let nobody know. I understood why she stayed there; why she let him treat her like that; why she lived with no affection from him. It helped me realize somebody else went through this.

I like Toni Morrison's books because they have that southern tint to them. I can understand that lingo. It's like I lived there. I lived on those dirt roads most of them walk on. I know what it's like when the older people in the town put a label on you. And you might not even know you may be labeled from a child. They might have seen you the day you was born and gave you a name and you don't know why you're called that. Like Milkman didn't know why he was called Milkman. . . . That's how it is down there, you know; that's just how we are. . . . My mother didn't know how to read and write, so I know what's that like to have a parent that don't know how to read and write, and they sign an X for things. . . . I know what it's like when people don't know where they come from. My mother has no background. All she knows is that she was given to a lady named Miss [X] when she was first born, so her name is [X], and she married my father when she was fourteen. . . . They made up a birthday for her, you know. So when I read these books, I can relate because my mother was one of these type people that just came out of nowhere.

I use my own vanity and say that she was an angel from God, that God just put her here for a purpose 'cause she was so perfect. And she endured so much hardship and never complained. And she had twelve kids, and I asked my mother one time, I said, "Ma, how do you keep shoes on twelve kids' feet?" And this was after I'm in the city and stealing this stuff, and I'm like, "It's hard for me to keep it on two. How do you do it on twelve?" She say, "You just do it." You know, my brothers and sisters tell stories of how they had to wear cardboard in their shoe. And like I said, when I was younger, we didn't even have to wear shoes to school, and this was everybody in the town, so I assume everybody in the town must have been the same level of poorness 'cause nobody wore them. And that surely saved on shoes in the summertime 'cause you didn't have to wear them. . . . And then we all went to church on Sunday. My mother was a deacon in the church, you know, and I'm like, how can my mother be a deacon and my daddy run the juke joint and sell bootleg liquor and have gambling houses? But they never fought. She put up with him coming home drunk every day, you know, picking him up off the side of the road, all skinned up where he done fell and skinned hisself up. And if somebody bring him home, he lay on the front porch and piss all over hisself and mama say he wasn't coming in the house, and let him lay out there until that drunk wear off. You know, this was everyday life. But it was beautiful, and I wouldn't trade a day for nothing in the world.

And when I read Toni Morrison's books, I see this. I can go back there, and I be happy 'cause I can relate. I can actually see the dust flying when they're walking. I can see their bare feet. You know, I can see the people sitting on the bench on the church porch or on the porch, the way all the people gather together. And when somebody say, "Oh, that's such and such's son. Their daddy was crazy," I know what they do 'cause I remember that.

When I went to my mother's funeral, I told you I got there the morning of her funeral. The purple jogging suit I wore from jail is what I wore to my mother's funeral. I didn't have time to change clothes. And as I was going in the church, this lady, Ms. [Smith] said, "That's [X's] girl, the one been locked up, up north." . . . All these years, I will always remember her for saying that when I was going in that church. I heard her through that crowd. The church was so packed that people had to stand outside. And through all them people standing outside, I heard her say that as I was going up to the church. "That's [X's] girl, the one that been locked up, up north." And even though I knew everybody knew I had been in jail, that was the furthest thing from my mind what these people think of me right now. You know, my mother is laying in here, and they say she's dead. This is all I'm thinking. That's the furthest thing from my mind what these people think right now, but I know these are those kind of people. I'm the one that got locked up, up north, so I'm something to see when I come home because I'm the one been locked up, up north. . . . I had a brother that had been locked up down there, but it's different when you leave and go up north and get locked up. When you go up north, you're supposed to be successful. You don't go up there and get locked up. You go up there to be successful. And especially a girl. Especially a girl. You know, I was supposed to have been successful, and I worked hard in those tobacco fields, and I worked hard in those cotton fields. I was conditioned to hard work, and I still am. That's why I believe I can endure almost anything because working in them fields was hard. And a lot of people don't know about that.

But see, when I read Toni Morrison's books, and I think about how Pilate and her brother had to survive after their father was killed, I know what that's like to have to survive. You can do it in them woods if you know them woods. But you got to know. A person from the city couldn't go live in the woods. They wouldn't know what to eat and what not to eat. But I would. They wouldn't know how to kill a chicken. They wouldn't know how to survive off of the land. But I would. So all those things I love, I learned. You know, they wouldn't know how to kill a snake with their hand. But I do, 'cause I been doing it since I was a child. See, and when I read her books, and I read little stuff like that in the books about how Pilate kept them bones in that bag and things like that, all through the book I'm waiting to figure out what this is. I'm thinking it was an animal bone 'cause you could keep animal bones like that. 'Cause I've kept animal bones. . . . We're not afraid of stuff like that where other people would be like, "Ugh, that's something dead!" We're not afraid of that because it's a history to that, how they die, why they die. You know, we look for the history to that. But that's why I love her books 'cause she takes me back.

Beloved is another story that blew my mind, the way she went back and brought this baby back. This baby was angry because it didn't get a chance to live. This book was great. I think I heard somewhere where *Beloved* was actually based on a true story of a woman that killed her kids to keep them from being sold into slavery. But [Morrison] took it and showed, well, what if this baby could come back? What would this baby do? How would it feel? And the baby made the mother wait on them. You know, she just came in and took over the house. But the mother knew who it was. The mother recognized, even though she came back a grown woman, and the shoes that had never had dirt on them or anything, the shiny shoes she wore, it's little details like that that I love in a book. I read *Beloved* once, and I'm thinking of going back and reading it again because that's the thing about her books: if you read them again, you'll get more and more. It's like it never stops.

That's how I am about *The Song of Solomon*. I keep getting more and more and more. I keep seeing whole sentences or whole scenes that I didn't see the last time I read it. . . . This book has so much for you to pick apart, so much! I gotta read it again 'cause I gotta get a better understanding of what Macon Dead saw his wife doing with her father. I can't get a clear picture. I think she was sucking his fingers or I thought she was having oral sex with him, but she was doing something so gross that he never touched her again. Then there's the issue of her molesting Milkman, you know. Would you consider that child molestation? Or do you look at her state of mind, where she was thinking because Macon wouldn't mess with her no more, that she was using her son to get some kind of pleasure? . . . And then the friend, with his crusade that he was on. And how did he end up killing Milkman for that? Now that's a part I haven't been able to understand. . . . That is so much in there to pick apart.

. . . I like to read self-help books, but a lot of self-help books turns into religious books. It's like the answer to it all is to turn to religion. Like whatever you can get from a book that says how to bring yourself out of depression, it's always gonna go back to God. So you might as well read sections in the Bible about how to lift your spirit, or how to pray to God to take these pains away from you, or how to get through the pain just by holding onto God's hand. So the self-help books bring me back to the Bible. I don't like that they always turns to religion because I know how to incorporate religion in my life. . . . I know about the spiritual realm. You tell me about the humanistic realm. You tell me how to go about it on this Earth. . . . Help me deal with my cousin that keeps pushing me down, you know, so I won't hit her, or so I won't try to hurt her back. God will take care of my soul. But I need to know on a day-to-day level, realistically.

If I see a self-help book, I'm gonna pick it up and I'm gonna read it, just to see what it's got to say. But I can get maybe three or four pages and realize whether it's bullcrap or just stuff for the weak-minded. I can pick it up in a minute and decide it isn't for me. It isn't strong enough for me. Because a lot of people haven't been through so much, so this book can catch them early and can help them. But after you've gone beyond that, you need something bigger. Like, let's take, for instance, abuse, domestic violence. . . . When you've been beaten for fifteen years, that book that tells you, "Once they start shouting, leave" or, "If they hit you once, they'll hit again," it's no help for you because you've already been in it for fifteen years. Now tell me how to get out the anger. This is what I need. I don't need this book that's going to tell me, "Once an abuser, he will hit you again. Go to a shelter. Save money." You know, it's too late for all of that at that point, so that book won't help me.

. . . Everything I read makes me think how stupid I was to stay in it. How all these avenues was there for me to get out. See, and it makes me think that the average young woman would probably be like me. Of course, there are stronger young women who would get out immediately, who's been taught that you don't let nobody treat you like this. But the average young woman would do what I did, would stay in it for love, for family. And that's where something is needed to tell them, "No, it's not gonna get any better." And these books say that, but when you've been in it for ten or fifteen years, you need a book to come at you like your best friend. You need a book that come at you strong like you care, a book really to snatch you out of it.

I don't really like those *Chicken Soup for the Prisoner's Soul* books.[14] They're just mediocre jargons to me, just sayings and poems and little stories. . . . It didn't have like a soul. . . . I thought it was gonna give me some food for thought. I need a book that I can carry around with me in my head, and I couldn't carry that around. Nothing profound was in it. You know, nothing stayed with me. . . . I couldn't tell you one thing I read in none of those *Chicken Soup* books and I read about three or four. I keep trying them and they all keep doing the same thing for me: nothing.

There's a book I like about Madea. Tyler Perry was a homeless man in Atlanta. He made plays where he plays Madea. Yeah, he wears this old crooked wig and this big old dress. He got *Madea Goes to Jail, Madea's Family Reunion,*[15] all of this. Well, he's wrote a book now with all these thoughts and just answers to simple questions.[16] Now, I like that book because he was a homeless man, and he can tell you some things that are real about life. Like, he tells you simple things about how to use Vaseline to keep warm. How to put it on your feet with your socks, and it'll help keep the heat in your feet in the winter when you're cold. . . . Even though he's a millionaire now, this is stuff he remembers from being homeless. So this money haven't made him forget where he came from because he wrote this book on simple things, advice he give about how to talk to your teenagers and things like that. . . . It's not sugar-coated. It's just down low, just life. *Chicken Soup* feels pampered, I guess. You gotta hit me harder than that for me to feel it. To me, a person that can take a *Chicken Soup* and think it's the all in all is shallow. They don't want to penetrate any deep. They want to just feel on the surface like that. They don't want to hit any deeper. I want [a book] to stay with me. I want it to impact me. I want it to make me think. I want it to change something about the way I view tomorrow. I want it to have that kind of effect on me that I change the way I see the next person, the way I treat that next person.

Now *Bastard Out of Carolina?*[17] I have tried to get so many people to read that book! But it's a hard book. . . . It was a lot close to home because I was molested when I was little girl, and I never told anybody. I feel so sad for [Bone]. I have to tell myself she's a character, but to me she's a little girl still running around in North Carolina somewhere. . . . I lived that book. I felt like it hurt me physically when he raped her that day in that house. . . .

You read this book, I ain't got to tell you my story. . . . All I got to tell you is, "This is me."

The only difference is I never told my mother. But when I told my sister, my sister got me out of there. But my mother never knew 'til the day she died. I never told her. And it was a guy that lived with us that was like a brother to me. . . . So now I'm real cautious of my girls. Real cautious. I watch everything. I have a brother that molested a kid, you know, and I tell everybody he's in contact with. . . . Even my mother knew he had done that, and she asked me to forgive him and to stop doing that to him, and I told her, "I forgive him, but I'm not gonna let him do this to no other kid. If I know he's with some woman and she got little kids, I feel like it's my duty to let her know he did this." . . . He's my brother, and I still love him and everything, but you got a problem. . . . That little girl was nine years old. You got a problem. And she was your niece. You have a problem. And that problem ain't just went away because you got caught or because mama know or because everybody in the family know. You still got a problem, and if people don't watch their kid around you, you'll do it again.

That would be a good book to read with [other prisoners] because I believe nine out of ten of the women could relate. And if not relate, if any of them got little girls, it'll be informative. It'll be a way they can see that they never saw before. They'll be able to see through the eyes of that child. They'll be able to see through that drunk mother that's not paying attention. They'll be able to see that man, what kind of character he might appear to be. . . . This one counselor, every time I saw her I'd be like, "Have you got that book and read it yet?" Because I knew if she read it, she'd share it with her group. . . . Every woman should read that book just to be aware that it can happen like that. That a man that you love or think you love could be mistreating your child behind your back. . . . I think it should be in the men's penitentiary too. I think it might make men be better fathers. . . . If men could see that book, maybe they won't be so quick to walk away from their little girls and let another man raise them. Or even if they let another man raise them, maybe they'll have a relationship with their child where that little girl can come talk to them, or a little boy can talk to them and be able to tell them.

. . . The first time I read *Bastard Out of Carolina*, my whole focus was on the little girl. Now I want to go back and focus on the mother and the man . . . [and] see if anything else in there can give me a clue to how the stepfather got like this. How the mother got like this. Why she let her daughter go through this. . . . I gotta find out what was going on with this lady so that I won't be so judgmental towards the next woman who lets a man beat her kids or who let her boyfriend molest her children. . . . Now in my head, this mother is just like nothing to me because she let this happen to her child, 'cause she knew it was happening and she still chose this man over her child. She don't know how hurt that child was that she chose that.

. . . And there's another book around here that I gotta read. Every time I see somebody reading it, they're crying. It's about a little boy that was abused. *A Child Called "It."*[18] . . . I know a lot of people in here that are child abusers, and I got this wall against child abusers. Like, how could you do this? So I want to read this book to look at the person that's doing the abuse so I can better understand where they're at in their head. And that way I won't prejudice myself against the abuser. 'Cause I'm sure this book is gonna give some background into what happened. . . . Now for me, for instance, I feel like I emotionally abuse my kids by going in and out of jail. But I thought all this time that by me letting them live with my sister who was stability, they was okay. . . . I would like to see a book on that, children whose mothers are in prison, how they come up, their feelings. You know, I'd like to see a *Chicken Soup* for the soul of children whose parents are in prison.

. . . I haven't read a book yet that wrote a true story about prison. They send out this horrific picture, I guess to deter people if that's the purpose. . . . A true story would focus on the women and the things they do in prison. It would focus on everybody trying to get the next good book. It would focus on the groups and the programs that they have. It would focus on people getting bad news from home that somebody done died, and how the chaplain goes to them, and how the other women rally around them. It would focus on how when women go to the board, and they're denied their freedom, how it takes other inmates to help them get through. Or to see somebody with worse time is what gets you through that. And the officers don't just shut you down, "Well, so what?" You know, they don't have that attitude. They have more compassion than is thought. It also would focus on the disciplinary procedures in the prison. You're not thrown in a dark hole when you get in trouble. Yeah, you're locked in a place called "the hole." But it's not a dark hole with no mattress where it's pitch black in there, and you're just in a room with concrete. You get a bed. You get a mattress. You get a shower. You get books to read. Other girls can bring you books to read back there. So it's not like nothing that they show on TV.

. . . I'd love to read a book about a booster. I'm thinking of trying to get a book out. I've never read a book about somebody that was caught up in that. And that's a whole world that people really don't even understand. If I could read a book like that, it may help me understand how I function and why I function the way that I do. And I try to find books about booster stories, but I've never been able to find one that goes in depth to the mental state of a person that's caught up in that. I ask around to see if anybody's seen anything or read anything. A lot of times, I'm ashamed to ask because I don't want anybody to know that I'm trying to figure me out. Or that I'm really trying to get help, because that's what my ego keeps saying. In here, that's like a status quo if you were a great booster, but I have to let somebody know I don't want to be this no more. I want to come out of this.

5 Bobbie

—∽—

Life Narrative

"I've been overcoming all my life"

I WAS BORN in Cleveland. I was raised by my mom and my stepdad first. [When my parents divorced,] my biological father wanted custody of his kids, but he didn't want me. . . . He took the oldest kids and left me with [my mom]. And then she got married to my stepdad. . . . I thought he was more my real dad. I mean, he never treated me any different than he treated the rest of the kids. In fact, sometimes he treated me better. So I guess he was a good relationship.

Then by the time I was in kindergarten, they separated. So I went to live with my grandmother and my grandfather, my mom's parents. They died when I was in the sixth grade, a couple months prior. I lived with my stepfather 'cause my mom was always sick. . . . [But] my stepdad got killed, so I ended up staying with my mom. Then my mom got sick and went to the hospital. Her next husband decided that he didn't want me in the house. So I was shifted from place to place to place to place. Stayed with a cousin, a brother, a stepbrother. Back to the cousin, back to the brother. Then I finally went back home.

My family was totally dysfunctional. Basically, I never had a childhood. 'Cause I always took care of the two boys and the little girl under me. And then after I got done taking care of them, it was like somebody else's child came along, and then by the time I was twenty-one, I had my first child. So it was like I skipped over childhood. . . . It was rough. Real rough. . . . I'm only two years older than one [younger sibling], three years than the other one, and four than the other one. So it was like, I'm their age raising them.

We ended up with my mom, and one time I remember my mama asking us whether we was hungry. And they all looked at me. They shook their heads. And I said, "Yes." And she's like, "I'm not talking to you. I'm talking to them three." And I'm like, "You have to remember. They've been with me all their life." I mean, I was always the constant thing in their life so they was used to depending on me. And then we moved in with my mom and my other stepdad, and he tried to cause a wedge between us, which actually didn't work because now my little sister and my one little brother that's right under me, they'll send me money, and they'll write me, and they ask my daughter how I'm doing and stuff like that. I have twenty brothers and sisters from my mother and biological father. But those are the only two I'm close with. I had twenty-one. One died.

School came to me easy. It was like when we were small, I had an older brother that wanted to be a teacher. So we played school quite a bit, and if we got things wrong, we got hit with the yardstick. So we learned real good how to add, multiply, subtract. School was real easy for me. It's easy now. I mean, I go to college. [Other women] all cram, you know, they study for the whole week. I'm always the last-minute study, and I still get a C or a B, and they all tell me they hate me [laughing].

... Violence has been a big part of my life. . . . I've got whupped with extension cords. One time with a bullwhip. I watched my mom and my stepdad fight. My mom and my dad fought. And then my kids' father and I fought. My stepfather, my father, and then my kids' father did the beatings. My older brothers, I watched them beat their girlfriends.

My father's side of the family, they drank. My aunt drinks. My uncle drinks. My father drank. My stepfather drank. My brothers and sisters have drank, used drugs. I even drank and used drugs. My kids' father drank and used, but it's just like a normal thing to do. I was involved with marijuana, opium, hash—God!—heroin, crack, cocaine, pills, uppers, and downers. Just about anything you can name, anything that didn't involve shooting up 'cause I was scared of needles. But anything smokable or takeable, I used them. I was eleven when I started. Ten when I started smoking cigarettes. Eleven when I started smoking weed.

The first time I came to prison, I had a chaotic life. I was using crack. I was helping people sell crack. I came to jail for possession. I did six months. . . . Prison is like, oh my god. It's so filthy, and it's so old and raggedy and pipes burst, and people were sleeping under sewage pipes, and I was one of those people. And one time the sewage pipes broke, and it flooded the place, and people was walking with feces and urine, and it was just nasty. That was just a dirty place. . . . When I was in [prison] the first time, I was younger, and I knew it wasn't a joke, but I played it like it was a joke 'cause I was only there six months. So I went through it, and I didn't have to really focus on anything.

But when I went home, I turned my life totally around. I stopped getting high. I didn't hang around the people, places, or things anymore. I got my own apartment. I was doing real good. I got my disability. I let my niece stay with me and her boyfriend. . . . And they said I was driving the car and they sold drugs out of the car, which was a lie, but I'm here anyway 'cause I have a record. . . . With me having a public defender, and after his statements he made after my trial, I do believe he was working with them instead of working for me. . . . That's my public "pretenders." 'Cause you're just a name. Okay, they don't even know who you are. . . . They don't fight for your case. They just go through the motions. They want everybody to take a plea, which just kind of sucks.

. . . I was clean for six years before I came back this time. I've done the rehabs. I've done the readings. I've done the AA things, the NA things, and it's like I'm fed up to here with all that mess because it's like—don't get me wrong—AA is good for some people. For me it's not good. They tried to tell me I was alcoholic when I knew I'd drink three drinks, and I'm done. Okay. I mean, when I went to NA, I was okay, I know I'm an addict. I know what I should do, what I shouldn't do for me to stay clean, so I'm cool. I don't need the meetings 'cause meetings depress me. It makes me want to use. I went to three different rehabs. I still got high after each rehab. I didn't stop until I wanted to stop. For each addict, it's their choice to stop. . . . Until you're ready to stop getting high, you're just not going to stop getting high. Prison made me stop. Plus me being away from my kids for that six months. I had never been away from my kids.

And now these three years is really killing me 'cause it's like I've never been away from them this long. . . . Being in prison this time is hell. Even though my daughter is twenty-one and she's taking care of her little brother, I have to ask her to send me money. And the child shouldn't have to take care of her parents, you know, especially when their parent is able to take care of itself. I mean, that's bad for me. I hadn't seen my kids in over a year, and they finally came to see me. My son is thirteen. He'll be fourteen in June. My son has grown. He's taller than me. He has a deep voice. I missed all that happening. . . . I missed my one granddaughter's birth, and she was one by the time I met her, and it was like I missed a whole year of her life. . . . My children are my joys. My daughter has her brother and her two kids she takes care of, and she goes to college, and she works a full-time job. I am so proud of her. My son is on the honor roll. I'm real proud of him 'cause I'm like 100 percent with education. Education, education, education. I have my kids knowing that education is the key to any successful thing they want in life.

. . . Me, they tell me I'm a strong individual, which I mean, I can shoulder a lot, but I do have a side where I just can't take it no more. And I do get fed up. . . . Basically, I grew up hearing [that I'm strong] because whenever my sisters and brothers wanted something from my mother, they would come to me and tell me and I'd go and tell my mom. That was for older and younger [siblings]. I shouldered everything. When my mom passed, I was put in the place of being the executor. And I was on drugs, so my sisters and brothers fought, and I ended up still being the executor, although we never settled my mom's whole situation. . . . It's to the point where it's just like I take care of everybody. I'm a take-care person. I take care of this one and that one and that one and this one. And then this one person was asking, "Well, who takes care of you?" and I was like, "I don't know. I think I do. I'm not sure. Hmm. Maybe I should find somebody to take care of me, too." And I still haven't found that person. So it's me.

This time I got three years, and my older cousin, she was here when I first got here, and she told me, "You will go to school. You will do this. You will get in this group and you will do this, that, and the other." . . . And when she left, she made sure she tells some of the other old-timers. And my one mother-sister,[1] she went home, and she said, "Well, I'm leaving and you have to do this, this, this, and this." . . . I go to college [in prison]. Yeah, I'm just very active. . . . I've participated in just about all the groups. I'm the vice president of education in Toastmasters.[2] I've done Coping, Anger Management, Family Relations, Self-Sabotage, Smoking Cessation. I'm in Prison Media Literacy. That's where we watch movies and then we critique them. We have very educated conversations about them. This guy comes in and he brings movies in. Then we talk about them. We saw *Eve's Bayou* and *We Were Warriors*. Those are the only two so far. We meet once a week, every Saturday.

Then we have this other group, Cleveland State students come in, and a group of ladies that are in the Prison Media Literacy group, we get together with them, and we're coming up with a way to put a face on Northeast Pre-Release so people won't just think that it's a prison. Yes, it is a prison, but there are people here. We're human. You know, just 'cause we made a mistake, and we end up getting caught, everybody breaks the law one way or the other. They just don't get caught. So for the people that do get caught, it's to show people that felons are just normal people. You know, we made a mistake, we got caught, we went to jail. That's it. We're not like the leper people or you know, like, "Oh, my God! They've been in prison."

We're gonna do a play. We're gonna try to get a book together where it's like a lot of the ladies' thoughts and how they feel about overcoming. So we're gonna get poetry, stories, all those kind of things from the ladies of Northeast and put it together. We'll act the part out. . . . I already put something in there, but I have to make it deeper [laughing]. I have to dig deeper. It's a reflection of your life and how you overcame.

See, 'cause the way I started it off is like I've been overcoming all my life. I overcame when I was born; I was born with a hole in my heart. . . . My mom was like, "Okay, so what? You have a hole in your heart. You can still do this, and you can still do that." And my pediatrician told her not to stop me from doing things 'cause that would make me an invalid. So therefore, she never stopped me. And I did it all [laughing]! I was just a little go-getter, getting in everything. Anything my brothers could do, I felt I could do. My sisters, I never wanted to imitate them 'cause they were like prissy and real girlie girlie.

. . . A lot of people say women end up in prison because of a man. Some-times that's true, and then sometimes it's just the economic situation. The way of life that they have. True enough, there's a lot of women out here because there's no self-defense law in Ohio. And it's easy for people to sit up and say, "Oh, you should have left him," but I been in that situation. It's not always easy to leave an abuser because you have guilty—like me—I had guilty feel-ings because I know how it feels to be left, and I know how it feels to not be wanted. So therefore, I just couldn't leave him, you know what I'm saying? And then there's women are here because it was either a you or me situation. Self-preservation. . . . And then a lot of people are in here because of the way the laws are. They're not geared for women. . . . And then in some instances it is because of a man. Then in some instances, it's because of economic stand-ings, education, where you grew up at, how you grew up.

We [prisoners] just made mistakes, and anybody could end up in our situa-tion. You could end up getting in a car and getting in a car accident. There's a young girl here. She's turned twenty-one in here. She came in here when she was nineteen. She had three different jobs. She fell asleep behind the wheel and got in a car accident and hurt somebody. Okay, so it ended up she did hurt somebody. I feel that they should have had her make restitution to that person. But I don't feel they should have put her in prison. See, when she came to prison, she was very, very naive and innocent. And the things that she seen, it took her innocence away, and that's sad 'cause prison shouldn't take anybody's innocence.

. . . If you just downright go out here and rob somebody at gunpoint, okay, go to jail. But if you make a mistake, I don't think this is the answer. I don't think this is the answer for people with drug problems 'cause they don't do nothing and they turn that door into a revolving door. I think that they should have to go somewhere where they're going to get treatment. Make some lockdown facilities. . . . Give them some kind of treatment and then give them some kind of work ethic or some kind of work-study where they can go out and get a job and start living a productive life. And then along the way help them get housing or help them get on their feet. And then let them go into the world. Other than that, if you just have somebody in jail, you send them back out to the streets, what are they gonna do? They're gonna turn around and come right back. A lot of people look at jail as somewhere warm to sleep in the winter, three meals free. Clothes, even though they're uniforms, and a warm place to sleep. And that's a lot of the drug offenders come back in the winter just for that. They get caught for like six month crimes. Okay, I do a little petty this and I get six or nine months. Okay, I do this, I get a year. They just turn this door into a revolving door. And it's sad. It's real sad, and nobody in here's even looking at it. The elected officials want to put us in jail, but now they're overcrowded so they don't know what to do. . . . It's not solving anything. It's just making more problems.

What's next for me is I'm gonna go home. . . . I want to relocate. I want to get married. And just enjoy the rest of my life. I like to smile. I like to have fun. That's what I want to do. Enjoy life, period. Just being alive, 'cause I consider myself really blessed.

—m—

Reading Narrative

"Everybody don't end up with a prince"

I READ EVERY day. Anytime I get a chance. Like today, I don't have school, so I probably would . . . read in between when I get up, and then go to my lunch and come back and sit on my bed and read. Everybody always says, "All you do is stay on that bed and read." And I'm like, "Well, I don't get in trouble this way." It's easy. So I read, like, pretty much all day unless I have something else to do.

I got all kinds of books at home. There I have religious books. I have different kinds of Bibles. I have *Habits*.[3] It's an Islamic book, and it tells you that this one said this, this one said that. And the Qur'an. Then I have romance books, you know the Harlequin Romances. And then I have how-to books. How to build a deck. How to fix this. Not that I fix anything; it's just that it's good to know if I ever need to. How to lay tile. I know how to do that. I've done that. I mean, I try to stay well-rounded. Medical encyclopedia. Which pills is which 'cause I was into drugs, so I always studied all my drugs. I just got a roundabout collection of books.

Here I like urban literature, sometimes romance. Harold Robbins, I like him. Jackie Collins, I love her. Autobiographies. I'm really into black history. Anything that deals with black history. . . . It just depends on my mood. 'Cause one day I came in and I had a black history book, I had a romance novel, and then I had a drama, and the girl looked at me and she said, "God, you're well-read." And I'm like, "Yeah I'm well-rounded here."

I like anything that deals with what happened back in the day, you know, back during slavery times. During the South and North war, the Civil War. What went on in the '60s and the '50s and the '20s. I'm just interested in it all. They have a couple of reference books over there [in the library] that's real, real thick. And then one is called *Black American History*.[4] I read that; you have to read it over in the library. They have books about Colin Powell, a lot of the sports players, actors.

. . . I just like go over to the library and pick up the little paperback books from the Cleveland library and read those. . . . I look for black American literature first. If they got something new, I grab that. . . . Brenda Jackson's good. Donna Hill's good. . . . They're basically romance books with a little twist. . . . If there isn't anything new, I'll go to Harold Robbins. But now I've read all his books. I've read all of Jackie Collins's books. I've read Dan Brown's books. . . . Now I have *Dreamgirl*[5] about the Supremes and Mary Wilson. Then I'm reading an urban book, *Bad Girlz*[6]. . . . So, I'm switching it up.

. . . I read the urban books before, then I stopped reading them, and now I'm reading them again. I stopped just to get a break from them. The same old thing all the time. . . . Where I'm from, we don't really have urban books, and now that I know that they're there, it's like oh, I can't wait to get home and get some money 'cause then I'm going to order this, and I'll order this, and I got to read this, and I gotta read that, and it's like I'm excited. . . . I like all of the urban books I've ever read. I've read Triple Crown, I've read urban books, and I've read Black Expressions books.[7] I mean, when they're talking about what's going on in the streets, how life was, how it could end up—some of them end up nice, some of them end up not so nice—but I mean, it's the reality part about it, 'cause there's something I can touch base with. A lot of the ladies order urban books, so I borrow books from them and read their books 'cause I can't afford to order them while I'm in here.

They have a ban on the urban books, which is totally uncalled for because it's like regardless of what you read, it doesn't mean you're gonna go out and do it. . . . I can read the *Black Dahlia*[8] book but it's not like I'm gonna go out and kill anybody, 'cause that's not in my personality. . . . I don't understand why we can't get [urban books] when we can get Mario Puzo, and his is about gangsters and the Mafia and priests that have kids, that sleep together. And I read about incest. I can read about murders, but I can't read about drug dealing and murder on the streets. It don't make sense. . . . They're afraid that the drug dealing and the street life will get ingrained into your brain and that's the way you'll go out there and live. . . . [But] that's not gonna happen. I mean, common sense will tell you that these books are books. They may pattern after somebody, but they're not anybody. They're fictional.

. . . Okay, and then [urban books] are dealing with everyday life that a lot of people just live. They're real. I don't feel like I'm in a fantasy world reading that. I don't feel like I'm a six-year-old, you know what I'm saying? Some books make you feel like you're in a fantasy world. *Alice in Wonderland.* Nobody lives that life! *Cinderella.* Nobody lives this life! Oh, god—the one with Julia Roberts, *Pretty Woman.*[9] Nobody lives this life! . . . I could never get into *Alice in Wonderland* or *Sleeping Beauty.* I mean, come on now. Everybody don't end up with a prince. So I can't get into those unrealistic books. I want something that deals with regular, everyday life. It's always nice to read about somebody who looks princess. The poor person gets to be like the pretty woman. That's always cute, but it's not realistic. I like realistic books.

The urban books, you can identify with that because that's street life. It's like that's how it is on the streets. It's part of life. It's a life that I've never personally lived. Well, kinda sorta I lived that life [laughing]. But mine wasn't so hardcore. I'm from a smaller community. Everybody knows everybody. I mean yeah, I had a rough childhood, but for the most part I was taught don't break the law, dah, dah, dah, dah, dah. Go to church, blah, blah, blah and was raised Baptist. But I guess [urban books] are a part of life. I'm into things that faces reality because even though I would love to live in a rose-colored glass world, I am a realist so I know that this happens.

I like *Payback Is A Mutha*[10] because it's about karma; when you do wrong to somebody, it comes back on you. I'm a firm believer in that. You reap what you sow. It's about street life, and I can identify with it 'cause it's about live people. But I also can look at it as a learning experience. . . . *Sheisty,* that's another book that came from Triple Crown. *Sheisty* and *Sheisty II.*[11] It's about these girls, they was from the projects, and how they came up. One ended up getting killed. . . . I can identify with the characters in this book because they're all black, you know, so when I'm reading it, I'm like, okay, yeah. And the setting is a real setting. It's not like one of these fairy tales, the Huxtable family.[12] Now, that's not what's really happening in the world. That kind of stuff don't really happen in the projects. But see, I'm from the middle class so I can see the smoke both ways, you know what I'm saying? I can deal with the poor people because I understand their fight. I can also deal with the rich people, and I understand that they fought hard to get to where they are.

G-Spot[13] was a good book. There was this young girl, and she started going with this guy that owned a bar, and then inside his bar he was selling drugs and doing porn movies, and it was a gambling house. He was just breaking the law all the way around. Plus he had a nightclub, and at the end he thought that she disrespected him some kind of way so they drugged her, and they ended up putting her in a porn movie. . . . It just showed me that you have to really know the person that you end up with because that person could be really, really evil and you not know it, and you shouldn't just go with some-body for the money. . . . Some women allow that kind of treatment. I wouldn't allow myself to be treated like that. I don't care how much money you have. You are not going to mistreat me. I'm mine. Because I've lived through that. You know, I've lived through abuse. I've lived through being treated badly. I refuse to go back to that. I won't allow that to happen to me anymore. And if I see it happening to me, I know how to get out of it. I know how to walk away. At one point in time I wouldn't walk away because I know how it feels to have somebody just walk away from you and leave you hanging. So I had trouble walking away from people. Now today I don't have trouble walking away from anybody. I can walk away.

I like all the urban books I've read, but there's one I couldn't get with, and that was *Slipping*.[14] That was about somebody smoking crack. . . . I'm six years clean, so it didn't upset me so much to read about crack because . . . that's part of my past. I've done that. Got over it. Now I have to watch . . . for my triggers and things, but it doesn't bother me just reading about it. . . . [But] with me being here, with me hav[ing] already done that, they weren't really portraying it the way it should have been. I mean, they made it like he smoked it once and he was hooked, and that's not how it goes. And so it was like, okay, I can't get into this one. It wasn't right.

. . . Jackie Collins books, now those are just like fantasy books, okay. Oh, god! The money. The glamorous life that they lead. For me, it would be a fantasy to have all that money and live that life. . . . You read about these rich kids that's flying around in BMWs and Mercedes and driving around in limos and carrying on. It's like, hmm, that's a nice way to live! . . . I've never been rich and famous, and I'll probably never know these people, but they show me where rich people still have problems too, and . . . we're all the same.

Some of the urban books is like fantasy, too. It's just about drug dealers, and all the money that they have and how they treat their women. . . . What a way to live! That would be nice. But then you have to deal with the police, and I guess I can see the reality in the urban books more so than Jackie's because urban books are more like me and where I'm used to being or what I'm used to doing. And I'm in prison [laughing]. And then in the rich people books, they don't never get caught. . . . In the Jackie Collins books they use drugs. They've had overdoses. They've had murders. They went to trial. They got off. They all cheat on each other. . . . I mean, they break law after law after law, but they never get caught. The police are never involved. There's never anybody going to jail. There's never anybody going to prison. [But] in the urban books you go to prison. You go to jail.

. . . Reading is an escape for me sometimes from my reality to somebody else's reality, you know, escaping from my life to get to somebody else's problems. . . . Sometimes when I'm reading a book, it's like I just tune you out. I tune out everything around me and everybody. When I'm lonely, I want to get romanced, so I read a romance novel. If I'm feeling thuggish, I get my thuggish feeling out of the way with a black or a Mafia book 'cause I love the Mafia. If I just want to be mischievous, I read Jackie [Collins] 'cause they're always mischievous. It's just different books that make me feel different ways. [When I feel thuggish,] I put myself where the characters are so it's like, okay, you're dealing drugs, I'm dealing drugs. The Mafia, you're killing people, I'm killing people. But I wouldn't really be doing it, you know what I'm saying? I'm just standing back there watching what you're doing. It's exciting. I read urban books or Mario Puzo for that. I've read all his books up here, *The Family*, *The Godfather*,[15] all those. . . . [Urban books] deal with black people and Hispanic people; [Mafia books] is dealing with Italian people. They're all immigrants. We all migrated one way or the other to America. . . . They call black and Hispanic people "thugs" and they call [Italian people] "Mafia." Same thing, two different words.

I read Mario Puzo's *The Family,* and that book was crazy. It was about a Roman Catholic priest, a Spanish priest, ended up in the Vatican. He had three kids by this woman. He took care of her really, really well. But when she had her kids, he took the kids and he raised them in the Vatican with him. And they had their little section of the Vatican where the kids stayed. And as they got older, they got little apartments. The daughter ended up sleeping with her brother. . . . She got pregnant by her brother. . . . Her other brother got killed 'cause he slept with his little brother's wife. . . . That stuff happens. I understand it. I know it. I lived through it. It happened to me so it's the same part of life.

I read for escape, enjoyment, to stop being lonely sometimes, to know there's other people outside of me that are like me. 'Cause I read books about abused women and stuff like that. Dysfunctional families. It helps me understand that I'm not the only person that went through the stuff I went through. . . . Like this girl the other night, she gave her icebreaker, which is the very first speech you give in Toastmasters. She gave an icebreaker, and it was this white lady, and I'm just sitting there looking at her like, "God, you're telling my life," 'cause I mean, we went through the same things, did the same things, had the same things happen to us. 'Cause I was molested at the age of five by three different family members. At the age of five, she was molested. So it was like, okay, I identify with that. She started using drugs early. I started using drugs early. I identified with that. She was in an abusive relationship. I was in an abusive relationship. I dealt with that. She broke the law. I broke the law. We're both in prison. I identified with that. I said, "Welcome to the struggles of the sisters. . . . I swear to God, you was telling my life story." I said, "I now have another sister; that's you," and she was like, "You know what? That meant so much to me." . . . A lot of women that's in the prison have been molested or raped. A lot of women is either on alcohol or drugs and have been in an abusive relationship. We have a lot of the same dysfunctional characteristics as each other. It's a whole city of women just alike and it's like, wow! That's deep. I never realized that.

. . . I read Mary Monroe's *God Don't Like Ugly*.[16] It was about a little girl who was abused, and she never told anybody except her friend. . . . It was another one of those karma books because her friend had did all this devastation and killing people and carrying on, and then I believe she lost her child and she was having trouble with her husband. She was just like, okay, God don't like ugly. You know, don't be ugly because then she would notice that ugly things would happen to ugly people. And it don't mean your looks. It just means your actions, your ugly ways. And then in the second book, *God Still Don't Like Ugly*,[17] it just showed how she went on with her life, and how she tried to make it. I like both of those. Those is real 'cause they had abuse, domestic violence, dysfunction. Yeah, I can identify with that. I've been through all of it.

. . . I read [Joyce Meyer's] *Battlefield of the Mind*. I like that a whole lot. Because at the time I was going through a lot of things, and I know what's right, but I was doing what was wrong. And then she explained how your mind has a battlefield. You know, you have a fight with good and evil. And it was like, okay, this makes sense to me. A lot of things that she said to me in that book, it made sense. So it was like, okay, I'm not crazy. I'm not weird.

[At this point], I think I've been self-helped enough. I just got to go with the flow here. I'm just taking each day as it comes. Each moment as it comes. Each hour as it comes. . . . With self-help, they want you to do this and this and this and this. And be on schedule for this, and I'm not a schedule type person. It's too structured. . . . I know my life, okay. I know the depressed areas. I know the happy areas. I know it. I don't need to be reading about it. I'm one of these type people who if you try to drill something in me, I put up a wall, and I'll fight you every step of the way. But if you just let me just go with the flow and ease into it here . . . then I'm okay.

. . . I wish they had more real religious books or religious subjects in the library. Dan Brown just blew me away with his *The Da Vinci Code*.[18] I loved that 'cause it had a lot of truths in it, and a lot of people think that it's not true, but it is true 'cause the Roman Catholic Church in Rome does have a lot of old documents that tells about our past that we don't know anything about, but the older people like Da Vinci . . . knew about them. It made me think about how the Bible was created by a man. That the only things in there is about men. It made me think about how there was twelve disciples, but there's only four of them in the Bible. So what happened to the rest of them? Where are their books? Where's Jesus's books at? I'm sure his mom was a smart woman, so if Mary was intelligent, why didn't she write a book? Mary Magdalene, she was following Jesus, so why wouldn't she know anything or write anything down? And then all the women in the Bible were whores, queens, and Mary. Other than that, they do something devious. I mean, Eve had Adam eat the apple. Okay, first sin of the world. . . . And everything in the Bible is like woman is on the negative side and the man's on the positive side, so it's like, okay, so we're just evil, which is not true. All women are not evil. We can be evil. We can be vindictive, but we are not all born that way. But from the way the Bible reads, it's oh, if you're a girl child, it's bad, and I just can't get into that. *The Da Vinci Code* showed that there's another way to look at the Bible. And where are the books that are hidden? . . . There's some of the Dead Sea Scrolls that the Roman Catholic Church doesn't want anybody to know because if it wasn't, they would be printed and put into a book like the Bible is. King James had people translate the Bible into what he wanted it to say. The Bible is in order to shock and control people, and that's what he did. He controlled them with the Bible instead of telling the truth.

The way I feel is that most of the religions come to the same point, but they just get to it in different ways. . . . I was raised Pentecostal Baptist. I have a sister that's Catholic now. When they had her daughter, she became Catholic. I'm Muslim. I have a couple of brothers that are Muslim. For prison, you have to choose a religion. Well, you don't have to, but they'll ask you what religion you are. So Muslim was the faith that I wanted to follow. But I like to broaden my horizons, so I might not end up being Muslim. . . . I'm still in search of. I know there is one God. I don't believe that I have to go through Jesus to get to God. I believe that I can just pray to God.

I believe that there's angels and there's demons and there's evil spirits. I believe in ghosts, and the reason why is 'cause I saw some in my lifetime. My grandmother's house did have a whole bunch of ghosts in it from the old days because her house is on the Underground Railroad, and down in her bedroom, it's like I would see things in the closet at night, and it would scare me so bad. . . . I would see like shapes of people that was real, real light, and you could see through them. As a child, I had visions. I mean, God would always show me things before it happened, and then it would happen that way. Then I got deep into drugs so I lost my vision.

. . . E. Lynn Harris is my favorite author 'cause he's real, and *Invisible Life*[19] is the first book I've ever read about homosexuals and something that happened to them that was good and not bad. . . . That was like, god, when is somebody going to write a book about that? . . . And you know, I'm pretty proud of him for coming out and doing a book like that because it's like, it's about time. I mean, you've got to say there are gay people in this world. We got black people's books. We got Hispanic people's books. Got Italian books. White people books. Why can't we have gay people books? There are straight people's books, so it's about time for some of them. Now I'm waiting for a lesbian woman to write a book. . . . It's always male/male. . . . In the urban books, [gay characters] are undercover. They're on the down-low, so you never know that they're gay. But in E. Lynn Harris, you know that they're gay. . . . Now kids can grow up and read and see that everybody needs love, not just a certain group. . . . A lot of people misjudge gay people. . . . But I look at it this way. Hey, to each their own. If they're not hurting anybody, everybody needs to be loved. Everybody wants love. That is one of our main things that we all crave: love. Why don't you let them love each other? What's the problem?

6 Melissa

—⚬—

Life Narrative

"They're trying to brainwash me and rebuild me"

I WAS BORN in North Carolina. At the time when I was born, my mom was still living with her mom, and she was separated from my brothers' daddy. My brothers are nine and ten years older than me. Somewhere down the line, my mom had a nervous breakdown, and they had to go live with their dad, so on my birth certificate, their dad is my dad but he's really not my dad. 'Cause my mama was messing with this guy, he was a preacher, and he was also married, so it was kind of a big scandal back then. I mean, even if I was too young to remember anything, I've heard about it. And as I got older, I was living with my mom and my grandma, then my grandma moved, so that left me with my mom. Then she had to work and I stayed with my aunt, you know, until my mom got home. Then after that, I've just been living with one relative from another, and I used to come home a lot on weekends.

. . . When I was probably about five, I started staying with my aunt, and I guess that's where a lot of abuse had started for me. Me and my cousins, we had found some *Penthouse* books and *Playboy* books and stuff like that, and you know, we was trying to experiment what they were doing in there, so I guess we caught ourself having sex. And my uncle seen what we were doing then, and he started making us do other things. And he was a drunk and stuff, so it was always some chaotic bull around there. So then, that went on from when I was about five 'til when I was about thirteen. . . . I guess somewhere down the line, they just kinda let me run wild or whatever, 'cause I can remember them always saying, you know, "I'm not your mama. Well, you ain't my youngun no way," so it's just a lot of abuse that I can remember, a lot of verbal and physical abuse and mental abuse.

. . . Probably when I was nine, my cousin's girlfriend was living with my mom, so she was babysitting me at the time, and [my cousin] used to put my arm behind my back and he made me start smoking some weed. So the first time I ever smoked any weed, I was nine, and then I never really messed with it again probably 'til I was about thirteen. . . . When I was about almost fourteen to maybe sixteen, I was real lonely. I smoked a lot of weed. Then by the time I was fifteen, I tried smoking cocaine. . . . I used to just stay drunk all the time, because I started drinking when I was eleven. . . . So after [my mom's boyfriend molested me], I started smoking weed a lot. . . . I really didn't have to go out a whole lot because my family, they deal in drugs, so I always have kind of a connection to get them. If I didn't have the money to pay for them, I would have oral sex with my cousin, you know, to get it. It was really nothing to me because I could remember when I was little having strip shows behind an oil drum, and they would throw chains and stuff at me. So I guess I really started feeling a lot of guilt and stuff because I knew things weren't right, because my friends at school, they would all the time be talking about their boyfriends and this, that, and another, and I never could relate, you know what I'm saying? Because it was always my cousin. And you know, one of my cousins, he was real jealous to where I couldn't get close to nobody.

During the time I was living with my aunt and her abusive husband, I went and stayed with another one of my mama's sisters, and she had three kids herself. But she treated us all the same. I mean, she punished one, she punished the other one. So there wasn't really too much abuse there, and there was, you know, some love there and stuff. And I guess staying with her I got most of the principles that I do have today. What little bit I do have I got them from her, and the respect and stuff, you know, I got from her. So you know, I was passed back and forth between those two aunts.

Then I went to go live with my uncle. And living with him, he was kinda strict and everything, but his wife, she kinda wasn't so hard on me, so I was stealing my uncle's weed and smoking it, and I started smoking cigarettes. And I had started junior high and I would be cutting class and stuff, and then I got mixed in with this girl. . . . I always felt that when it come to a guy, I had to do whatever he wanted and somehow or another it was all right because all my life from the age of five up 'til thirteen . . . I could probably name about twenty of my cousins that I have had sex with or had something to do with as far as sex. So I mean, none of that wasn't new to me, and having an experience with a woman, you know, that was something new to me even though it was a whole lot confusing and stuff.

. . . I started smoking weed, and fighting, and cussing out the teachers, so they didn't know what to do with me. So I came out and said, "Well, I shouldn't be staying over here anyway because I should be living with my mom." . . . So I went back and started staying with my mom, and my brother moved in so he was watching me. We fought all the time, I mean fistfighting, you know. . . . My brother, he is an alcoholic. He used to come all drunk and stuff and you know, he used to beat on my mom and beat on me and stuff, so it was a lot of abuse from him while he was drunk and everything. . . . Back when I was younger, my brother tried to have sex with me, too. . . . He was probably about fifteen, sixteen, seventeen at the oldest.

And somehow or another, my mom was seeing this guy, and he was really nice to me and stuff, and he would come get me and take me to his house, and this, that, and another, and then things started with him. I remember him trying to kiss me and I would try to keep my teeth closed so he wouldn't stick his tongue in my mouth. That was a big mess. I got raped and molested by him and everything else. But you know, I never said anything. So finally my mom just left him alone. She didn't know what was happening and I was too scared at the time to say anything.

. . . When I was about sixteen, I took to the streets. . . . My main thing when I went to the streets at first was not to get money. You know, that was not my motive. My motive for going to the streets to begin with was I wanted to find somebody to love me. So I would get in a car with these people, I'd do whatever they asked, they'd put money in my hand, then they would put me out. And then that really hurt me, so that gave me something else I had to deal with, you know, on top of trying not to get caught from my family. Then, you know, I'd get in car after car after car and you know, still the same thing. They put me out, and you know, that's not what I wanted. I didn't want their money.

They put me out of school when I was sixteen 'cause I was so hard to handle. There was nothing they could do for me. . . . There was a trailer park up the road from where we stayed and I had met this guy. And this is when I was fifteen, and he was living with his girlfriend, and I was always a people pleaser. Whatever they wanted to do, I was all right with it. I was game for it. I don't care what it was. Steal the old lady's panties, burn them while they're on her, I mean it don't matter. I was down for it. So I stayed with them and was called the trailer park whore, the trailer park trash, because I believe I probably slept with about every guy in the trailer park, married or not, black, white, widowed, crippled, crazy. I mean, it didn't matter.

And I had kinda got back on drugs again, so we all went and did a breaking and entering and when it all came down to it and the cops pulled me, I told them about it and I was put on probation. Well, probation didn't work out so well and I had went for a party one night. And they had put something in my drink. And they took me home 'cause they said I was acting real crazy and stuff, so they took me home. During that time I tried to kill my brother, I tried to kill my mama, I busted out windows in my mama's house, I tried to kill myself. She called the police, and they took me to [X] Treatment Center. And I stayed up there for about three months.

During that time I had met this guy, you know, and he was the first guy that had really ever paid any attention to me besides the people in my family, so I mean I thought I was really in love with him and I needed to be with him. But things didn't work out, so I took back to the streets, and I really got hooked on cocaine. I started shooting cocaine. The police were looking for me, so I would leave and go from one side of town to the next to avoid them. I had failure to appear because I didn't show up for court. . . . I ran from March to May.

Then the guy I was in love with, I had really respected his mom, so she talked me into turning myself in. So I did. I winded up staying a month in jail. . . . I dried out in jail, and it was real hard, you know, because I didn't have anybody. I didn't have drugs. Drugs had become a comfort to me. They helped me deal with myself, deal with the world around me, and I didn't have any of that no more and I'm in a place where I don't know anybody, I'm locked in, and I don't know anything. And when I went to court, they gave me my four years. It was up under the old law, so they sent me here. I stayed here for about six months [and then] I got out.

. . . I had got back up with the guy that I was with, and me and him stayed together for a few months. I was just smoking weed and drinking then. We broke up and I started going with his best friend. . . . After a year of being with him, I left. I went back to the other guy I was with. I stayed with him for about a year, just drinking and smoking weed. And you know, life was just really boring to me. It was just a drag not doing anything. So then, after that, about towards the end of the year of me staying with him, I met my co-defendant that I'm in prison with now. . . . Me and him hooked up and were staying together. I got back on the streets while he was gone. This time I had a motive, I had a mission—well, a different motive, a different mission: I had to get my cocaine.

Then some things with some guns and some robberies had went down, so we left and went up to [X]. I felt like I needed to go with [my co-defendant] because I had freedom, I was out on my own, I could do what I wanted to do. And the crime scene, I had a love for it, you know what I'm saying? Going into a store and shoplifting, I mean, it was something I had to do. . . . I did breaking and enterings because I got a rush from it. . . . We were robbing stores up there, and then we winded up getting caught, and I stayed in jail for a year. And I went through a lot of depression, and a lot of being suicidal and stuff. And then they gave me thirty years, fifteen years for the armed robbery, seven years for common law robbery, and eight years for common law robbery, which I'm still on my armed robbery sentence now, and I've been here ever since.

And I've been in a lot of trouble since I've been here. I've smoked weed since I've been here. I've made wine since I've been here. I mean, I was only twenty. I had just turned twenty when we got locked up. . . . Some of the time in prison's been easy, and some of it has not been easy. You know, it's like certain things that you don't know about crime before, you know now, because now a person can tell you about their crime, and you can find out just by talking to them why they done it. . . . There's a lot of women in here that are revengeful, that are just hateful and full of anger, because I'm one that's full of anger. You know, from my past and stuff like that, and I get real rebellious. I mean, when I first got here, I would not do nothing they told me to do. I stayed in lockup. '95 and '96, I lived in lockup. They let me out for a little while, I'd go back. And I tried to get my stuff together in '97, and that worked for about a year and a half, then '98 I started back smoking weed, and that run all the way until '99. But I haven't smoked any weed or anything since August of '99. And now I'm in a therapeutic community where I'm try-ing to get myself together, work on my behavior, my attitudes, and my drug problem and stuff like that. Because I do want a better life when I get out on the streets.

The one thing that really scares me, though, is that even though I wouldn't do it, is that you could come into prison naive as hell, like I did. I mean, sure, I was down for whatever. Let's go rob a bank, you know, I was down for it. I mean, I was young, I was eager for people's attention. I wanted to be needed, I wanted to be wanted, you know. I didn't want to be lonely. I didn't want to be a castaway. But now, I mean, when I came into this prison, I really didn't know anything. I have grown up in prison. I have matured a lot. I still hold on to the inner child in me, I mean, don't get me wrong, 'cause I am still a baby. But the only thing that really scares me is that you can master crime. . . . Take for instance, like, we have all these people in here that are in here for murder. You see how they got caught, you know how they got caught, you know what I'm saying? And then you sit and you analyze their crime, so now you know if you want to go do it how you do it without getting caught. And I think it's sickening because someone that was in my situation, I don't think they should have sent me to prison. Know what I'm saying? North Carolina needs to build something else for people twenty-five and under to send them to. Because I could come out of here being a bigger criminal if that's what I chose to do.

And I know half the shit, I would get away with it. Because I know what they did, I know how they did it, and I know where they messed up.

. . . Now I'm in the LATCH program: the Last Alternative Therapeutic Community of Hope. It is really structured. I have never lived in anything like it before. . . . It is really hard for me. 'Cause all my life, basically I've done what I wanted to do. There was nobody there to tell me not to do it, you know, there was nobody to say, "Don't go do this. Don't go do that." And if they asked me to go right, I went left on purpose, so I mean, nothing was ever said about it. It was like, let her go. But being down there? Whoa, it's different. I mean you have to be out your bed at 6:05. You can't lay back down on your bed 'til 8:30 at night. You get ten phone tickets a week. You have certain times to take showers, certain times to use the phone. . . . I mean, it's just really hard. I don't know if they're not understanding or if they do understand and they just keep trying to push me because they know that I've done things the way that I've wanted to do them. And I am really a messy person. I do not make my bed, I do not clean my locker out. They've been on me about that lately, so I mean, it is a big change. . . . They have all these rules that you have to abide by. It's crazy to me sometimes.

. . . The only time I've really asked for them to please put me out the program is when I've had to deal with my inner issues. When it comes time for that, for me to have to take a look at myself, I don't want to be there. That's why sitting here now, I guess it's because I don't know you, that I've told you all that I have because I don't even tell my counselors a lot of that stuff. I mean, it's really hard when you have to sit and you have to look and then, it's like I don't never really do anything about my revenges. I just hold on to them, which they tell me is dangerous. Like, I hold revenge against my co-defendant for me being in prison, and I'm angry because I'm in prison. You know, I've missed a lot of my life. Everybody else's life has moved on. They've gotten older. My nieces and my nephews, they're getting older. They don't even know me. I mean, my mom's out there. She needs me and I hold a lot of resentment and lot of anger in from that, you know. And right now, their main thing is trying to help me to deal with that so that I don't come back to prison.

One thing what they have started on is helping me to realize what anger is. I just know that I'm angry, but I don't know what to do with it. I don't know what it is, you know what I'm saying? . . . Way back when I was young, I used to have a real bad temper. And I had to go see a school psychologist and they sent me on to the other psychologist, so I mean, the state worked with me on and on and on, and that's really all they worked with me was my temper. But now I kind of hold my temper. Sometimes I just want to go bust the wall. But I have to hold that in, and that makes me even more frustrated, and it puts me more in a rage. Sometimes I don't want anybody around me. Don't speak to me. I don't have nothing good to say. And a lot of people that don't know me, they think that, oh, you know, she's just trying to be a badass today, and that's not it. It's that somebody's gonna piss me off and I don't know what to do with it. I don't know how to deal with it. So I just sit and be in a rage all day, feeling like I could just kill everybody in the world, or cut one of my fingers off, you know what I'm saying? 'Cause I mean, from these marks right here on my arm, that comes from me being angry.

. . . Once I realize what anger is, which is taking them a little longer because I'm just so bottled up with rage, and I try to talk about some things and some other things are there, . . . once I realize what my resentments are, why am I angry anyway, then they're gonna teach me, you know, what to do with it. Then after that, I'll be able to sit and figure out, like if somebody hurts my feelings or whatever, I get angry. Instead of saying, "Fuck you. I don't want nothing else to do with you. Leave me alone," they're trying to teach me there's other ways to go about doing that. If I feel hurt, then that's what I need to do is sit down and deal with the hurt, then the anger may not come, and then when it does come, it won't be so bad. I can just look at it as anger and send it on. I'm just trying to deal with one thing at a time so that I can get myself together. . . . I'm angry about a lot of things, you know. Like the first time my brother ever got drunk and slapped me, I'm still angry about that. Him hitting on my mom, I'm still angry about that. And when I was seventeen, I almost killed him for hitting on my mama. And then I'm angry because I almost killed my brother. Ever since I can remember, I know I had to be about seven or eight years old, I had been trying to fight him, fight him, fight him, to get him off my mom. And I had just got out of prison and I told him, "I don't mind drinking with you. We can have a good time, you know, sit and watch the videos, play the Nintendo, just me and you being that I'm home and you're celebrating, you got a new woman and she's pregnant. Just leave mama alone."

Because me and my mom, we did not have a good relationship before I came to prison. She was every bitch in the world to me, she was every whore, she was nothing. You know, the things she done for me, I felt she had to do them. And if she didn't do them, it was like, oh, you're gonna do them, you know, and I would always find something to hang over her head. Oh, you don't want to do it, okay then you do this. And when I came to prison, a lot of that changed because I learned then that a lot of people's parents didn't do nothing for them while they were here, and I was like, "Why your mama don't do nothing for you? Your mama got to do something," and they was like, "My mama don't have to do nothing for me." I was like, "But you're the same age I am," and they'd say, "I moved out when I was sixteen and I been on drugs and stuff. My mama don't have to do nothing for me." So that kinda wised me up. And then being around older women and stuff. You know, so then I learned how to appreciate my mom, and I started to learn how to love her.

So when I got home, I was trying to talk to my brother about it, 'cause my mom was the only one that came to see me. She was the only person in the world that I had to look after me and stuff. So I asked him to leave mama alone, but he got drunk, and as usual, he wanted to go beat up my mama. And I told him, I said, "I'm not gonna fight you tonight. If you put your hands on her, I'm gonna try my damnedest to kill you." So he reached over to grab her and I stabbed him in the stomach. And I had stabbed him in the liver and he almost died. So now he has a scar from the bottom of his stomach all the way up to his chest. I hate that that happened, because I do love my brother, even though I could kill him sometimes. You know, it's like I told him, "Every time you get ready to get drunk and you think you can put your hands on my mama, I want you to look at your stomach." Because I mean, I'm like that now. I feel like if anybody messes with her now and I get out of prison, then I'm scared I will do something to them 'cause for my mama, I would come back to prison. She will be the only reason I will come back to prison.

Right now I'm having a really big issue as far as with my brother because of a lot of shit he put me through with alcoholism and stuff. Because he used to come home drunk, and he used to try to fight my mama when I was too little to do anything. So I can remember standing at the stove trying to cook him some eggs and grits because he's drunk and that's what he wanted. And you know, him laying on the floor, and me having to feed him and stuff, and when I think about it now, with me having so many resentments towards him, I probably would have choked him with that spoon if I would have knew anything at the time. And it just makes me real angry and real resentful, and I know I have to work through a lot of that stuff.

. . . I feel if it was my brother and he loved me, how could he want to have sex with me? And then it makes me angry with myself because I was prostituting before I had really even knew my ABCs! Or even how to spell my name. And I stay angry about that. Then if he was my brother, how could he put his hands on me to hurt me? How could he hurt my mama, you know what I'm saying? . . . Now I will not sleep up under the same roof with him. I will not be in the same house with him by myself. . . . I won't even let him come up here and see me. I don't care who he comes with, because I'm scared I'm not gonna be able to handle it. . . . Me being as angry as I am, I know I'm not gonna be able to sit there and talk to him sensible. I'm gonna be like, "Well, why the fuck did you do that to me? And this, this, this, this, and this," and on and on and on, and then I'm gonna get in trouble. And I'm not looking for no trouble today. I'm trying not to. But once I feel like I can work through all that, then I'll be all right.

And another issue I'm having is my self-will. . . . Mine is real big. I guess I tend not to have friends and never get close to many people unless I know that—and this is just something I'm just now learning about myself—if I know that they'll do what I want them to do. It doesn't have to be anything bad; it could be all good things. But as long as they do what I want them to do, then we can be the best of friends. But if you're not gonna do what I want to do, then we can't be friends. . . . I guess that's why I don't have many friends on the compound, and my counselor tells me I pick and choose my friends wisely. No matter if the person treats me like shit, does whatever to me, stabs me in the back every time I turn around, it's okay with me because in the end, she does what I want her to do. And I mean, it's a lot of sick things I'm finding out about myself, but today it's okay because I'm gonna try and work through all that and get over all that.

I'm learning a lot about myself that I did not know. Like they keep telling me, you manipulate your way through this, and you manipulate your way through that. I was like, no, I don't. That had kind of hurt my feelings and made me mad with them saying that, but then she had explained to me all manipulation is not bad. Some of it is good. So then I had to find out all my bad manipulation and all my good manipulation. You know, and then, try to stop manipulating and then just try to go about doing things the right way, and if I don't know the right way, I just leave it alone. . . . I find myself when I go to the infirmary though, when they don't do what I want them to do, I get real pissed off with them. They won't give me the medicines that I want, they won't give me bed rest when I want it, and I just get pissed off with them. . . . I just go ranting and raving, and then I throw off on them. Because I'm sitting up there making myself look like a ass, I'll throw it off on them, you know, like it's all them and not me. . . . Yeah, I see now. I do be trying to get over on people. On those I know I can get over on, I do. I ain't gonna sit and lie and say I don't.

. . . As far as me being able to manipulate people so well, and me being a woman, and me knowing the power that I do possess, sometimes it scares me, and I won't do nothing with it because I know what I'm capable of doing, and I know who I'm capable of doing it to. You know, I know who I'm capable of getting over, I know who I'm capable of not getting over. . . . I never plan to be with another man because of all my abuse and with being in prison now. But the one thing that really, really scares me, because I know with me being a woman and with all my charms and my seductions and my manipulations, I'd be scared of what I would do to one. And it wouldn't take long for me to block out everything that I've learned, block out the person that I am, to become somebody else, because I have endured so much pain from men. . . . I don't think I would ever try to manipulate a woman like I would a man. 'Cause I've dealt with men all my life, you know, and I've sat in prison for so long and I've went back over everything that has happened from a man, so now being that I seen how they got over on me, I know how to go back and reverse the tables and get over on them. That really scares me. . . . I've never really told anybody this, but I think that's my main reason for wanting to keep my back turned away from them.

Even some men that I work around with in here, I will only get so close to them. It's like this one officer, you know, he really believes in me. I've changed a whole lot, you know, I've turned all the way around. And I care for him as an officer and his duties towards me. It's not no love thing or nothing like that. . . . But I try to keep a little distance away from him because I know how to get up under him to get what I would want. . . . We have a segregation quad down the hill, and they're just locked in all day. And nobody can't take them anything. . . . If one of my friends was in there and I wanted her to have a book, and maybe some hair gel and some toothpaste and the senior officer was saying no, I could go to this man, you know, and I could get him to take stuff up in there. And I would be in the wrong because I shouldn't have did that to him. So I stay away. I try to keep my distance. . . . I don't want to do things like that because I feel like if they let us get away with the small stuff, then we'll go back to the big stuff, and then the big stuff's gonna carry on and I'm gonna be back in prison. Because when I think about it, I manipulated my co-defendant so bad. I mean, some of the stores that we're in here for is due to me. He did not want to go rob all these stores, [but] I manipulated him and he went and did it. He did not want me to go, but I manipulated him and he let me go. Places that we went and broke into, he does not like doing breaking and enterings; I manipulated him and he went and did it. You know, I mean, it's like a lot of stuff this guy was against, I talked him into it and he went and did it.

There is no way in hell that I would ever go back out there and do that again, because I consider myself lucky, especially being as young as I was. . . . It wasn't nothing but God with me, 'cause phew! I should have been dead. A lot of people say when you go to jail and go to prison, you're just being saved or whatever, so maybe that was one of God's ways of trying to save me. 'Cause I know even when I was on the streets, I feel a lot of times that people tried to save me, and God hisself tried to save me, but I wasn't taking no heed. So this was the last resort, 'cause I can't get out and do what I want to do, 'cause my mom has even tried to put me in drug rehabs and stuff before. I'd climb the fence, climb the wall, go down the elevator, go out the door, I mean, they could never hold me. Okay, you can hold me for about two weeks and then it's over with. So nothing really worked until I came here.

The only drug I think is gonna be a problem for me to stay away from is marijuana. Because marijuana has been there for me. I mean, when I had no one around, marijuana was. I could smoke a joint, lay down, and be content and not have nobody bother with me, me not bother with nobody, and you know, just have fun and laugh. I needed marijuana to make me feel good about myself, and that's another thing that my counselor's trying to work with me with, to help me find other things that's gonna make me feel good about myself. 'Cause ever since '96, it seems like I've always been able to go about nineteen months on the grounds without smoking, and then it's like, bam! Everything hits me all at one time, you know, and I just go back to smoking.

And now, for the first time, it's been twenty months, and it's not an easy street. It's really not. You run into situations where you don't have enough money, then you have to wait in all these lines, and you know, then people wanting your money and they want to smoke your cigarettes and I mean, Thursdays are really frustrating 'cause that's when they pay us, and then half the time, they act like it's their money that they're giving you. The most you can get paid off a job is $1 a day. The next pay is 70 cent, and the next one is 40 cent. When the sewing room was open, they paid you by the hour, like 13 cent a hour or 28 cent a hour or something like that. The most you could make down there was $15 a week. But now they've closed that down because they're getting ready to open up a license plate place. But I never really got into any of those jobs because they just did not interest me. You know, I mean, and don't ask me what kind of job I'm gonna get when I get out 'cause I don't know.

One of my plans, though, I plan to be out of prison by the time I'm thirty. By the time I'm forty, which will be ten years later, I plan to have my own house—built, bought and paid for, my own land, and whatever necessities and accessories I'm gonna have to go with that. By the time I'm fifty, I plan to have some kind of a building, a big building, and I'm gonna name it The Last Chance, 'cause I want to go out and help anybody twenty-five and under. I don't care if they've been in trouble ten times. I want this to be their last chance before they come to prison or their last chance before they spend the rest of their life in prison. I know it's gonna take a lot of money because it's gonna be a very closed-in facility. On one side will be the living quarters.

One side is gonna be all the schools they're gonna need, and on the next side is gonna be a very big variety of jobs, for those that want to be doctors and lawyers and nurses and stuff like that.

. . . I read a article in *People Magazine* today about the Impact drug treatment. And now I'm thinking that when I get out of prison, I might go up there and work and get a lot of experience from them then come back to North Carolina and try to do something. . . . This man is talking about opening up another Impact house up in California, and he's gonna be looking for about four hundred or something recovering drug addicts to help run the house, and I was like, bingo, there goes me. I'm trying to get my counselor to at least get his address and stuff so I can write him. Let him know I'm incarcerated, what I'm doing now, so maybe once I get through the prison system, if I needed help getting to California to get on my feet, this man will be like, "Yes, I remember you. I don't have a place or nothing for you but scrubbing floors, but you're welcome to stay." I'll scrub floors, don't matter to me. At this point in time, I'm willing to do anything—the right thing, not wrong thing. . . . They really know what they're working with with me, and we're fixing to go out and start our jobs sometime next month, so then they're gonna try and work with me, and they're gonna try to put me in school. Right now, basically what they're trying to do is brainwash me and rebuild me, is what they're really trying to do. I hope it works!

I think the reason why a lot of women get into crime starts from loneliness. They get lonely, then they don't have a man to depend on, so then they start depending on the drug. . . . Then before they know it, they're in prison. Because half of these little over a thousand women that are in here, they're in here because of a man. I know there was plenty of times I took the rap for a man and winded up in jail. And too, if people would just start with them while they were younger, 'cause I mean, in North Carolina, they do nothing! Only time they really ever do anything to you is if your parents push it and then they put you in juvenile. Or if you wait 'til you kill somebody, and I mean, oh let's go put you in juvenile, then we're gonna send you to prison. I mean what's the use then? And then with the other young people at home, killing each other, I mean, damn! Something ain't right, something's not right in the home. Something ain't right somewhere.

If I knew that I had a kid with a behavior problem, I'm gonna do whatever it takes. If I had to lose my job and go on welfare, I know I've got to do what's best for my kid. I'm gonna do whatever it takes to get them that help, you know, so if things turn out and they wind up in prison, then there's nothing I can do, because I did all I could. That's why when I get out, my main focus is going on younger people. A lot of people that wind up in prison is because, a lot of the women that I know of, they didn't have nobody to take care of them. They come from a dysfunctional family, they were adopted, they were left here and there. So someone has got to go in and start from there. . . . You're gonna put me in juvenile, you're gonna put me in jail, you're gonna put me in prison, I mean, what's the use?

That's like I was reading that article from California. People that started getting busted with drugs up there and trafficking and all that, they're starting to put them in rehab centers instead of sending them to prison. They should do something like that in North Carolina. 'Cause I mean, there's a girl on the grounds, she got caught with cocaine. And just because she's been here so many times, she got a eight-year sentence now. How is that gonna help her? I mean, she's thirty-eight now, and this is her fourth time here. What's gonna help her this time that didn't help her the first time, but now you've given her eight years? So what's gonna help her except for she's gonna be in prison for eight years? She's gonna turn out to be this angry person. She's gonna hold a lot of resentments, and ain't no telling what the hell she's gonna do when she get out! So I mean, where is there any justice at in the system?

Then you put a sixteen-year-old girl in here or keep her over there in lockup because she's fifteen, then put her out on the grounds when she turns sixteen. You hold her 'til she's twenty-one and let her go, but what did you teach her except to be a better thief, a better criminal, a better killer, better to go and rob people and places? I mean, where did you get rehabilitation at? . . . All these young people, they go home and they come back. Okay, well they were here before, and they had five hundred write-ups, and you looked over all of them. You know, and you just sent them right on home. You didn't do anything with them. You didn't try to sit them down and talk to them. There's no groups here for them. There's nothing for them to do but run with the older people and learn the things that they know. . . . The officers, they don't care. I mean, you live in prison, you die in prison. It doesn't matter to them. So people get out and they come back. They get out again and they come back again.

I mean, especially if they're young, anywhere from sixteen to twenty-one, they don't do anything. They don't have any groups. Okay, they have little functions at night where they say, "Okay, we're gonna have a youth offenders meeting with the church people and give them a little snack and send them on back down to the dorm." Where are you getting rehabilitation at? I don't understand. Half of the time you have to fight to get into school. I don't understand. Where are you getting rehabilitated? It's fine and dandy with them if I go out there and sit on the compound all day long and do nothing. They don't care. You can go to the infirmary and get you a medical where it says you don't have to work and just sit out on the compound all day. . . . Half of them is on mental health just to stay high. There's nothing to do in prison. They have nothing to do.

. . . That's why I hold this grudge against the prison system because when I came in, if I didn't have the little bit of a backbone that I did, then I would have been in a world of trouble, you know what I'm saying? . . . And the prison system, they don't care. "Oh well, she did that because she wanted to." No, she did that 'cause she felt that's all that she had to do. I mean, they just have nothing for the young people that come to prison. . . . The prison system's just screwed up. The whole justice system is to me. That's why when I get out, by the time I'm fifty, I know I can't turn everybody's life around, but if I had five hundred people, if I turned one life around, that'd be fine with me. Something needs to be done. So I'm gonna try to help as many as I can.

—⟨⟨⟨—

Reading Narrative

"From her life story to mine is not that much difference"

I NEVER REALLY read 'til I came to prison. And I was in prison probably about three years before I even picked up a book and really read it. I mean, I might read a book and it'd take me a month to read it. But now it takes me about two days to read a book.

A lot of things that I know, I know from reading books, whether it be drama books or suspense, true crime, biographies, or whatever. . . . Sometimes if I read like a drama, I can feel like I'm there, or like with Jackie Collins, you know what I'm saying, it's some of those things I want to do from the way she puts her characters. And suspense books are something more just to be interested or whatever. The other kind of fiction books I read are Nora Roberts, Jackie Collins. And I read some Sidney Sheldon.

. . . Sometimes when you read true crime stories, you can feel what's going on.[1] How they were feeling, and everything. . . . Some people just live to read true crime! . . . I mean, especially if she can relate that to her crime, of course she's gonna want to read it. And other times, people are just nosy. I mean, like *Invisible Darkness*,[2] okay, I recommend that book to everybody on the compound so everybody's been trying to get it, and a lot of people that's read it have been recommending it, so I mean, sometimes, when we stop and we talk about books, that's what we're talking about. We really get into deep conversation about it, but like, if it's a Jackie Collins book, you'll be like, "Oh yeah, it's a good book" . . . and then you go on about your ways. But you tell them about a true crime book, oh, hold up! Everybody's fixing to stop and listen and get in on that one! . . . Everybody on our quad . . . when we came in [after the first meeting for the research study], they was like, "What books did ya'll get? Did ya'll get anything good?" We said, "Tonight was our first night. We didn't get no books to read, but we're gonna get three." "Well, which one you gonna let me read?" I was like, "I don't even have the books yet [laughing]!"

. . . I'm not really into reading no book about no man, for real. . . . The man's the hero in a romance novel, and some of the other books, they're always detectives, or they're the cops, or they're the investigators, or they're the brutal murderers and stuff like that. . . . I pretty much read a lot of true crime books about women. . . . As far as the men, they want to go back and blame it on, "Oh, something godawful happened to me during my childhood." . . . With the women, I can understand. . . . Women have these things happen to them, and they just bury them. I mean, we're not allowed to talk about them. We're not allowed to deal with them, and we're fragile anyway, so all that builds up and then more experiences happen and happen and happen, you know what I'm saying? But I feel like as far as a man, he don't care. I mean, so what [that] it happened? I feel like they'll be like, "Okay, so what? I'm still a man." I mean, who knows really when all of them get together what they talk about? 'Cause they say talking is good therapy. They might be like, "You know, man, what my uncle come and did to me when I was little?" And then he might be like, "You know, that motherfucker's in a wheelchair today. I ain't got to do nothing to him." Then all the men can sit and relate to that.

But you don't see a bunch of women sitting around talking about all the things that happened to them. 'Cause we weren't allowed to talk about it. . . . It's one experience on top of another experience on top of another experience, and they just keep on going. I think that's something just womenhood come up with. "Oh, don't worry about it baby, it's all right. Don't worry about it. Just don't even worry." I mean, why not worry, 'cause it's bothering me? "Oh, ain't no need to talk about it. I know, I know, I know, it's okay." So we tend to bury that stuff and keep on going.

I just don't believe all that stuff about the men. For real, I just think they're full of shit. . . . The first thing that men holler after they get in trouble are things that happened when they were little. But a woman don't really go into all that. . . . With a woman, it might take a little while to go back that far because they never talked about it. If they were angry or something had happened to them and they were angry about it, they were never able to feel that. If they were hurt, they were never able to feel that. They wasn't allowed to feel. It's like times I know I went and said, "Such and such done something to me." "Oh, don't worry about it, don't worry about it. Come here," you know, and they'll love on you for a few minutes and then you're gonna shield me and it's not gonna allow me to feel what I want to feel. And then other times, I mean, you're hollering and you're raising hell, and this, that, and another, okay, that's still not gonna allow me to feel what I'm feeling, because I'm wondering why you're mad. What did I say that make you mad? You see, women are never allowed to feel what they want to feel until you're grown, and then a lot of them have to go through this treatment to find out what your feelings are and go through all of them. . . . "You need to dry your eyes. You ain't got time to cry! That's nothing to even be crying about. You know, you just need to go on and forget about that. Don't be crying! Go in there and wash your face. Don't be crying." A man, he can get all his stuff out. A woman was never able to.

. . . I wonder in reading the Ted Bundy book if everything was so dramatic and everything. Being sodomized and beat and stuff when you were growing up, how could that lead you to kill a string of women? I mean, something don't make sense in there somewhere. I think that maybe if your mama did that to you, then you just took it out on that string of women because won't no other woman gonna ever do you like that and you're gonna prove yourself that nobody's gonna do you like that, so then you go and just kill them all. I don't know, men are sickening to me anyway. I've had too many experiences and I don't, uhuh [shakes her head no]. I've had enough.

. . . [Discussing *On a Killing Day*,[3] which features Aileen Wuornos, who claimed that she killed seven times in self-defense]: I know from experiences that I've had with men, even through prostituting, there comes a time when you have just had enough! I talk to my mom, and I tell her, "I'm happy with being with women. I'm better off with being with women." . . . Because I've been through so much stuff. If a man was to come up to me and hit me just playing, you know, like a boyfriend or somebody I'm gonna go out on a date with, I'd probably kill him 'cause I would think that he was trying to beat me and abuse me just like the other ones did. . . . My biggest fear with men is to just not get close to them, just don't be around them, be around them as less as possible. You know, because I don't really feel like I can handle it. Something might trigger in me and that might be the end of his life or mine, so it's just best that I don't do it, 'cause I've got this thing against men.

I just now recently got to where I could talk to the men that work here, so I could imagine how it would be like on the streets. I mean, if I gotta work with you, that's fine. If I don't want to be bothered, don't bother me, 'cause I have this real bad complex. And I think what done it for me, out of all the abuse and stuff I've been through, is spending all this time in prison behind a man. This is it. I'm through, 'cause I would probably kill, too. I think that's another reason why I might be interested in reading [Aileen Wuornos's] story because men, they go on these bad ego trips! They do. I mean, they got to beat you to prove they're a man, you know. I mean, and then another thing that really gets me is, I mean, how sick are you to say that you get your thrills off beating a woman so you can get yourself up? Where did all that come from?! . . . Men are just sickening!

. . . [I like reading true crime books] because it's just knowing that you're not the only woman in prison, you know [laughing]. Then you can be like, oh, shit, I didn't know she did all that, you know, oh, my God! How can a woman be that way? I think it might, too, wise you up to women. Because some women, you think they're so sweet and nice and everything, and actually, the way they make the characters in the book, those are really how people are. . . . I think it's just good to know what people are capable of. . . . From reading a lot of the true crime books, there's only certain places I will go. 'Cause when I was on the streets, a dark patch of woods and there could be a house a mile away, I mean, it's so dark you can't even hardly see where you're going, I'd walk by myself. . . . But knowing what I know today? Unun. I'm taking a knife, a gun, or something with me. If I've got to go, and dear God, I'm not gonna put myself in a predicament to where I will have to, if it is a must, it's got to be a life or death situation for me to get out there and walk the streets at night. And half the time, in the daytime.

. . . When I had read *Fatal Seduction*,[4] I wanted to write to the girl that the book was about and when I got out of prison, I wanted to go see her in prison. I felt that we had something in common, or maybe she done the things that I wanted to do, or she was the person that I wanted to be and I just felt a connection there, or something. And too, I wanted to go and talk to her and find out how has her life been in prison. How has she survived all these years in prison? And I wanted to hear from herself a little bit of the extent of what did happen. With the lesbian girl, I, oh Lord, I really, really felt her. I mean, it's not just because she was a lesbian but because she thought that this girl loved her, that they was going to have everything. I mean, both of them had the same dreams, they had the same ambitions, they was gonna have this, they was gonna have that. The girl was in love with her, and at that point in time, she was willing to do anything for this girl. . . . I've been in situations like that. . . . You know, when it was something that she didn't want to do but she loved this girl so much. I know how it feels to do something for somebody that you love so much you'll do anything for them, and then after the deed is done, they don't want nothing else to do with you. I really felt that. And I could just see myself a lot of times when I just got strung along. She strung her along long enough to get what she wanted right then. Then she pushed her off to the side, and then when she was ready, she came back and got her, and of course she was always there. You know, I can really feel a lot of that.

After I read that, and the girl went to prison and stuff, and it was like, how she hadn't been in any trouble, and how she'd been doing good and she was working as a library lawyer, and how she had turned herself around and she was waiting to get out of prison, and how she had made all these changes and stuff and how she was stronger. I think just seeing her picture in that book, you know, I don't know what it made me feel, because I know this girl is in prison trying to do all this and do all that, and all behind this woman. But then, I also had to look at it like maybe that was done to her for her to get her life together, because she did start getting into a lot of drugs, and she was getting into some minor trouble which led her on probably later to major trouble, so maybe it will help her more than it won't. Same with me. . . . When I had read that part about that girl, I was like, damn! 'Cause I just never really thought that nobody in the world could be as stupid as I was. Here's another girl as stupid as I was and now she's in prison. Just like I am, maybe another state, another town, another time, but we're in prison today together. I mean, that really made me feel good reading that, to know that I'm not the only dummy.

If you look at [true crime books] in the wrong way, and you read things the wrong way, you can be like, "Shit, well I know I can do that 'cause I'm better than her." But if you have a open mind and you're reading things the right way and stuff, you can be like, "Out of all this that's happened to me, look what this girl has done!" . . . I stayed in trouble a lot. I did not want anything out of life. But after I read *Fatal Seduction* and I seen how she had turned her life around and everything was so uplifting for her, I think that's what gave me really the inspiration to try to do something. I mean, hell, if she can do it, I can, too, 'cause from her life story to mine is not that much difference. . . . The majority of it was down pat.

I read *Charmed to Death*[5] probably last year or the year before. It normally takes me three days to read a book, but especially if it's a good book, it only takes me about a day or two. I think that one, it took me about a day and a half to read it 'cause I was just so amazed at how this woman was! It was shocking! She is a true, live criminal! She is out there! God! She did all kind of things. Like how she did her insurance scams and stuff like that. . . . She is smart! Now she was on her toes! . . . She is . . . one of those people that are like a great manipulator. If she hadn't have done all the killings, she could have been anybody and anything that she wanted. She was too smart for her own good. I believe that's why she got caught. . . . I have never known or read a book about an older woman like her. . . . She done married this rich man and it seemed like she always could get whoever she went after. It's like they were always drawn to her. . . . But you know, just all that killing, I don't understand why she would do all that killing when you're doing all these insurance scams to have all this money. And I think that she treated her kids kinda shitty. I think it talked a little bit about the problems that her kids were having and stuff, behavior problems and other little problems. . . . I felt kinda sorry for her son. I did, I felt sorry for him. . . . And with her being as old as she is, I don't see how she would ever get any rehabilitation from nothing. You know, because that is something that she's just been doing on and on, I mean, I really don't think there is nothing they could do for her 'cause she's a sick person!

Cruel Sacrifice,[6] with the little girl Shanda, I couldn't believe that she was as young as she was and the types of stuff that she was into. . . . I can remember as far as with me, it brought back a lot of memories when I was that young, and my way of thinking and stuff, but I don't believe I would ever have done this to anybody. . . . It's really sad and I guess when I was reading it, I wasn't expecting them to get that much time like they had got, but they really socked it to them. And I thought maybe because of their age or something they really wouldn't get all that much time. And then to know that all that stuff was going on in the little community all right there together as far as with the girls being lesbians at so young and into witchcraft and Satanism and stuff like that, 'cause in the little area where I grew up in, it wasn't all that stuff.

The sick part in the book is when they were talking about Melinda with her dad. It really didn't go into detail I guess because Melinda wasn't willing to say that anything had happened between her and her dad. But her dad is sick! He was a sicko! From all the stuff he did, after reading all that and then Melinda growing up in that, when it got to about her parents and stuff, I really started paying attention to Melinda's character to see if they would say anything about her, because it seems like she would have a lot of dysfunctions going through life and stuff.

I would like to meet all of the girls involved. I guess because they're so young and a lot of things that the book was saying that they went through and that they felt, I have been there at some point in time in my own life, and I have this thing for young people anyway. I guess because I got locked up when I was so young. If I could go to the prison where they're at and meet them, I would like to know how has their prison experience been. Another thing in the book as far as the family, they were like, "They're up here doing all this crying now but they wasn't crying when they was killing my friend or my daughter or whatever. They wasn't crying then when they was killing the girl, Shanda. And now they want to be on the stand and now they want to cry." That kinda brought up some feelings for me towards the family because I mean, especially with some of them being older, I know that at some point in time in their life they've done something and then had regrets for it later. And then while you're doing it you don't care. So I feel like they should have at least, I mean, I know they took a life, but them girls were so young. It sounded like it all just turned out to be a fun thing or whatever and then the older girl, I just think things went too far. You know, they didn't mean to kill the girl or nothing like that. Things just happened, which I know they have to be punished for what they done, but just because at the time when they were doing it, if they had remorse, they wasn't showing it and they wasn't feeling it, didn't mean that a whole year later they wasn't going to.

'Cause I mean, when you sit in jail for a year and have to put up with all that up there, eventually you'll feel something. And a lot of times, your main thing when you're in jail is you focus on what you're in there for. I mean, you tend to start feeling something then, if you have a heart, you know, you'll feel something then. I stayed in jail for a year, and your mind goes back and forth. You feel sorry for yourself, you feel sorry for the people, you think of how you could have done things differently. So I feel like their remorse at the end was genuine. Laurie and Melinda, they really, oh God, they lived messed-up lives! You know, one's got a crazy daddy and the other one's mama is, "Christ is everything," so I mean, if I could put myself in their shoes, I probably would feel pretty much the way that they were feeling, because I also come from a dysfunctional family.

As far as the molestation part and doing things for attention and just being in with the crowd, I could really relate to Melinda because I was with this girl at one time—I was thirteen—and to be honest, the more I think about it, the only thing that probably saved her life or saved her from a lot of torture was the fact that she had moved. Because me and her were seeing each other, and she filled in a lot of voids for me, and I felt like Melinda did, you know, she's mine. And there was this other girl that had came in the picture and that was liking her and stuff, and it was just a constant battle between all of us. I didn't have a dad that I was close to or whatever, but I would have people that would be in my life and I got attached to them and then they left. They'll write me for a little while, and then all of a sudden it wasn't nothing else about you; you were just pushed back off to the side.

And then, like with Laurie, with her getting into the witchcraft, I had run across some friends that was into the witchcraft and some of them were into Satan, but I would never do that because when I was being brought up, my grandmom was a firm believer in God. She just beat that down on all of our heads and stuff. But as far as the witchcraft, I've mingled with it or whatever, to be with my friends, and just like Laurie said, to get the attention from other people. And then as far as Hope, I've been in her situation before. I've done things I didn't want to do, or I've done things just because I wanted to be a part of them. I wanted to fit in, too. And then, as far as Toni, there was a lot of things that had happened to where I was just there, and I didn't want them to happen, and because everybody else was so much older and so much bigger, you know, I backed on out of the way and let them do whatever and just didn't have no part in it. So it was like each one of the girls, a part of my life was in there, too. And that made it real interesting to me.

It lets me know that I'm not the only one. And when I'm reading books like that, when I can fit my life so much into theirs, and then they wind up being in prison, I would like to go and talk to them and see if their prison life has been the same. To me, it would just be some type of a bond. Because even though these are four different girls, I'm pretty sure that at one point in time I played each part of their life. Each part of their life has been a part of mine. And it's very few people that you find like that. I mean, to actually find somebody that has lived a part of your life, actually been there, you know, then it just feels like you can bond with them. There was other things that I would like to ask them about their crimes. Like when things got to the point to where it had started getting out of hand, why didn't they stop then? . . . I could probably feel wanting to torture her a little bit, because . . . back then I was really—I didn't know it—but I was real revengeful.

. . . Maybe if somebody wrote another book they would bring more out about them. I would like to ask them about the prison that they're in, you know, how are they coping with the prison? And even though their time's been cut in half, how are they coping with having to do all that time, because even coming in at a young age like that, for a while you can be settled and be where you're at, but on other days, it's like I know they feel like they just want to go, you know, they could be so much better and do so many different things.

And as far as Melinda's mom, here this woman is trying to work, she's trying to provide for her kids. She feels like she has to stay with this man, he's doing all this stuff to her, and she's still trying to make it. That, you know, I really have sympathy for her. Because I've also been in situations where I felt I had to stay. You know, that was the best thing for me to do right then was to go ahead and stay. And you know, that's really a messed-up feeling to be somewhere that you really don't want to be, but you love this person, and I know that that woman had to go through a lot of therapy. She had to have, 'cause I was in a relationship here on the compound for about two and a half years and I'm still trying to get myself together from that because somewhere along the way, I lost myself. I lost who I was. I lost the things that I like to do, things I like to talk about, I mean, just everything. I just totally lost me trying to make sure this person was happy, doing for her; 99 percent of my life consisted of her. And things just wasn't working, so I'm getting myself together now from all that. And I know that woman had went through a lot of stuff as far as her kids, 'cause one of them . . . was still going through therapy. And I mean if my cousins were molesting me like her daddy was, I think that it would be similar feelings.

. . . It was a lot of emotions. Some of them are sad, you know. Some of them when I was reading and thinking about them, I used to get high so I wouldn't have to feel that way, or I'd want to cut myself so I wouldn't have to feel that way, or I'd want to kill myself so I wouldn't have to feel that way. Today I wouldn't do it, you know, so just reading that let me see how far along I have come up from that, that I can look at that, recognize it for what it is, what it was, and move on.

I'm reading a book now, it's *Don't Call It Love,*[7] and it's like a therapy book, and it's got a lot to do with molestation and stuff like that. I'm reading that one; no, I'm not gonna say I'm reading it, I'm reading a page [at a time] out of it maybe. Because it's really hitting me. You know, a lot of things that I didn't think of, a lot of regrets that I'm starting to have, and a lot of resentments, I'm going through a lot of those issues right now. A lot of people when they've been molested, it talks about how their life has been, and it was mainly saying like out of seventy-some people, they think it's like sixty-some, or whatever, they had a percentage, and they tend to have a lot of behavior problems when they grow up. And they tend to be addicted to a lot more things than drugs, you know, and I'm starting to relate to that, because there's some foods that I find now that I'm addicted to, there's some books that I'm addicted to, there's just a whole bunch of things.

. . . And as far as my behavior, it's like you wasn't able to say anything then, you know, with the people messing with you and stuff, so it's like you try to put a cap on that. It's like when you were growing up you were trying to reach out to people and of course, if I don't tell you, you're not gonna know what's wrong with me. And of course, if I've been threatened not to tell you, then I'm not gonna tell you. So therefore, it's like a constant battle with the child all the way up 'til they get older. So then, when they get older, they just act out a little bit more and maybe take things a little further. But I'm starting to talk about a lot of my stuff now. I mean hopefully, I will get over it.

When I'm addicted to books, I'm through with the book, but I'm not willing to pass it on no further because I've done some possession of the book. The book is mine; I'm gonna claim the book so I've done become addicted to the book. And then another compulsive behavior with books, I might read five books at one time, and my counselors tell me that's not good for me because I try to take my focus off of whatever it is that I'm supposed to be doing. Like, if I don't want to think about the incest from me and my cousins, I'll want to read *On a Killing Day*. Then after that, if I start thinking about something with my brother, I might want to read *Cruel Sacrifice* because when I was thinking about my cousin, this is the book I had started reading. Now that I'm thinking about my brother and my cousin, I'm gonna move on to something else. And if I don't want to think about both of them while I'm reading the books, I'll just leave them here with this book and then I'll go to this book.

And then a lot of times I tend to have a block on things. I block myself out, because I've learned that when I was little and growing up, I detached my feelings, and I detached myself from what's going on around me. A lot of times my counselor will ask me what I'm feeling and I'll say I don't know. "What you mean you don't know what you're feeling?" And I'll tell her, "I don't know, I'm not feeling nothing." And then it's like, well, you have to feel something, so I'm starting to get in contact with my feelings. And I went through a bad week where I was expressing my feelings maybe in the wrong way, but I was expressing them. So I'm trying now to get a better lead on my feelings. I guess that's another reason, too, why I would want to go talk to those girls in *Cruel Sacrifice* is because it didn't really talk about their feelings. What were they feeling? It didn't talk about what they were feeling while they were in jail, and how they were feeling about what little bit of time they were in prison. You know, how do you feel that you have to do all this time? They wanted to talk about everything that they did do, but then it was like, when it got to the end of it, that stuff wasn't important. And I think it is [important], especially for somebody that stayed in jail for a year. I mean, you have feelings. It's like good for them to talk about those feelings because a lot of times if you don't talk about them, you hold those feelings in, you have resentments, and then you have more problems.

And too, like somebody else that might read this book, they might be like, "Yeah, them bitches got everything they deserve, you know, since they did that little girl like that." . . . I think that someone that likes to read books that's never been introduced to crime about anything, if I was ever to meet one of those people, and I would be like, "Yeah, I spent about eight years in prison," they'd be like, "Eight years? You should still be there. What you out for?" because it's like I don't have any feelings. And then, like in this book when the girls were crying, it was like, "Well, they shouldn't have been crying. They wasn't crying [when they committed the crime]." I mean, if that's what they were feeling, then yeah, they should have been crying. That should have been recognized a little bit more. . . . I mean, these girls could be doing just like I am, you know, trying to turn my life around so I don't have to live by all this when I get out, even though I'm still gonna have to look at it in the face. But even if they are, I feel like half of the community, or maybe even no one in the community, would be willing to give them a chance. "You killed this girl in cold blood, and you done spent all these years in prison. You didn't care then, so don't be trying to come tell me you care now." People that does not deal with crime or know anything about crime, they're not gonna know, except for what they read.

. . . It's like those people never really took time with their kids to teach them anything. If I had kids, even if I had young kids, that book would help me to at least start teaching them about the things that's going on out there. . . . They need to be talked to a little bit more, maybe helped out a little more instead of like with me, when I got older, my mom just let me go. "Oh, you're thirteen now, just be careful, you know, don't stay out too long." . . . My mom didn't know how the world was changing.

. . . I'm a good writer. I love to write poems. I write poems all the time, so when I get out, I ain't gonna lie, when I get out, I plan to sell them 'cause I think they're just that good. I won't care if I take only $10 for one. And then maybe one day I'll write a book. I think I probably might want to write one about me. I think my life was interesting enough [laughing]. Everybody's attention would be there. I mean, who wouldn't want to know about a young girl having sex with her family members, at first not being forced, then being forced, then not being forced, you know what I'm saying? People in the world love that stuff, so I think they would. If I was to ever write it, I would be comfortable enough with it to attach my name to it. My mama would probably have a heart attack.

7 Valhalla

—〰—

Life Narrative

"I've been like a ball that someone threw
and I've been bouncing around ever since"

I WAS BORN in Toledo, Ohio, in 1978. My parents were high school sweethearts. I come from a very close extended family. I have one brother. He just turned twenty-eight. My parents raised me 'til I was about six. My parents split up. Then me and my brother and my dad lived with my [paternal] grandmother, who basically raised me until I was twelve. When I was twelve, we moved to [a small town in] Ohio. My dad basically was gone from six in the morning until ten at night. He was a very heavy drinker. Me and my brother, for a couple of years we pretty much raised ourselves.

. . . My [paternal] grandmother is Orthodox Greek, so she raised me to be very, very maternal. From a very young age we were taught to cook and to clean and to sew and to be a little more subservient. And then my [maternal grandmother] burned her bra and fought for feminist rights in the '60s and '70s. My [paternal] grandma, she's a real Betty Crocker. Real sweet. She's round. She don't like no anger, no yelling. But my [maternal] grandma, you can't tell her nothing. If I don't like what they got to say, stand up and make a scene. No one's gonna tell me what to do, you know. Power to the people, that kind of stuff.

. . . My [maternal] grandma, she's the coolest lady in the world, but she's a little crazy. She's manic depressive. My mom's manic depressive. I'm manic depressive. I am the only one who actually accepts it and understands the severity of it. They just don't, you know, they're a different generation. They're not going to accept it. I know what it is, so I know what to look for, and I know my downfalls, and I can see things coming. They don't at all. From what I understand, my great grandmother from Poland was a raging alcoholic . . . and she was manic depressive.

. . . While my mom was raised, she was treated one way, and her brother was treated another way. Basically, all the negativity in the household came on her. Her parents divorced when she was young. So my uncle got away with murder, and my mom couldn't do anything. Then [when I went to stay with my mom,] my mom turned it on me. You know, the house had to be cleaned. If anything was wrong, it was my fault. My brother, she'd ground both of us, but he would laugh and walk out the door. Very different set of standards.

Eventually, I just got sick of it, and I got up and left. I moved here and there. My mom got pissed off 'cause I was living with friends of the family, and she threatened to turn them in. So my dad came and got me, and we lived with my dad, had nothing to do with my mother. Well, I went back to visit her at Christmas. I hadn't seen her in like six months. And she had this new boy-friend. He was a lot younger than my mom. He's only four years older than I am. And all of a sudden she was totally cool, you know. She would drink and smoke pot and have her friends over, a whole different person. So of course, being fifteen, I came back.

He ended up being a very violent man. Not when he was sober, but him and my mom were both really bad alcoholics, and he is crazy when he was drunk. He was a maniac. He's violent, he's mean, he's psychotic. He will do crazy things. Punches holes in the wall. Cuts himself up. You know, that's the first time I ever saw anyone ever hit another adult. I saw him hit my mom. So for the next six months, my life was—it probably seemed more like a year—my life was a mess. I mean, there was fighting all the time, and I had not grew up with that, so of course, we were getting in the middle of it and getting pushed around. . . . [Once] I saw him—he was a whole fifty pounds heavier than my mother—jump on her back, knock her down. They both fell on the floor, and she hit a coffee cup, pretty much cut her ear off. I called the cops. . . . My mom said nothing happened.

. . . And that kind of stuff happened for about the next eight or nine months. Me and my brother had our own rooms. We pretty much put all the stuff in one room, and we had to, like, live in this other room. You know, we just had a bunch of blankets on the floor and our TV, and we would party and stuff. And we stole one of them huge dumps from the neighbors and put it in front of our door so they couldn't come in. [My mom's boyfriend] was very violent. Traumatizingly violent. And I have never experienced violence in my life until then, but I have violent tendencies now, and I don't know if it's from that.

. . . When I was sixteen, [my mom's boyfriend] kicked us out for the week-end. When we came back, she had moved and she didn't tell anybody. . . . I got arrested for underage consumption, but while I was in jail, they realized that

I had no parents around. So I sat there for three months. They had to wait for someone to get guardianship. My [maternal] grandmother took custody of me for a year, then I moved back with my dad when I was seventeen. I stayed there 'til I was nineteen when I moved back to Toledo, where I stayed ever since.

. . . Usually the people you come across, most people are way worse than my situation. And my family's good to me. I'm well-loved and well-liked. I didn't grow up on the streets. I haven't been abused my whole life. No one molested me. Nothing like that. My mom's boyfriend was an asshole and tried to beat up my mom. I got in the middle of it, basically. If I would have never got in the middle, nothing would have never came down on me, but I could never stand there and let it happen.

. . . I have a fantastic family. My parents, we're really close, but they're my friends. My parents were total wild hippie party people. They're not very parental. My brother is my best friend. I mean, we're as close as you could possibly imagine being. . . . I have nine uncles. I was the first girl born in the United States. I have a lot of cousins. I'm the oldest one. We were raised very, very close. We all hug each other every time we see each other, every time we say goodbye. We call, and all my aunts, uncles, cousins, they all write me letters. . . . When I was ten, my cousin was born. I was there at her birth. She's like my sister. . . . A couple years later my cousin [Paul] was born. He was also raised in the household. He's like my little brother. All my uncles are very supportive. . . . I have a very, very good family, and they all support me. Nobody has turned their back on me. And I have quite a bit of time.

. . . I've had extremely good friends. I've had a fantastic life. Very adventurous. I've been all over the country. I've traveled like road trips, and you know, millions of parties and lots of friends. . . . So I've had actually a wonderful life. I mean, ups and downs from what most people have had. But I've had some unbelievably fantastic experiences. I've come across some wonderful people.

. . . I did good in school when I was young. After about third grade, I started having a lot of problems. I was very, very outcasted, extremely outcasted. I had no friends. I started cutting myself; I was kind of suicidal at a very young age. I didn't know I was manic depressive. My parents didn't know. It was just, that's just the way Valhalla is. You're up and you're really down. . . . You know, I just always thought I was crazy. As a little child, everyone just always said what a psycho I was. . . . I was really ADHD, extremely bad concentration, especially when I was young. It went downhill from there, really bad grades. . . . It was a very well-off neighborhood where my grandmother lived. . . . I went to a school with all white kids whose parents were doctors and lawyers. My dad was a maintenance man with a beat-up Volkswagen bus, okay, so we did not have money like all these kids did. I was very self-conscious. I was very introverted. People would pick on me; I was the one kid who moved into the school and they focused on me. And it just snowballed from there. I was very outcasted, picked on, spit on, tripped, made fun of. Really bad. I still have issues with it.

Things got better when I moved away from that school. And after that, I kind of every year got more and more popular and outgoing. By the time I graduated, I went to the prom with the prom king, you know, so a whole different world. But when I was a sophomore, I was doing a lot of drugs and partying. You know, we had no supervision. I went to school the first day. Skipped five days, went back, suspended for ten days, and I didn't go back again until March. So that was my sophomore year.

After moving [in] with my [maternal] grandmother, who kept a real close eye on me, they put me in the Ohio Education program. It's a program where they put you in school for a couple of hours a day, then you go to work. It's kids that basically they don't think are going to make it. I was a very smart girl. I had extremely good comprehension, you know. I didn't want to be there. I wanted to do what I wanted to do. I didn't care. Well, I did really good. I got straight A's. I did graduate. I ended up making up the lost time. I missed a whole year of school but still graduated on time. So I did really good there.

. . . [When I was nineteen,] my boss's wife killed herself and put me in the suicide note. She said I was sleeping with my boss, which was totally untrue. . . . [My boss] said I can't work with you because of this letter . . . so I lost my job. . . . My dad basically made it seem like it was my fault, and he was embarrassed by what had happened. . . . I'm flipping out, and I'm losing my mind, and I'm crying, and I'm going through a crisis and I don't know what to do with myself. And then my boyfriend broke up with me. He was calling me a junkie whore and all this other stuff, and I couldn't take it, and I took a whole bottle of 250 uncoated aspirin and downed a bottle of vodka and just waited to die. . . . And I got my stomach pumped, I'm tied down, tubes in everywhere, catheters, needles, and my brother is the only one that came to the hospital. And he cried and said, "How could you leave me?" I was released to him on the condition that I turn myself in to some place. So I went 'cause I knew something was wrong with me that I would want to end my life. I didn't want to die so much as I wanted to shut my brain off because my head, I felt like I was losing my mind. Everything was spinning, and I was wanting to bang my head against the wall. I didn't know what to do. I just wanted to shut it all out. And that's the only thing I was able to do, 'cause I wanted to sleep and not wake up anymore.

. . . So I turned myself in to a hospital, which has a mental health unit, and that's when I found out I was manic depressive and I had raging thoughts and I was severely manic; I was in a phase. I had an inability to handle stressful situations. And once it started, it went on like probably a week and a half that my head was just going, and I was losing my mind. My emotions were up and down, but I didn't know that there was a name for what was wrong with me. And when I started reading about it, it was like everything I ever felt was right there on paper. And it makes me understand my mother and my grandmother more.

. . . I met my husband on September 6 and married my husband on September 17. November 1, I found out I was pregnant. . . . When you're pregnant, you are mental, and I wasn't on medication or anything. It affects you, especially my first pregnancy. I didn't really know him that well to tell him about being sick, and I'm uncomfortable, and I have hemorrhoids, and I'm constipated. All these things, and my emotions are messed up. I started to despise him and hate him, and I left him. I moved out and moved in with my mother. I had the baby and then everything got okay. He was very patient. . . . He still came to see me every day and gave me the car. Paid for everything and just waited for me to come back. And I did.

When my son was probably three months, four months old, I was pregnant again. On my son's first birthday, I had another baby. I had two babies in a year. . . . I'm tired. I haven't slept. Both of my kids are sick, not sleeping. . . . I collapsed on the doctor's floor. It was just so much to deal with, you know. . . . My friend came up there . . . and he brought me up some pain pills. And I felt better. He brought me some more and brought me some more. And brought me some more. I was a heroin addict when I was a teenager, but I had quit when I was twenty. My husband did not know this. . . . So I'm starting to use these drugs . . . and he was very naive to drugs. Well, it got really bad, and after about a year, I must have been doing OxyContin and . . . I started using heroin. I'm trying to hide this from him. I'm slowly destroying our lives, selling stuff off, and you know—I don't know how to explain all that—he just didn't see what was going on. . . . I was a drug addict and nobody knew. I maintained very well. I kept my house clean. Took good care of my kids. I wasn't dirty. I wasn't prostituting. My husband had a really good job. But I did all the finances, and by the time we were done, I had bankrupted us.

I didn't have any money. I was addicted to heroin. So I decided I'm going to go steal somebody's purse. So I chose this lady, and I asked her for directions. And she turned around to point, and I grabbed her purse and took off in the car. Well, what I didn't know—I don't know how I didn't realize it, but at the time, I swear I didn't—I didn't realize she was hung up on her purse, and I drug her thirty feet in my truck. I didn't know it until I got arrested 'cause three days later I got caught. I went on a high-speed chase. I hit a telephone pole going sixty miles an hour. Bad accident. Police come . . . and take me to the hospital. I'm 118 pounds. Hadn't had a period in a year, you know, heavy, heavy drug addict. . . . I find out I'm pregnant, probably four months pregnant. . . . I'm flipping out. Now I want to kill myself 'cause I know what I've done, and I know what's going to happen. Heroin withdrawal is no joke. You know, this baby is in utero; this child is going to suffer. I had to call my husband from the hospital. I was handcuffed to the bed. I had to tell him I'm going to prison and I'm having another baby. You know, I'm leaving him alone with two infant children, a one-year-old and a two-year-old.

So I go to the county jail, nineteen days in the county jail, and I'm going through withdrawal. And they're telling me there's a 90 percent chance I'm going to lose this baby. I don't know if the baby is dead inside of me. I don't see a doctor. Nobody's doing anything about me. So finally my lawyer got me out . . . on a medical furlough. I went home for eight months. I did everything right. I didn't do any drugs. I stayed home. I gained eighty pounds. I had a healthy baby, and she was beautiful, and she's smart, and she's fine. The scariest moment of my life was having that baby. . . . [But] she's walking now. She's talking. She's fifteen months old. She's smart, she's learning, she's fine. . . . She was three weeks old when I had to go back to court, so I haven't seen her since she was three weeks old.

On my boys' second and third birthdays, I got sentenced to five years in prison. I have adjusted very well [to prison]. I'm actually an easily adaptable person. . . . I've been moved around my whole life. You just get used to it, and I'm not afraid of change. I actually like to move around. I was at eleven different schools. When I graduated high school, we looked on the Internet and found a job in Montana and got a bus ticket and packed up our shit and moved to Montana. You know, moved to Florida for six months to hang out with a punk rock band. I have no problem with change. It's really easy for me to move around. People tend to like me. I'm very open, and people feel comfortable around me. I was raised with all the hippie love stuff, you know. My friends call me Moonbeam. . . . So I have tons of friends. I'm not trying to toot my own horn, but I tend to be a very popular girl. 'Cause I'm just real nice, I'm real friendly, so I know everybody. You're not supposed to, but I have a girlfriend.

. . . There's so many people that have less time than me that want to get into these programs and groups that someone like me who's got three or more years, they tend to just push me out. They say, "Come back when you have less than three years." So there's not much I can do. I go to [NA] meetings every once in a while. I'm the rec[reation] aide, so I do all the movies and stuff in my unit. . . . When I have less than three years, I'm gonna reapply for anger management, victim awareness, a drug program, maybe a parenting skills program. . . . [But] I'm really not bored. I read a lot. I read a *lot*. I love to read. I watch movies. I have all these projects. I'm real crafty. When I go to my cell, I make flowers and sew. I keep myself really busy.

. . . From my experience, there's different reasons why so many women end up in prison. Drugs is a huge, huge, huge part of it. Drugs is definitely by far the biggest problem. There's girls who have been doing drugs since they were little kids. Lack of love is a big part of it. There's so many people here that do not know what it's like to really be hugged. You know, there's women here who are the nicest girls in the world. My roommate, sweetest little girl, twenty-two, no one's ever touched her feet. I don't know if that means anything to you, but to have been having sex since you were fourteen years old and no one's ever touched your feet. No one's ever gave her a backrub. She's had plenty of sex but no love. No affection. I mean, there's a lack of human kindness, compassion. . . . And there are girls that are here for prostitution because they were molested, and no one ever said it was wrong.

Also, uneducation runs rampant. . . . The math I learned in third grade, these women are thirty years old and I'm just explaining to them over and over and over again, and they're not getting it. . . . Girls that are twenty-one, twenty-two-years-old, to me should be setting the world on fire, but they can't even hardly read. They can't spell. They don't use correct English. They say "mines." What the hell is "mines"? . . . It just breaks my heart that these women come in here and they cannot read. I don't know what my life would be like without reading. It's just like the world can be so closed off to you, so why wouldn't you go do drugs? What the hell else is there besides TV and getting high?

. . . . Drugs are such a big problem because life is hard. Life is scary. Mental illness runs rampant and people do not know what's wrong with them. They don't know because their parents have no idea. They don't understand the extent of mental debilitating illnesses in this country. . . . My parents, they didn't know I was ADHD when I was a kid. They didn't know that if I would have took Ritalin, I probably would have did better in school. They didn't know. I know. I'm educated. I will educate my children. I will watch my children. If I'm not sure what's going on, I will get them help. . . . When I was at home, before I got married, I had no insurance. I went to a [counseling] place once a month. They said, "How are you doing? Do you feel suicidal? Homicidal? How's your medication? Here's a prescription. See you next month." When I had my own insurance, I went every week for an hour and a half, and he listened to me. He discussed. If I had problems, I could call. I got help from that man. He was an antidepression specialist who specialized in dual diagnosis. He helped me a lot. Just simple things, like the fact that green lights help with depression.

Most women here, something's wrong with them: depression, anxiety, violent tendencies, anger, abuse. But they don't get help. . . . In the world we don't take care of people that need it. I mean, the fact that people who are here with a drug offense can never, ever get government aid to go to school? That doesn't seem right. They're the people who need it the most to change their lives. It's disgusting. It disgusts me. I'm lucky. I've got a wonderful husband who will support me the rest of my life. . . . My family will always be there to help me. There's a lot of girls in here who walk out to the street, and that's what they walk out to and they have no options. They're going to wait tables or go back to walking the streets because there's no help. You can't get a student loan if you have no backing. You can't walk off the street from a shelter and say, "I need a $20,000 loan to go to college to better my life so I have a future." You need the government to help you with that. And now you can't. It makes no sense to me. It's the old thing: you keep a down man down.

Different cultures, especially African American culture, has put such importance on how good you look when you step outside that your kids get that [idea]. And the best way to make money when you're poor is to get your hustle on. They're not shown anything better. There's no programs in the poverty-stricken areas to show any kind of enlightenment. There's no Zen. There's no meditation. There's no circles and flower children in those kind of places. You go to an alternative, upper-crust white school, they have all that stuff. They take yoga for gym. You don't got that in the lower, poverty-stricken communities. . . . I was always told that I would be successful and that I was smart and that I was beautiful and there was opportunities out there. And lot of them don't always get that. This girl is a real close friend of mine. She's twenty-two years old. She's got scars on her from being beaten with an extension cord when she would get in trouble. . . . I've been spanked once in my entire life. [I] [n]ever put my hands on my children. . . . It's like, violence begets violence begets violence, and people raise their kids and think it's okay. I just hope that because we're a more educated society that it will get better.

I'm very day-to-day here. . . . I can accept that this is my life. This is my home. This is my family. This is my girlfriend. This is my job. That gets me through. When my mind travels outside of the gates, I fall apart. I cry. I get lonely. You know, I have a child out there I don't know. He does not know what it's like to have a mother. That really upsets me even thinking about it. . . . When I get out of here, what I'm going to do is spend every waking moment of my day staying sober, 'cause out there it's not easy. I mean, I know I can do it, but I'm scared to death of it. I stayed off heroin for five years, but once it was back in my face, I was on it off and running. And it destroyed not just my life; my whole family's been affected. My mother, my father, my brother, my husband, my children, my grandparents have all been affected by this. I will do everything in my power never to have to do this again. If I have to put myself in rehab a hundred times, I will do it. . . . I would like to do a program now and start applying the skills that I'm learning 'cause I'm not doing drugs but I'm still a drug addict. And it's not like everything's gone away. I still have the thoughts and the cravings and I would like to know better ways to deal with it.

. . . I'll tell you a realization I've had recently. I'm very hippie love, you know, very open with sex. It's been part of my life. My parents were far from prudes. Far from it. So I've had a lot of sex. I've slept with several men, a lot of women. I've never done anything I didn't want to do. You know, you can do what you want to do; as long as you're consensual it's fine. Well, a couple of weeks ago, this girl was leaving. So a couple of these girls had a threesome while two other girls watched. I wasn't there. I was invited but I didn't want to go. And it really bothered me. It disgusted me. It made me lose respect for these girls, and I was thinking about it and I'm like, why am I feeling this way? 'Cause it never would have bothered me before. As long as it feels good, we'll have fun. Do what you're going to do. But it really bothered me. I didn't look at them the same way. It disgusted me. I felt like they had lowered themselves. I've been high almost every day since I was thirteen. You know, I was always doing something. Acid, coke, crystal meth, PCP, LSD, ecstasy, whatever. I've done it all. Lots of it. So I was talking to my best friend here, and I was asking why it bothers me. She said she thinks I'm learning to love myself. And that was a great eye-opening thought and it really has stuck with me. Since I was a kid when I started doing drugs, maybe I've never learned to love myself. You know, I'm really trying to look deeply into my soul 'cause I don't know who I am, 'cause I've been clouded for sixteen of my twenty-nine years.

. . . I've always been real proud of myself in having no boundaries and not judging anybody, but maybe there's not anything wrong with having boundaries and being judgmental. 'Cause you know, maybe morally that isn't right. Maybe it really isn't okay for me. I'm the biggest open-minded person alive. But maybe I have more morals than I really thought that I did. Maybe I have more self-respect than I really originally thought that I did. . . . I'm really nice. I'm so nice that my friends are like, "Can you just stop, because people take advantage of you." And when I was seventeen, [my friend said], "I think you are the way you are because you were so lonely, and nobody liked you when you were a kid." That I have a need for everybody to like me. And I do. She was right. 'Cause I still do it. I know that it's kind of manipulative because I know what people want to hear. I know how they want to be talked to. I know that different people like to be treated in different ways. And I can change like this [snaps fingers]. If I want anybody to like me, I can make them all love me. . . . I'm getting better about it now. I don't need everybody to like me. They still do for the most part, but I stand up for myself more now. I don't care so much about hurting your feelings as much as I used to. I used to be, oh, if someone didn't like me, it just, oh, I'm so upset about them. But it's not so much like that anymore.

And her saying that I'm learning to love myself has really made me look deeply into maybe I am [learning to love myself], 'cause I'm thinking. I'm aware of what's going on every day. I remember yesterday, the day before, the day before that, and there's no blank period. I have to feel it all. I never had any boundaries. Everything was okay. Maybe that's why I've bounced around the world. I've just been like a ball that someone threw fifteen years ago and I've just been bouncing around ever since. And maybe this is going to teach me to stop and say this is the way it is, and I'm not okay with everything anymore. You know, I'm not going to just accept everybody. If you're gonna be walking down the street blowing people for money, then I don't want you in my life. Before, I was never going to judge you, but now I am, and now maybe I don't think there's anything wrong with that. Maybe I am allowed to have boundaries for myself and think that things are not okay. It's not okay for me. And maybe it's not okay for you. I'm allowed to say that. And I never thought I could. I can say, "No, I don't think it's right."

. . . So I'm learning, like the talents that I have now. I had no idea that I could do the crafty things that I can do that other people can't do. I did not know I had that in me. The patience that I have now, I never knew that I could be so patient and so tolerant. I thought I would be so bored my whole life. . . . I'm not bored at all, and I'm in prison.

Reading Narrative

"The books I've read are like my friends"

READING IS A huge, huge, huge part of my life. This has been a long, lifetime love affair. . . . When I was a kid, books were everything to me. Everything to me. That was my life. I didn't have any friends, but I had my books. I spent all my allowance on books. All my presents were books. I was a library freak when I was a kid. I read *Babysitters Club.*[1] *Sweet Valley Twins* and *Sweet Valley High.*[2] I mean, I was obsessed with the series books. *Where The Red Fern Grows.*[3] I've read that book so many times. *The Outsiders.*[4] *Chronicles Of Narnia.*[5] *Alice in Wonderland.*[6] *Flowers in the Attic.*[7] . . . In school I would get in trouble all the time for having books in my schoolbooks. . . . They called me "Bookworm." Like, they would see me later bartending and stuff, and here I am, I grew up and I'm gorgeous and I'm stacked and they're like, "Hey, it's the bookworm!"

. . . Reading is totally, totally an enjoyable thing for me. . . . It's my down time. It's my alone time. It's what I do just for me. I'm a very, very giving person. I'm always doing something for somebody else. It's a known thing. You can come to Moonbeam for anything. You want your hair done. You want to watch a movie. You want me to make you something, anything. I'm always helping somebody with something. But reading is what I do just for me. That's my selfish time. When I'm reading, I don't want to be bothered. I have that about two wonderful hours a day, 'cause a lot of time I read at night when everybody's in bed. You know, I'll sit there and listen to my headphones and read. In the mornings sometimes I read. It depends on what I'm doing that day, what the weather's like.

. . . I'm an avid reader. Very comprehensive. Eclectic. I can read really fast and I comprehend it very well. My roommates trip out 'cause I open a book that's this thick, and the next day I'm closing it. . . . A lot of people will ask me to tell them about books 'cause I'm a good storyteller. . . . My family's from Athens, Greece, and I grew up with mythology as a part of my bedtime stories and stuff, and explanations for why the seasons change, how Persephone went to the underworld, and Demeter, and how winter came, and stuff like that. And one of my first roommates here, I would tell her stories every night and put her to sleep.

But it's not easy to discuss things like literature with people. I love to talk about books. 'Cause I've been in book clubs when I was going to college. I didn't graduate, but I was in all the book clubs and reading seminars. . . . But

I can't talk about books here 'cause I read some highbrow books. You know, I tend to read some books that are a little above a lot of people's levels. Now my girlfriend's a really smart girl, so me and her do discuss books. She likes vampire books and stuff like that. Ann Rice. Some of them are really good. They're not cheesy.

My grandma likes to read, and I read so fast that she would buy a book and say, "Read it. This is good." And that was one thing that kept me going with the books. I read a couple of hers and it became a thing with me and her. . . . It's like something we share. If I read a good book, I will tell her. If she reads one, she will tell me. I call home every week to my grandma and we talk about books. I just read a book called *The Glass Castle*[8] and I called my grandmother and told her to get it. If it's a real good book, I'll tell her about it and she'll read it, and she'll give it to my cousin 'cause we all can talk to each other about it. We've been doing that for years. [We've talked about] *Fall on Your Knees,*[9] *The Book of Ruth,*[10] *She's Come Undone.*[11] And another book by Wally Lamb. . . . There's been so many I can't remember many of them. . . . But *The Glass Castle,* she couldn't put it down. She had to finish the whole thing. My cousin was supposed to go to a party, and she's nineteen, and she was supposed to be there at 8:00, and she didn't get there until 11:00 'cause she couldn't put the book down. Six hours she sat there and read the whole thing!

. . . I've read pretty much all of the Oprah books for the last couple of years. They're really good books. I mean, they're really rich. It's very intricately made-up characters. They're not simple, but they're not a real difficult read. I used to go through them pretty quick. . . . My grandma watches *Oprah,* and she would write them down. And then I would be the person who reads it really fast, and if it was really good, I would say, "Yeah, you should read this. You'll really enjoy this."

. . . Given what's here, I read whatever strikes my fancy. The library is not really well organized, even the card catalogue. . . . You really have to pick up every book and read the back. . . . I'll read it and flip in it and read about the author, and I'll say, okay, that looks good . . . I do inter-library loan every time I turn around, but it takes forever . . . and it's so hard. I would like some kind of list of books in categories, like mystery novels, science fiction novels. . . . 'Cause it's hard to pick a book if you don't know it's there. You have to know a title and the author for them to get it for you. There's no computer that you can look up and say, "Well, I want books in science fiction and by this author." . . . Even if it was one book list they had in the library, that would be a really good thing for someone like me who, by the time I leave here, I'm going to have read every book in this library. I got three and a half more years left, and

I've read a big chunk of the books here, so I try to get them from the public library, but I can't pull something out of my head. I call my grandmothers, and they read, but they don't read like I read, and they're not on the computer. It's not like I can call my grandma and say, "Get on the computer and find me a list of books about this." It's just not that simple for me.

. . . There's a lot of romance [in the prison library]. A *ton* of romance. The crappy, romantic dribble is okay once in a while, but I flip through it and it's like cotton candy. It's good for a minute, and it tastes really great, but there's no substance there. When it's gone, it's gone, and there's nothing left. . . . There's basically a thousand books and each are all the same, you know what I mean? She don't like him. He don't like her. But they get together, and they're having some sex. And they give the description of the sex. They fall in love happily ever after. You know, different environments but basically the same thing. The tall dark handsome stranger with the tight pants, and she hates him, but her breath quickens. It's just all like the same book but the words are rearranged. I'm not learning much from it. . . . There's not a whole lot of thought put into it. I mean, they're good books. They're enjoyable. They're just a little simple—cotton candy for books.

But if you read *Grapes of Wrath*,[12] there's a book that's going to take me longer to read it 'cause I'm going to absorb it. You start to feel the people. You can put yourself there. . . . I think that would be the best book I ever read, and that was because it was just so devastating. And when I finished it, when I put it down, I was stunned for a while, you know what I mean? There were parts that bothered me. They still bother me a little bit. That's what got me wanting to read more of the great American classics. My husband had it, and I picked it up a few years ago, and I couldn't put it down. It just broke my heart, you know, but I couldn't stop reading it. It was just like suffering just to survive. The strength that these people, they never gave up no matter how things got, and it made my life seem phenomenal, you know, how easy I've had it. Things like that, they make me appreciate what I have. . . . I hadn't really read much about the Depression. . . . I kind of stayed away from the '20s, '30s, '40s, '50s. They never really interested me. I read the '60s and '70s kind of stuff. But when I read that, it really made me look at things differently. My grandparents told me about the Depression, but they lived in the city. To see it from that point of view and how hard it was starving to death, that was one of the most influential books in my life. . . . I'll never forget it. And it's so well written.

I really do appreciate good writing. I mean, there's a difference between an entertaining book and a well-written book. You know, the book that takes me longer to read, I know it's better written. Some books I can fly through. I can skim read. I don't skip pages, but it just flows so quick. But something that's hard to read, it seems like you've got to go back and read a sentence. I have a vast vocabulary, and I get a lot of it from the type of books that I've read. . . . There's so many things that I've learned that I would not know about just from reading a book about something that was fiction.

Some of the books I've read are like my friends. There's characters I've met who I keep with me inside of me. There's a book called *She's Come Undone* by Wally Lamb. Phenomenal book! One of the best books I ever read. . . . Not the most deepest book in the world, but you know, I felt for this girl, and I was rooting for her the whole time. I've read it like three times. I've recommended it to other people. It really impacted me 'cause I can feel her hurt, her pain. . . . Her dad . . . had to leave his wife for a rich woman. The little girl moved in with her grandma, and her mom was in the mental hospital. . . . Her grandma had an apartment upstairs and these people moved in. . . . It's a young married couple, and he raped [the protagonist], and it kind of flipped her out. . . . And the next couple of years, she withdrew from everything. Stayed in her room and watched TV, ate until she was just humongous and fat and mean and angry. . . . She had this fascination with whales, and she read this thing where the whales were beaching. So she got a cab to Cape Cod and went to see the whales, and took all her clothes off and went out to one of the whales that was dying and looked and it was dead. She looked in [the whale's] eye and so she tried to drown herself. They found her and put her in the mental hospital. . . . It took her five years, but she finally got a good doctor, who was a hippie doctor who wanted to rebirth her, start over from the beginning. So he took her into the pool, and she was in the womb, and he would talk about "the little baby is kicking now" and stuff like that. At first she thought it was ridiculous, but they became really close, and she went through her entire life. When she was raped, it was really hard, but she got past it. And she lost all this weight. . . . She got out of the mental hospital and looked up this guy [from her past]. . . . He was mentally abusive, she fell in love with him, she got pregnant, she had an abortion. And that was pretty much the end of the book.

The writing was just phenomenal. I felt all of it. I mean, from the abandonment of her dad, to her mom going to a mental hospital. Nobody understands, she's the only child. She got picked on a little bit in school. The rape scene, the way it affected her, and then there was a part in the book where . . . [the protagonist] had been closed off for years. She just stayed in her room and got fat. And when the guy came to redo [her grandmother's] wallpaper, he was whistling, and he was a hippie. And she's like, "Well, why don't you invite your wife and your baby?" 'cause they were camping. . . . And she saw the love that they had for each other, 'cause her mom and dad weren't like that. She had never seen a real loving relationship. But she seen them together, and it affected her. They made her feel beautiful, and they're smoking pot and they're talking and laughing and she had a shit-eating grin, and it made me laugh out loud when I read it. She had a moment of happiness and I was happy for her. 'Cause she was so depressed, and she finally seen it. It is out there: there is love and affection. These people don't have anything, but they got this. And it was just an emotional roller coaster, the book. . . . When she was older, the need to please and to mold herself into what she thought everybody else wanted her to be, I could kind of identify with that. I could put myself there, and I felt what she was going through. It's one of the best books I ever read.

. . . I read 'cause I get lost. I'm there. You know, I get lost in that world. I really like fantasy books, too. You know, knights and dragons and wizards and stuff like that. . . . I read *Dragon Source*.[13] It's a huge book this thick, and it's all about these gamers, and they get transported to the middle earth, and it's like a series of three books put in one book. I really like a science fiction book. Love 'em! . . . In the county [jail], you can only get four books a week. So I was looking for the biggest books I can find 'cause I read really fast. The biggest book happened to be a science fiction book, and I loved it. . . . I think it's because they're so far from any kind of reality that I know that you just get lost in that world. . . . My family played imaginary games and pushed Santa Claus and tooth fairy and stuff like that. I've always been a very imaginative child, so I have that movie playing in my head. I can see all these things happening, and I get lost in it. You know, they're riding the dragons. They're casting spells, and some of them are extremely complicated. But it's fun reading. It's a great adventure and quests. It's not so emotionally draining.

. . . I read all the *Harry Potters*.[14] Fairly enjoyable. . . . I've read every Stephen King book known to man. I've read everything by Dean Koontz. . . . And one of my favorite authors is Tom Robbins. I love Tom Robbins. I love Tom Robbins! Here they have *Skinny Legs and All,* but I've read *Still Life with a Woodpecker, Jitterbug Perfume,* a bunch of them.[15] He's got some really out-there stuff. His sense of imagination fascinates me. He can put a whole chapter in the spoon's perspective, you know, and the spoon is talking to the plate about going to New York City. Some people find it stupid, but I just find it extremely entertaining. I have a very good imagination, so I like books that take you away. There's a lot of eclectic writers; you're not going to find none of that stuff here, you know, new alternative stuff. Ginsberg, to me, like phenomenally good writers, you don't see a lot of it here. There's really a lot of crap. A sixth-grade reading level is like the norm here. If most of these girls read a Tom Robbins book, they would be lost.

. . . I'm never really into the cop stories and stuff like that. If it's about the cop's point of view and the investigations, that really doesn't pique my interest as much as the weird murderer killer who's torturing people. . . . I'm trying not to be a morbid person, but if it was something that was really twisted, I would definitely read that. I don't even know why, but I love horror. I love it! . . . I really like the weirder side of life. I like twisted things in the world. They interest me. I'm a very bright person, but I have a very dark side to me. When I was a teenager, I was real gothic. You know, I always had black hair and black clothes and went for the vampire clothes. . . . I've read quite a bit of Ann Rice . . . and I've read James Patterson books, Tom Clancy books.

I've read all V. C. Andrews's books, too. Very popular here. Very popular here. . . . They're good. Very predictable and simple. I mean, it's probably sixth-grade level. I can read a V. C. Andrews book in an evening. . . . [They're so popular that] they're worn out. Probably 'cause there's always a damsel in distress. You know, a horrible family. . . . Orphans and stuff. Some people feed off tragedy. It seems to be more interesting than happy life, sunshiny cloud kind of stuff. Plus a lot of women here, they can relate to tragedy. And the women in these books, their lives tend to be worse off than yours are, so then it makes you feel a little better.

. . . I love *Wicked*.[16] It's the life story of the Wicked Witch of the West. The green, mean, horrible witch. I look at her totally differently now. Her life was full of tragedy and pain, and she was born green with pointy teeth. . . . Her dad made these ruby slippers. They're beautiful, sparkly, ruby slippers that he gave to her sister, and she was jealous because her dad didn't make her any shoes. . . . And she was in love at one time, and her lover was brutally murdered in her apartment. And there's another thing about animals and Animals. Animals with the lowercase letters are animals. Animals with the uppercase letter, they think. They're professors, and there's like a big revolution going on with the emperor, and he wants the "A" animals to be put in bonds. It's fascinating. . . . I actually recommended it for my cousin's birthday. I wanted my grandma to give her a book, and I had her get that book 'cause she loves *The Wizard of Oz,* and she's real theatrical. . . . I recommended it to people here, but I think people get frightened by how big it is. You know, people tend to go for smaller, and I'm just like the opposite. I hate reading a book that takes me an hour. I feel like it's a tease.

I didn't read urban books until here. . . . There was girl who lived a couple doors down, and I read like four of hers before she got moved out of the unit: *Diaries of a Chocolate Cruise, Diary of a Street Diva, G-Spot,*[17] and there was another one. . . . They're really good. It's something that is so far from anything I've ever known. You know, I grew up in upper-middle-class areas. There was a pool in my backyard, and I had super white hippie parents that wore Earth shoes. We never lived in the ghetto. I never rolled the dubs and put spinners on my cars. I don't know nothing about pimps and the crack dealers on the corner and placing all your happiness on how nice your boobs and fur coat is. But it's interesting. . . . For me, those books are pure entertainment. And maybe a little understanding of the culture . . . 'cause it's so far from anything I've ever experienced. To be honest with you, really the only black people I've ever known were drug dealers. I'm not racist, but I hung out with a bunch of hippie skater kids all my life. I went to golf clubs. I get tattoos and piercings, and I like heavy metal music.

. . . Urban books aren't allowed to come into the library. . . . The powers-that-be find them derogatory. They don't understand what would be interesting in it because the people who decide what we can and cannot get tends to be a white man. I'm sure it's not a bunch of urban project women with a bunch of kids. You know, I'm sure it's highly educated men that went to a good college and had a good life, and they don't understand. That book's ridiculous to them, and it's disgusting. So why would they allow it to come in?

. . . There are certain books you just cannot demand. Like you can't get anything on Wicca. I don't understand why. I believe that's total censorship. I don't see why you can get the stuff on hookers and rape, and you can't get something that's about nature-based religion. It's an ordained religion now. It doesn't make any sense to me. . . . These people freak out. If you're reading a book about Wicca, then suddenly you're a Wiccan and you're casting spells on people. It's just ridiculous. . . . Where you're going to rest your eternal soul, that's a choice that you should make on your own. That's how I was raised. . . . I'm a great spiritual person, you know, and I don't really follow one religion. I just take little bits of what makes sense. I've made up my own way of looking at things.

. . . I might not read as much [when I'm released] because I have three kids, and I'll have a job, and I have a house to take care of. But that's one thing I never will let go of is my books. My husband likes to read, too . . . and we have a huge bookshelf that's like from there to here, and it goes all the way to almost the ceiling, and it's just covered from here down with books for the kids. And I've got boxes of books. That's one of the things that I cherish is my books, and I read some of them over. My grandmother can never understand why I reread books. But to me it's like visiting an old friend. I love to go back there. *The Lion, the Witch, and the Wardrobe.*[18] I don't know how many times I've read it, and *Where the Red Fern Grows*. I know they're kids' books, but I still enjoy them. . . . I got *The Chronicles of Narnia* in here. It takes me an hour to read one of them, but sometimes I like to revisit.

8 Jacqueline

—◊—

Life Narrative

"I refuse to be another statistic"

I WAS BORN in Youngstown, Ohio, in 1965. My parents got married, from what I understand, a few hours before I was born. They were teenagers. My mother was sixteen, and I believe my dad was eighteen or nineteen. I had two brothers and a sister that grew up with me. I'm the oldest. I don't remember my father living with us. My mother remarried when I was twelve or thirteen.

I was the oldest, and I never felt like I was a child. My mother put a lot of responsibilities on me very young. I've been cooking and cleaning since I was six years old. My baby brother, I'm like five years and some months older than him, and I remember changing his diapers and feeding him and washing his diapers in a toilet. . . . I've been taking care of somebody since I was five years old. I always had to be the one to take care, and I'm even doing it still here in this prison. I'm always putting myself last.

. . . And I got beat a lot by my mom. My mother beat all of us, but I think I got more so than the rest of the kids. And I hated her for a long time for that. She would tell us stories. Well, I would hear things about what it was like for her when she was growing up. And what she was telling us was she was abused also, even worse than what we were going through, but we never believed her because my mother come from a large family, and none of the other children went through what she went through so we thought she was making it up. And I didn't find out until three years ago that everything my mother said was the truth. So she was a victim of abuse that had kids as a teenager, and it wasn't until she told me, "I raised you all the best way I knew how" that I understood that's all she knew. So the cycle continued.

[When I found out,] I told my mother that I knew she was telling the truth. The oldest boy in the family died almost four years ago, and he went to his grave hating my mom because of the abuse. And I just wish he was alive for me to tell him that all this time she was not lying. It made me understand,

and it made me forgive. And we try to have a relationship now. You know, it's hard sometimes because, I mean, she don't want to believe that she did the things she did to us. It hurts her that she did that. And I tell her, "If I didn't forgive you, then we wouldn't have a relationship." . . . I do understand now, and I try to tell myself that my mother has some psychological issues because of what happened to her, and so I overlook a lot of stuff.

When I was, I don't know, I might not have even been five years old, my aunt's boyfriend took me in the basement and sexually abused me, and I didn't know what he was doing. All I knew [was] it was wrong, and I never told anybody 'til I was twenty-eight years old. . . . My maternal grandfather abused me sexually for years, and I thought that I was bad 'cause I let him do that to me. And then another thing is, I don't hate my grandfather. I love him. He's dead, but I thought, how can I love somebody that did that to me? What's wrong with me? Why don't I hate this man? Every man that has abused me sexually—my stepfather did it, too, and I don't hate him either. And I don't understand why, you know, what's wrong with me? Because as a matter of fact, when I found out that I wasn't the only granddaughter that he did that to, I got mad at him. I guess I thought I was his special one because he did that to me. It started probably when I was seven or eight, and it continued until I learned how to stop; when the other kids would leave, I would leave also instead of sticking around.

With my stepfather, I was in junior high school, and it was right before [he and my mother] got married. And she turned around and still married him. . . . It happened with my sister, too, and my sister was the one that told my mother. My mother wrote me a letter when I was in jail six years ago and told me that what happened was I was having sex with my stepfather, and my sister caught us. And I made my sister have sex with him, and that I initiated it. To this day she believes that. And I'm like, I was just a little girl. But in her mind, she says that if it didn't happen that way, then why would I, even after I got married and had kids, if I needed money or anything, I would go to my stepfather instead of her. Or if I was in trouble, I would call him instead of her. But I didn't ever feel like she would come to my rescue, so that's why I didn't call her. I called the person who I thought would help me. But in her mind, if he had abused me, then why do I want to be around him? So until this day, she believes that I'm the one that initiated with her husband, and I don't even try to talk to her about it because I be ready to do something to her.

I did very well in school. I always liked learning. I graduated from high school in 1983, graduated at the top of my class. When I started my senior year, I was number one in my class. And my mom and I fought a lot. She didn't want to let me do anything. My senior year I was like, "Forget this." And I would sneak out, you know, and get grounded for it. I got a job, and my mother and my stepfather wasn't working because they worked in the steel mill. My mother was hurt, and she wanted to basically take most of my money. She told me I had to help. I had to pay bills, and I did that. I helped pay bills for a while until I realized, you know what? I'm still a minor. You're supposed to take care of me. I'm not supposed to take care of you. But in the meantime, I still got brothers at home, and I'm buying them shoes, you know, so I didn't really save any money. And I was angry about that because here I'm going to college, and I have nothing. So before I graduate from high school, I get upset because another girl comes from another school on the other side of town. All during high school, I took all academic courses, honor this, honor that, honor this from ninth to the twelfth grade. This girl come over here, and she has home economics and art, and my grade point average was 3.83, and hers was a 3.93, but we're not on the same level, and they put her in the number one position and put me in number two. So I just said, "That's it." That's how I felt. How could you do this to me? I busted my butt for four years.

That summer was horrible 'cause I left home. And every night I didn't know where I was gonna stay. And I'm having a hard time getting work, and then when I go to work, I have no drive. No initiative. No nothing. I worked at the engineering department at [X Company], and I was just basically doing data input. Actually, to be honest with you, it's a blur, 'cause I remember going in front of the screen, but I don't really remember what I was doing. That's how much my life was so chaotic before I went to college.

At the University of Akron, I flunked out my first semester. I brought baggage from home, and I just stopped going to classes. I was kicked out after my first semester. Had to sit out a semester. When I first got to college, I had this whole new ahhhhh. This is gonna be a new beginning, and I can start over, and everything's gonna be fine. But I'm struggling. I'm hungry. . . . Then I start partying, and then I just was like, "F it." You know, I resented the fact that there was nobody to help me. And in my mind I felt like this: I've been busting my butt since I was in elementary school, and you mean to tell me can't nobody in the family help me do anything? I felt like somebody owed me something when in all reality, they didn't. But that's not the way I was thinking back then. I was angry. And I was angry that I had the parents that I had. You know, why didn't you save money for me to go to college? . . . The thing that bothered me the most, I felt like my mother hated me, and I was suicidal. Even before college, but at college I was, and I talked to somebody on campus about it, and they were telling me that until I accepted my mother for who she was, I would not go anywhere. And they were right [laughing].

Then I got involved with a guy, and it just made it even worse. And then I tried to take my life. I went into a very, very deep depression for months. They tried to put me in a mental hospital, and then my best friend said that she would be my guardian and got me out. And then, [my boyfriend], I started clinging to him, which was like the blind leading the blind. I went back to school, but I dropped out because I ended up pregnant. And then I was like, "Oh, this is another new beginning. And I'm gonna go to Louisiana, and everything's gonna be great." And it wasn't. And I kept having babies after babies after babies after babies. And life was hard in Louisiana. It was very hard for me. And I got married the same way my mother did, got married hours before I had my baby. Got married in the hospital. Had my daughter. It was hard. When I had my baby, my first baby, I didn't even have clothes to take her home from the hospital in. Do you know how that makes you feel? I had nothing. I had nothing. I had two outfits to wear the whole time I was pregnant. You know, there were days I didn't have no food.

And you know, I just kept thinking things was gonna get better, but my ex-husband, he's one of those type of people—he's not a bad person—he just believe you can live free. And during my marriage, I kept having babies. And I have to take care of us 'cause he worked when he wanted to. Didn't put his hands on me, but emotionally, oh my gosh. It was horrible. . . . The baby needs diapers, but he wants to buy clippers to cut his hair. . . . It was always what he wanted. His needs came before me and the kids. And I used to jump on him, you know, I would be so angry.

I finally went and got a job at Kmart, but I couldn't get with the racism. If I had to do it over again, I would rather deal with that type than the type that's in the North because at least down there you know where you stand. And up here they just smile in your face when they call you a nigger behind your back. But it was just the way the managers would talk to some of the employees. I remember one time the manager spilled her drink on the floor and told the one guy, "Clean that up." And [the guy] just ran, you know, just like it was still slavery time. And I was like, oh, hell no. You know, me being from Ohio, I'm not used to seeing that. . . . I tried to address the issue with [the store manager], and he didn't do anything about it. So I wrote the district vice president. . . . Then they started writing me up for things I didn't do to try to make me quit. And I told my husband at the time, I said, "They will have to fire me. I will not give them the satisfaction of quitting." So they finally made up a lie that the customers was complaining about me, and they fired me.

So we ended up coming back to Ohio. My ex-husband didn't want to work, and I worked and spent most of my money on the lottery, which I couldn't afford to do, but I did. So we were always getting evicted. And when he left, as much as I wanted him to leave, that was one of the most painful things, because my family was split up, and I had five little kids. And I'm super-woman, and nobody could see me not be superwoman. And I crumbled. I got addicted to crack and was on that roller coaster for ten years. And I almost killed myself in '93 or '94 through suicide. I was so angry when I didn't die that I pulled out a tooth. They had to strap me to a bed for three days and had me on a suicide watch. . . . [My ex-husband] came and got his kids and brought them to Akron. I thought he was taking care of the kids, but it was [his parents]. . . . They were up in their 80s when they took care of my kids 'cause their mother is strung out and their father, he's just in lala land.

I moved in with [another] guy. I got clean . . . [but] then I started using, and I eventually lost my son to the system. And I know where he's at: with a very good family, but I haven't seen my baby since he was two, and he's fourteen. . . . When I lost him to the system, I felt like that was God's punishment for me being unfaithful to my husband and having a child when I was still married. That's the way I look at it. I think about my son all the time.

My three older kids, they're twenty-one, twenty, and nineteen now. Two of them are in college. My oldest daughter was in college but she messed up. She's married and got three kids. And they're some of the strongest people I've ever met. And it's my babies that when I was still using, no matter how low I got, I would think about them, and I'm like, I gotta try. I gotta keep trying. I gotta keep trying. I gotta keep trying. I gotta keep trying. And I'm so proud of them. My oldest son has a full scholarship to Ohio State. He's a junior. My youngest daughter's at Bowling Green. They both have grade point averages of 3.0 or better. I'm very proud of them. I worried about them when I came to prison . . . [but] they have handled this very well.

. . . The last two years of my life, I haven't gotten high. . . . Whenever I was at my lowest point, I would never come out in public so you could see me, you know. So a lot of people don't believe I got high. What really made me stop was my boyfriend. I stole almost $3,000 from him. I never done that before. And it scared me. I said, if I do this, what am I going to do the next time? . . . The first year it was very tough not using, you know, dealing with my feelings. I've been medicating myself since I was a little girl 'cause I started drinking when I was little. My mother left us home a lot by ourselves so when she was gone, I started drinking, smoking weed. I was in elementary school. . . . So for the first time in my life I had to deal with emotions that I didn't even know existed. Because when they would come up on me in the past, I got high. I'm not gonna feel this. So yeah, that first year was really hard. The second year was a little bit better.

. . . I had a letter from my brother yesterday, and he said in his letter, "You really have a story to tell, all the things that has happened to you, and it's time to tell your story. . . . We have to tell others so that they don't make the same mistakes that we made." I sat there, and I sat there for a moment. And you know, he's not the first person that's told me this. See, I have a cousin, she graduated from Oberlin, and she's a professional woman. . . . Every time I see her, she says, "When are you going back to school?" and "You have a story to tell." . . . So when I read his letter, I said, "Well, when do I begin to tell my story, and who do I tell it to?"

. . . Sometimes I think about trying to be a mentor to young people. I don't know if I have the patience for it. . . . But it's really funny that my kids' friends, I always talk to them. And I talk straight talk to them. I don't sugarcoat anything because I don't want them to make the mistakes that I made. I tell them just like it is. And they always want to be around me [laughing] for some reason. They like honesty. My kids will even come talk to me about anything. I've been told that there are some things that I should have not discussed with my kids because they're children. But I'd rather them hear it from me than from someone else.

. . . My first reaction when I was convicted was, "Oh, my god. I'm a felon. What the hell am I gonna do now?" And I cried. And then I said, "There's gotta be some kind of light at the end of this tunnel. I have to find something positive." . . . I have never been in trouble since I've been in here. . . . I think for the first time in my life I started caring about me and loving myself.

. . . I go through major depression. Mental illness runs on my dad's side of the family, okay. There's a history of that. But there were times I would wake up when I was with my ex-boyfriend, and I didn't get out of the bed. . . . One day I was crying, and I told him that if my parents couldn't love me, how could anybody else love me? And you know what he said to me? He said, "So what if your parents don't love you? The question is, do you love [Jacqueline]? See, that's your problem. You don't love [Jacqueline]. That's why you treat [Jacqueline] the way you do." And it was a slap in the face.

And I also thought about there was a guy that I was with. We got high together. . . . And he treated me really, really, I mean the things he done to me, only me, him, and God would know how bad it was. When I would get high, I was so vulnerable. He could do anything to me. One day we both were getting high, and he was getting dressed, but he kept staring at me. I'm sitting on the bed. . . . And he was just shaking his head like this. And he said, "You know why I treat you the way I do? . . . Look how you treat yourself." He said, "You are so beautiful." He said, "I ain't talking about just on the outside." He said, "You are such a beautiful and giving person on the inside, too. And you're very smart." He said, "You can have anybody you want. You can do anything you want. But all you want to do is get high. And look at you. Look how you look." And I got up and looked in the mirror, and I saw a monster looking back at me 'cause I was so little, that big face all sunk in, skin dark. And there were moments in my life afterwards, like I would be getting high by myself, that I would look in the mirror, and I could hear what he was saying. And my son told me, he said, "Mommy, you don't see what everybody else see." And I never have.

When I almost died, they told me what was wrong with me. 'Cause I'm telling them that ever since I was a little girl, I would tell my grandfather—this same man who is molesting me—I said, "Granddaddy, I feel like I want to kill myself." And he said, "Oh, baby, that's just the devil. Just fast and pray." And that's what I would do. I would fast and pray for him to go away, and then he'd come back. And every time he'd come back, I would fast and pray. And when I was [suicidal] in '93, I'm telling them that I've been going through something like all my life. And then they finally told me [about my depression]. So for the last five years I have been seeing a psychologist on the streets. . . . She and I was getting somewhere. When I would relapse, I would lock out everybody else but her. . . . And we were gonna start talking about the sexual abuse. We would try to talk about it, and I would freeze up. And I had made up my mind if I'm gonna get anywhere, I got to start talking about this.

. . . I've been [in prison] two months, and I haven't had a [counseling] session yet. . . . This is supposed to be about rehabilitation, but what I'm seeing is if you don't find somebody in these places that give a damn, these women are still not going to give a damn. And they ask why [women] keep coming back. There's a lot of self-hatred in here, and there's not any kind of ray of light. And then you expect us to get out of here and be a productive member of society? Well, where are the tools at? What are you giving us to take out of here? First of all, somebody has to start telling you that you're not a bad person. You're a beautiful person. You're a human being. You know, God didn't make junk. Start teaching us how to respect ourselves, and give us some respect. . . . I understand that we're in a prison. I understand that. But why do you have to tear us down mentally? They're tearing us down mentally. And then you want us to go back into society. Why do you think people keep coming back in here? You're breaking us down while we're in these places.

That's not rehabilitation. We're being broke down. . . . I tell myself on a daily basis, "You're salvageable. You're worth being saved. You're better than this." I have to do that myself 'cause nobody in here is telling me that. Because I refuse to be another statistic. I have been enough statistics [laughing], and I don't want to be another.

—ɯɯ—

Reading Narrative

"I wanted his strength to jump out of the pages into my life!"

I LOVE TO read. I love to read. Always have. When I was a little girl, my mother would buy me those Dr. Seuss books, and I never wanted to go outside and play. So she would take the books and tell me, "Just go outside for a little bit, and then I'll let you have your books back." So I'd go out there, and I would be so angry 'cause I don't want to go outside. I don't want to be around anybody. I just want to read.

Ever since I was a little girl, reading was always my great escape into somebody else's world that I felt was better than mine, and it continues to be a very positive escape for me. It's my survival mechanism right now. . . . If I didn't have books to read, at this stage in my life, I would be in a straitjacket for real. . . . Because I escape [when I'm reading]. My mind is not here. I don't have time to think about I'm in prison. . . . I don't have time to think about I'm surrounded by people that I wouldn't even keep company with on the outside, and think about these idiots that's running the place. And I don't have time to really kick myself in the butt for doing this to myself. When I read, it's really like I'm in another world, and I'd rather be in that world than in this world that I'm in right now.

I read every day. . . . I'm a slow reader. I like to read my sentences over and over and take my time reading, so I could fully grasp what I'm reading. . . . My favorite place to read is my room because my roommate is not in there most of the time. When she is in there, she's talking, but I can totally tune you out when I'm reading if I don't want to be bothered. So I tune her out a lot.

They got a lot of junk books in the library. I call them "ghetto books" because they seem to stereotype the mentality that comes through the prison, like what's going on with our young people now in the hip-hop culture. They got a lot of junk books in there about the drugs and she was a stripper, and getting beat up by the boyfriend and having a lot of babies by different men.

There are women in here that like to read that kind of stuff. But they're so closed-minded. I don't think that the librarian really realizes that there are people in here that want to read something with some substance to it.

Sometimes I go to fiction, but . . . more often, I'm gonna go to the nonfiction because I love history and I'd rather read about something that actually happened than not. . . . I love to read black history. Martin Luther King and Harriet Tubman, Frederick Douglass. I love to read about Abraham Lincoln. I *love* history. I took black history when I was in the ninth grade, and I was amazed because it's really sad that they don't teach us about ourselves in the public schools. And I was amazed at what black people had done. You know, I was like, oh my god! We did that? And we did, oh my! So when my kids were little, I started teaching them about Martin Luther King, and it's really sad because a lot of kids my kids' age, they have no idea of the civil rights [movement], none whatsoever.

. . . Anything about slavery hooks me. I've read a book by Booker T. Washington, *Up from Slavery*,[1] and I was amazed by the inner strength that he had. It helps me. When I read about those people, I think about my ancestors and if they had that kind of strength to overcome, especially his book. And there are times I get angry with [the white] race. I really do. I get very angry. I get angry now at the things that I see because there's still so much racism and it's so subtle. And when I read his book, this is when I was going back and forth to court about my charges. And I told myself that no matter what happens, I was going to get through that. I couldn't get over how a human being had so much determination and had so many odds stacked against them and still he persevered. . . . And it's really funny, I thought about that book yesterday. I thought about how Booker T. Washington, the one thing that he did every day was read something from the Bible. He did that on a daily basis. And how he took advantage of most of the day, instead of having like idle time or sleeping a lot, he took advantage of each day.

. . . I like to read books like that. They give me hope, especially right now. There are times when I just don't know how much more I can take. . . . Things happen to remind me of what I have to face when this part is over, and it's scary, you know, that I've made my life that much more difficult, that I did this. So it's actually why I'm constantly reading, to escape. I'm escaping. Instead of using drugs now [laughing], I'm reading the books. But I'm trying to give myself some hope.

When I was a little girl, for some reason I never would read Malcolm X. For some reason, in my mind he was a bad man when I was growing up. So I finally, as an adult, read *The Autobiography of Malcolm X*,[2] and boy, he was one hell of a man! I read that book before I really got strung out on drugs. I think my drug addiction had just begun, and my brother had the book and I read it. I can't put it in words how that book made me feel. When I first started reading the book, I thought about what I was going through at that time of my life, with the drugs, and I felt inadequate as a human being after reading that book. Because I had become a slave to the drug. I was beginning to be a slave to the drug and I really didn't know how to make it stop. And I wanted his strength like to jump out of the pages into my life [laughing]!

. . . *The Autobiography of Malcolm X* let me know that I am somebody as a black person. And that all I have to do is reach deep down inside of me, and there's nothing that I can't do if I want to do it, if I just persevere. I mean, he was a drug addict, pimp, gambler, went to prison, did time. But while he was in prison, he made very good use of that time. And when he came out, he tried not only to help himself, but to better his people. And at first, he might have been going about it the wrong way. Well, he was. That's my opinion. . . . You know, there's racism on both sides. But then when he realized that he was being misled . . . even though he knew that it would cost him his life, he was still willing to be about the right thing for the human race as a whole. And that's what it's about. It's not about black and white and green and yellow and all of that, it's about us being a human race as a whole.

. . . I like autobiographies, biographies. If it touches on things from my real world and there's a positive ending, then that gives me some hope. See, I'm so used to pain that I have to find some way to not feel pain. . . . I like to read about happy endings. I like to read some positive things because there's so much negativity in my life. . . . I don't go anywhere; that's why I have books. Even at home, the books is what gives me the inspiration.

One book I've read that really, really touched me was called *Angel On My Shoulder*,[3] and this book was a autobiography of Natalie Cole. She was born, she would say, with a silver spoon in her mouth because of who her dad was. . . . I thought it was fascinating to grow up with a famous father like that, at that particular time when a lot of blacks didn't have money. She was born with money. Her dad was very, very rich, you know. . . . It seemed like her mother was jealous of [her husband] and Natalie, their relationship. As a matter of fact, when [Natalie's] father was dying, her mother didn't even let her know that he was dying, and her dad died while she was away. . . . That bothered her that she didn't get a chance to really say goodbye to her father. And her mother didn't want her to be a singer. You know, she didn't want her to follow in her father's footsteps. And [Natalie] talked about how her father had so much charisma. . . . And she talked about how she

156 Jacqueline

got on drugs. The first time she went to rehab, she borrowed money from her mom, and I think her parents had adopted a boy. And he was the one that told her you're borrowing your own money because their dad had left them money, but the mother said he left them nothing, which was a lie. . . . I identify a little bit with not having a good relationship with the mother, you know, but they finally were able to make amends. . . . She got off drugs, and her mom and her have a healthier relationship. She's been clean like twenty-something years.

I like a happy ending because it gives me some hope. It's what fuels me. I start thinking that no matter how bleak everything is, looking at that moment, I tell myself that I can do this. Whatever it takes for me to reach my full potential, I know I can obtain it. . . . When I mop the floors, it really tires me out. But I told myself yesterday, 'cause I'm trying to discipline myself, this will be the day that I start not only walking in the mornings, but I'm gonna walk in the evenings also. . . . As the floor was drying yesterday, first I said, "I'm tired. I'm gonna start walking tomorrow." But then I said, "No. I have to do this now." And I started thinking about how my characters in my books push themselves. So as the floor was drying, as tired as I was, I went on and I did my mile walk. And it made me feel really good. When I read a book, when it has a good ending, that's what happens. I tell myself, you know, no matter how bleak everything's looking right now, if I do this and I do that and if I do this, even though something negative might happen, it happened in the book also but they kept going. They persevered. They kept going, and I have to keep going. I have to keep going. I have to keep going.

. . . I love Terry McMillan; I love her books. They make me think of my family a lot when I read her books. *Mama. Waiting to Exhale. How Stella Got Her Groove Back.*[4] Her books also, they kind of make me feel like it's not too late, and I still have time to get it together. They give me some kind of hope. Because she has professional black women in her books and sometimes I can relate to some of the things that they have gone through or they're going through. Like when I read *A Day Late and a Dollar Short,*[5] it was three sisters and one brother. And the oldest, her name was Paris. Paris took care of everybody. Paris acted as though she was perfect and was trying to be perfect. But she had got hurt and the doctor had to prescribe pain pills for her, and she got addicted to the pain pills. And she had to admit to herself that she wasn't perfect and also to her family. She was very successful and at the end of the story, she overcame her addiction. So I liked that character. Paris had her own catering business where she cooked gourmet food, and she pushed herself. She pushed herself. She pushed herself. And I tell myself, you know,

I can't be lazy anymore. I can't procrastinate. I'm forty-one now. I have to push myself. I have to push. I have to push myself. And I'm trying to develop this behavior right now while I'm in here, you know. You take advantage of every minute of the day, you know, even if I don't feel like it. I have to push myself and try to discipline myself right now because I done wasted enough time. I can't waste any more time.

My self-esteem has been so low that when I read about people like Paris and Malcolm X and Natalie Cole that are real people, it builds up my self-esteem somewhat. It lets me know that as long as I'm still breathing, I still have a chance to make my life better. As long as I'm still breathing, I still have a chance. And it also lets me know that I'm a human being, and that everybody make mistakes. That I'm not such a bad person because I got on drugs, and I'm not a bad person because I was sexually molested. I'm not a bad person because my mother beat the crap out of me. I'm not a bad person. And it lets me know, too, that you could have done some things that are bad, but then you can fix it, and not just do bad things but do some great things. You know, Malcolm X did a lot of bad things, but in the end, he did a lot of great things. And that's what I feel, I can do some great things. I know I can do if he could do it. That's how it inspires me.

I also read a book called *Good Girl, Bad Girl* about Whitney Houston.[6] . . . When I read the book, I saw a lot of me. . . . Whitney Houston wears a mask, which I have done. She had this image of America's sweetheart, but Whitney Houston was a rebel. She was, and she's a fighter. . . . She's been getting high for years, but nobody wants to believe that. . . . And when she did her interview with Diane Sawyer in 2000 . . . my son watched it. My son said, "Mommy, when I saw that interview, guess who I thought about?" . . . I said, "You thought about me, didn't you?" He said he saw her strength, and of course the drugs, because people did not want to believe that I got high. . . . So when I read that book, it was like looking in the mirror. I think about Whitney Houston a lot. You know, because she's really going through something. But I believe with all my heart that she's gonna come out of this. I really believe that. 'Cause she's a very strong woman, and I pray for her all the time. You know, I just believe no matter how bleak it looks right now—that's the type of person I am—no matter how bad it looks, don't count me out because as long as I'm breathing, I'm not gonna stop fighting.

. . . Sometimes, when I'm reading my books, I'm living through my characters. I can really feel them. Like what I'm reading now. I'm reading a science fiction book called *Kindred* and it's by Octavia Butler.[7] And I haven't read anything like that before! I just went to the library two weeks ago and I picked it up and I looked at it and I was like, hmmm. . . . A part of me wishes that you can go back in time, and come back, go back and come back. That's why I like that book. I would want to go back to the slavery time, and I also would like to go back to the time before we were slaves. I would like to see Africa back then. Because most of the time growing up, you only see the bad part of Africa. Even like now most of the time. We're talking kings and queens, and I would like to see how that was. They say Africa had some of the first cities. I would like to see that, to know who I am. To know really who I am.

. . . When I realized that [the main character of *Kindred*] wasn't just [going back to the past to save] her family, it makes sense to me because I would have done the same thing. Because it's not just about us. It wouldn't be just about me and my family. It's about our race as a whole. But I have to wonder if a lot of us think like that nowadays. It's not the same as it was before. We're not the same people as we were before, like the civil rights movement and before. When MLK died, he took something with him. We don't have the spirit that our ancestors had. You know, they're rolling over in their graves. For one thing, we're not whole families. We're not a whole unit. And then the parents get strung out on drugs and the kids are left to fend for themselves, so many of them are ending up in foster homes and homes where people really don't give a damn about them. It's a new form of slavery. You're in it. Right here. This is it. Do you know how many of us are in here? Do you know how many of our men are in here? We have more men in prison than we have in college.

And Africans coming over here look at black Americans and think that we're crazy because there are opportunities that are here for us and a lot of us don't take advantage of these opportunities. . . . You can get loans and grants to go to college. You can get a good education. But there's also drugs that are put in the communities and in the ghettos. You got all these videos and this music talking about making fast money and "I'm in love with a stripper," and our kids are getting these things. And they're idolizing these people. And it used to be that a lot of the fathers were locked up, but now it's the mothers and the fathers. Eighty something percent of women are locked up because of drugs. It's like people don't have any hope anymore. They want to escape. They don't want to deal with life. They're looking for a quick fix, looking for a quick way to make money so that they can have nice things, instead of them realizing that if you obtain nice things quickly, then they're gonna go quickly. But if you obtain them the hard way, they will last a lifetime. Everything is [snaps fingers over and over]; everybody wants things quickly. Videos and the hip-hop culture glamorize street life. It's sad. That hurts me. There are times when I'm ashamed to be black.

. . . I would like to find some nice self-help books, something that would give me self-esteem and have a positive attitude. . . . What I'm learning is you got to help yourself. No one's going to do anything for you if you don't do anything for yourself. . . . I need to keep telling myself no matter how it looks, that this is gonna be okay. That I'm gonna be okay. I have to believe that. 'Cause if I don't believe that, then I will be just like those other women that keep coming back. And I cannot do that. I can't do this again. . . . I would like to read a book about positive thinking, self-esteem, learning how to deal with rejection because I'm sure there's gonna be plenty of it out there; how to toughen up my skin. As you can see, I'm a sensitive person. And not to take things so personally, I guess. I would like to read a book about forgiving myself. That's number one. I would like to read a book about letting the past go and letting go of the pain because if I don't let the past go, I know that I can't move forward. I know this, but how do I *do* that? That's what I want to know. How do I do that?

I would really like to read books about how the mind works [laughing]. Because sometimes the way I think I'm like, "Is this normal like this? Is it because of what I've been through?" Like I said, there's mental illness on my dad's side of the family and I would like to try and understand what is all of that about. I've been taking medication for years and I know I'm not crazy. I'm not crazy, but they say I have psychological issues. What do they really mean by that? And the way that I'm thinking, am I going all the way to the left sometimes?

And I'd like more books on black history. Let us learn about ourselves. Let us find out who we are. And maybe if we find out who we are, then we'll start loving ourself and want to be a better person, a better woman, a better mother, a better sister, a better daughter, a better member of this society and want to do something to right our wrongs, to make amends with what we done wrong to society. While we're in here, we have nothing but time.

9 Audrey

—ɯɯ—

Life Narrative

"That's a chapter that's closed"

I WAS BORN and raised in North Carolina. My mother, she had six kids. She raised all six of us by herself, and we was brought up to believe in working for what we got, and we did pretty much like help out around the house until we got old enough to get out and get public jobs. My childhood was all right.

[When I was in school,] about eighth grade, I think, I started messing up pretty good 'cause I was into boys. Oh he's cute, and this and that. And my mom put me in a girls' home, too. I think I was almost ready to turn sixteen. But that's the part, too, that I closed out because I can't even believe my mom even did me like that. . . . Me and one of my best girlfriends, we skipped school one day on lunch break. We went to this little place called Little John. It had a little short lot out there where you look at trailers. So we went out looking at trailers and stuff and we messed around, went to sleep on the bed. The trailers, one of them, they would always have the electric on, you had a television running, or a little air conditioning and stuff, and that would be all. We were cutting it up, sitting there talking, you know, like girls, dreaming about, oh, when we get married we're gonna do this, we're gonna do that, and we messed around and we slept, and the [school] bus was gone. So we went to across the street to the store. We had tissues in our bra like we was like big girls, we was getting married, you know. We went and told the guy we was getting ready to get married and our husbands wanted us to come and look for a trailer. I think they knew we was lying, but we had bras full of tissue [laughing]. She called one of her friends to come and pick us up. We caught up with the bus, I think it was about four cars behind. So my brother got out the bus . . . and he says, "Oh, you skipped school." I told him, "No, I didn't skip school. I skipped lunch." He says, "Oh, you're in trouble." . . . I said, "Now you know I ain't told," 'cause when we got our mail, we would always get it at the end of the road, 'cause we lived down the path. And if it was mail from the school

... we'd always tear the mail up and just throw it in the cornfield, just shred it up when he hadn't been to school in so many days and stuff.

... [The next day] we went to school, and when I came home, all my little stuff was sitting out on the porch, my little clothes, my little books and stuff. So I'm thinking my mama's doing spring cleaning, right? So I didn't see nothing but my stuff, though. So I get to worrying. My mom come out the door and she says, "You think I'm gonna work hard to buy clothes for you to run up and down the street in? You ain't going to school. No, what did you do yesterday? Riding in the car with that boy." Nobody didn't say nothing about it was a boy and two girls. I said, "But I wasn't doing . . ." "Oh, you gonna lie, too?" She told me I could take my stuff and get out. . . . I asked my brother, I said, "Why did you tell my mama that I skipped school?" "Oh, I didn't tell it." . . . I was gonna go down there and tell my mama about him skipping school all the time, right? So I go down there and tell her that, she says, "Oh, you just coming down here trying to start some mess." . . . I said, "But no, he really hasn't been going to school. Call the school and find out." "I'm not calling the school because I don't believe he's not been going to school. Somebody would have told me by now." And he really wasn't going to school!

So then she put me in a girls' home. I was staying with that same best friend, her, her mama, and her daddy, and her brother. And my mom called the cops and the cops came and got me at their house and took me to my mama's house. Then they took me to the girls' school up here. . . . I had to stay two months, but that was forever, it seemed like it was. . . . We was locked in. We had like a certain little time that you go outside and sit in like a little yard or something. Then we had to come in, and we had chores and stuff to do, then we had like a class where you had to read and stuff. And them people knew I was going to school 'cause I was reading better than pretty much everybody that was in there. But my brother, he sold my mama big time on that.

And that's something, too, that I wanted to talk to my mama about, too, but I don't think I will now, though. 'Cause I couldn't understand that. I'm talking about when the policeman come and got me at my best friend's house and took me back to my mama's, my mama was cooking fried chicken and collard greens, my favorite, and I thought maybe that's for I was coming home. She was like giving me a dinner, you know, then I'm talking about, "Well, you got to ride with me." And I'm in the [police] car, fifteen and a half, almost sixteen, and they're taking me to some girls' home. That was bad, too. And I hated my mama a long time on the inside for that. And I think it ended up being long before I got over the hating her part 'cause I couldn't believe she sent me to a girls' home.

. . . I went to [X] Junior High School but I quit 'cause I got pregnant. And I had my baby. Then I got married when I was nineteen, and I stayed married seven years. . . . But I think the marriage was dead something like maybe three years after it was supposed to been. And I got three children. They're twenty-three, twenty-two, and nineteen.

When I met my husband, he worked on a farm. . . . I think he was like a mama's boy more or less because when he worked, he would give his mama his money. He wouldn't think about he got bills and a child that he had to take care of. So my mom, she co-signed for the furniture we got in our house, to help us get credit, and sometimes when I couldn't make the payments, she made the payments herself, too.

And somewhere in there, I had been abused about twice. He had hit me but he said, "Oh, I'm sorry and I'm not gonna do it again," and I didn't do anything about it. Then he hit me for the second time, and I took him to court to press charges, and dummy me, I dropped the charges then, still trying to make it work. But it wasn't working. He said he wasn't gonna do it no more, and I believed him, and I was, like, shocked the second time he did it 'cause he said he wasn't gonna do it again. And when I dropped the charges in the court, the judge, he said hisself that once a man starts hitting a woman, he'll always keep doing it. I didn't believe that at the time 'cause I still took the charges off, but I do now.

. . . My oldest daughter she had nerve deafness in her left hear because he would be fighting me, and she would be like in the corner somewhere just shaking and stuff. And my son like to not ever got born because I was four months pregnant with him, and my husband jumped on me and beat me up with him, and I had to stay in the hospital about three months just laying flat on my back, used the bedpan and everything. [My son] was supposed to been born in November but he was born October the second.

. . . My mama told me, she said—'cause my mom went through it, being abused, with my dad—and my mom said, "I'm not telling you what to do 'cause you're grown, but I'm gonna tell you this, I'm taking the children." She took my children. Like she said, "If that boy end up and kill you in this house, then my grandbaby's not gonna be laying up in the house waiting for social service to come and get him." And when she took them, that really opened my eyes to see that he was not better than my children.

. . . So then I started changing. . . . One time, I picked up a baseball bat to hit [my husband], and I kinda like caught him somewhere in the mid part of his arm. I broke his arm. Then we was fighting and I had the rifle, .22 rifle. I was gonna shoot him, but he hit me with the rifle, and he broke these two fingers right here and they still don't go down. And I ain't got no teeth now thanks to the fact that he used to knock me in the mouth and knock them out. That's been seventeen, eighteen years since he knocked my teeth on my lip, and I don't have any teeth thanks to him from getting them knocked out. . . . And it got to the point somebody was gonna kill somebody. And I think he realized it might have been him, 'cause it had got to the point where I didn't care if it was me, 'cause I thought being dead would have been better than being in this marriage, you know.

But he left and went to his mama's. . . . I would take them over there because I didn't never tell my children that me and your daddy's going through this; that wasn't their business, you know, that me and [X] wasn't getting along because that was their daddy and I didn't want them to grow up to hate me, say, "My mom wouldn't let me see my daddy," so I didn't never talk bad about how me and their daddy got along. . . . Then one time I took them over there, he said he was gonna take the children away from me. And he said it was 'cause I was an unfit mama. And I was unfit 'cause of the fact that I was working around the clock trying to have something and did make a down payment on a singlewide trailer that I was buying to own, and he destroyed that. He burned it up one day. . . . I was working pulling tobacco plants, then at night time I swept. It's like a tobacco plant where they ship the tobacco and you pick the leaves and stuff out and then you sweep the floor of the dust. That night, somebody called to my job and told me my house had just burnt down, and it was him. He burned it down, and I tried to tell a policeman that he did it . . . but they said it was a accidental fire, a electrical fire, that's what they said, but it wasn't. I think he was messing around in that meter box back there.

. . . He filed for divorce and it became final last year. Yeah, because I had told him he better pick him a corner of the world and go to it and act like I don't exist, and I was gonna do the same thing, and I said I ain't paid nothing to marry his sorry a-s-s and I said I won't pay him nothing to divorce his sorry a-s-s. So he finally did it two years ago. Best thing in the world 'cause I know when I get out, I ain't really got to see him. The kids is grown now. If they go see him, they can. They can go on their own. If that's what they want to do, that's fine. I don't talk against him or anything like that 'cause he never really tried to hurt them except for when I was carrying [my son]. And that's his only son, and my children's the only children he got.

. . . Let me tell you, the most violence I ever had was staying at home. My mama, she had nice long hair. My daddy, he drank all the time. He stabbed my mama in her head nine times, and she grabbed the knife with this hand and like to cut these four fingers off her hand. . . . They had to shave all my mama's hair off except for around the cuts. That's why we knew it was nine because they couldn't shave all the way around the cut. And me and my brother, how we got [X]—that's my daddy's name; I don't say daddy. I call him [X]—but how we got him to stop trying to stab my mama with the knife, because my mama had got up on the bed, and we had come from school. We had took like a piece of pine wood and we beat him with that. Hit him in the leg and the knees so he could stop. . . . But he got his just deserts. He died about four years ago with cancer.

. . . They didn't know what pressing charges was when my mom and them was coming up. I don't think they did, 'cause I can't never remember her ever doing it. And I think sometimes she thought she deserved it. And maybe, in a way, I thought maybe when [my husband] was doing me like that I kinda like felt that maybe I am doing something wrong. . . . I mean, you think you're deflawed, or something is wrong with me. It can't be because I'm doing everything I'm supposed to do, but maybe I'm not doing enough, you know. [My husband] kinda like made me think everything I did was my fault. If he said jump—it's not really that he said it now—but I was supposed to say, "How high?" and go ahead and jump. Or I was supposed to just jump and don't ask no questions. And that's the kind of guy he was, you know. And his mom and dad fought a lot, too, when he was growing up.

. . . I had him on the visitation list when I first came to prison eleven years ago, and I don't know why I put him on the list, but maybe too because I thought maybe he might have to bring the children sometimes. But he never did. He came in '93 or '94, that's the first time I saw him in prison, and when he came then, I told him I was taking his name off the visitation list, 'cause my mama was bringing the kids in. He was up here wanting to really, "Yeah, look what you did, killed somebody yourself. After you're in prison you won't never get out of prison. I told you you wasn't no good, no way. I should have took my children." Well, I told him, I said, "I guess this will be the last time I'll see you." So when I got out of visitation that Sunday morning, I went back and I filled out the visitation list and put [his] name off of my visitation list. And he came this Sunday, believe it or not. And one of the officers here said that he was out there, and . . . he said, "What can I do to get on the list?" and they said, "Well, you have to ask her." I'm not putting him on the list. So there's no point in him or nobody really even asking me. 'Cause that's a part of my life that's a chapter that's closed. I'm not walking back through that book any more, 'cause it's a painful book to go through. And I finally got to the end of it where I could close it, and that's where it's to stay.

. . . I have talked to a counselor here. And then sometimes now I go over and I talk to Miss [X], because I'm not gonna talk too much of personal life with anybody on the compound 'cause they're really not your friend. You tell them something, they go back and they tell everything, and then they add more to it and take something from it. And the things that matter to me doesn't matter to the majority of the people here, 'cause I'm trying to, like I told my children, I want to be the best mom from behind this fence that I can be. And I'm gonna go home and be with them. . . . [But] this is what the majority of the compound is: "I ran around with this man here one night, and I remember we was in the motel and he was taking a bath. I took a stack of bills, I took his whole pair of pants and I went through it" and all that stuff. It's stupidity. . . . You sit here and you got the same niggers and stuff on your mind as you came in here with, and you go out with the same niggers and stuff. And believe me, I've seen repeaters after repeaters after repeaters back.

This here is where you're gonna, not really say grow up, but this here should be an experience where you really sit down and take a look at your life from this point on. Because this here is the lowest level I think of a human form that you could ever get, to be a inmate in a prison. But it's better than being a dead inmate in somebody's graveyard. . . . I've did AA [in prison] 'cause I'm a alcoholic. I've did day treatment. I've worked in the sewing room. I've worked on the yard. And that's what I'm doing now, cleaning up in the dorms. I've cleaned up in the blue building. I've worked horticultural. I got my certificate for completion of horticultural. I got my GED. . . . GED was about the best thing I did for myself, but I don't think I'm smart enough to go to Shaw [University]. . . . I might enroll. I don't know. I'm still skeptical about that. It's gonna have to take a big pitch for me: [Audrey], okay sit down, I believe you can do this. You know, 'cause I didn't think I could do my GED, either, and I passed that with flying colors.

. . . The thing is that I'm going through—'cause I got three more years here—I'm kinda scared. I'm not terrified yet but I think I'm gonna get there [laughing]. I'm just kinda scared 'cause I know the world's changed so much. . . . I got a little grandson. He's nineteen months old. So that's gonna be kinda like my little child; you never can replace growing mines up, you know what I'm saying, 'cause in my mind for a long time, I kept my children so small, and they're bigger than me and I'm looking up at my son, you know? But in my mind, I wouldn't let them get any bigger than what they was when I left. It's like I want to freeze that frame in time and just start back from there and go ahead. And I've sorely learned that I can't do that. They're adults now, you know.

[My sentence is] life plus twenty-five years for second-degree murder. This lady had came over to my house and I woke up with the noise, like as if my window was breaking, and the lady had threw a brick through the window. So I called the Police Department to ask them to come out there, 'cause I was telling them, "This lady's out there in my yard. She's out there." I mean, she was cussing me out: "You goddamned nigger this, you . . ." I didn't know who she was, but I had seen her to know that she used to go with this boy's brother that I was going with. . . . I leaned out the window and said, "What in the world is you doing?" She said, "You bring your ass out of that house, you damn nigger or I'll kill your damn ass." . . . I called the cops and they didn't come, then I called back again, and they didn't come, and by the time they got there, I was in the yard then 'cause she had throw a brick through the window. It's what crashed the window.

So I took a brick . . . and I started hitting her in the head. I don't know how many times I hit her, but I know I was cussing her just like she was cussing me, and I was telling her, "I don't know what the hell you're doing, trying to act like you're acting, coming over here. You ain't never called anybody no nigger." 'Cause I wasn't raised with color, and I said, "I don't see where you even come out your mouth with that, and then you're gonna break my windows out." And I was a single parent, like I said, trying to have, trying to have. And that pissed me off. Because I think I hadn't even had them windows in for about two months. I had just got them, bought them from the trailer place. And I was talking to her and hitting her with a brick. And she didn't die then, 'cause the cops came and they pulled me off of her, and they took her to the hospital, and the next day she died, that next evening.

And at the time, I didn't know what I was doing 'cause it was just so much fury and stuff. And I guess some of that anger that I always kept packed down, packed down, it just exploded. And I hate it was her. And I don't mean any harm in trying to say it, but I wish it could have been him instead of her. If I had to do time, I wish I was doing it for him, 'cause he's the one that really, really did me like he did, and hurt me like he have. But I can't change that. I can't go back and change it.

I talked to them, when they sentenced me for my trial. Her mama didn't say she hated me or anything, she just said that she told [her daughter] about hanging out with niggers. It was a plea bargain trial. They had told me at the beginning that they was gonna try me as a death case. Then they found out that we both had been drinking, but I had been drinking and I was in bed. . . . Then they also found out that the 911 dispatcher had the tape where I had called them twice for them to come. . . . When I called, I said my name,

I said the address, but the last time when I called I said, "This woman is out here, and she's really raising hell. Somebody better come and get her before I go out here and handle things myself."

. . . I had no right to take that lady's life, at my house or not at my house. But I don't think I should have pulled the time that I've pulled in here behind that because I wasn't out looking for nobody to fight with or nothing like that. She came to my house. But still, her life had a meaning in this world, and it liked to fuck me up real bad. For about the first three to four years, everybody thought I was really looney and I was on a lot of mental health medicine. I was about big as a damn house, 'cause I mean, that's all I thought about. Like when the breeze blow outside, I think, "That woman can't feel that breeze on her face." Or when I get up in the morning time, I could get up and I was in prison, but I would think, "That woman can't get up out that grave."

. . . I'm gonna tell you what I caught myself doing: I caught myself being a "in the closet" drunk. I'd go to work, come back home and I'd usually cook and the children would put the stuff in the microwave. But the lady across the street kept my children . . . and when I got in from work, I made sure that they had had something to eat and the lady, my babysitter, had done their bath and so they were asleep when I came in. . . . I'd come in from work, and I'd be tired, bone tired. But I couldn't come and say, "Ok, children, let's sit down. Look, I'm telling ya'll I had a rough day today at work. I don't even know how I can go to work tomorrow; will I feel like it?" Or, "Somebody said this that really cheesed me off," or "Somebody did this and it was really nice." I couldn't sit down and tell the children. I couldn't sit down, 'cause I didn't have nobody else grown 'cause I closed us off; it's just me and them. That was all the world, just us.

. . . So when I got them in the bed and asleep, we had a little screened-in porch, so I'd go in the house and get the little black and white TV out, and I'd sit it on the porch and I'd sit out there and drink bourbon and listen to the trailer park wake up in the morning, you know. Had the coffee pot to run about five, so nobody wouldn't know I was sitting out there drinking and stuff. And have some coffee, and then have their breakfast ready and stuff. And I told them about six years ago that I was a drunk, and they didn't believe me.

I've been to AA. But I really couldn't say I had a bad experience from drinking. I can't. I got one DWI one time for drinking, but most of my thing was I drank when the work was through, and the kids was straight. Then I did my little drinking. . . . I was off from Sunday to Monday. And usually those two days was kinda like carnival. Playing with the younguns on Sunday. See, I didn't take them to church, and that was wrong, but I didn't take them to church. And Monday, when I got them dressed for school and they went to school, I'd buy me some bourbon, and I'd drink 'til about time the bus got ready to come, and about time the bus got there I'd have coffee made and I'd be drinking coffee and have a little food cooked, then about five I'd get ready and go to work.

. . . My mama wasn't the kind you could talk to either about problems, and you know, I don't know about you, but you don't want people to think that you're a failure, you know, you gotta whine about everything. And then you hear stuff all the time, saying, "You be nothing. Yeah, I'm the best thing that ever happened to you. When I leave your ass there, you're gonna go down the hill." And you fight so hard, and you fight so hard, and you just, you fight, and you give out. You say, I'll be damned if I am, I'll be damned if I am, but it's somewhere in you it's happening what they're saying. But me, my pride stood up to the fact that I wasn't gonna let it shine through, the phase that they said I was gonna be. I said, I'm gonna pay the bills. The trailer I live in, I said, it's paid for, it's mine. It's paid for, so the next thing I was working on, I was gonna get a little lot to put the trailer on so we could have somewhere to say nobody can come and knock on the door and say, "Well your rent ain't paid, so ya'll need to get out," you know.

And like my son came home. He was third grade. He came home and he said, "That little boy at my school says my mama can't afford to buy me no Filas, 'cause we're on welfare, Mama." He said, "Why are we on welfare?" I said, "We're not on welfare. That's why I work." He says, "But why don't I have Filas like Gabriel does?" I says, "I'll tell you what, if you do your little chores"—he had his little chores to take the trash from here to maybe five steps outside the door . . .—and I said, "You can probably get you some Filas this week if you take the trash out and I don't have to remind you nine times." So he would do it. And when he got the Filas, then I was gonna let him have a little job assignment and pay him like five dollars a week, make it so they have to work to get what they want. So, I gave him a little job assignment. Now when he got his little Filas, I said, "Now you know you got to keep the trash and stuff out and I'm gonna pay ya'll every week." You know, that boy, I had to set up on every day to take that trash out 'cause he done got his doggone shoes [laughing]!

. . . Having my younguns, that's one of the biggest highlights of my life. And if I could run a movie screen, I think I'd watch it over and over and over. When I had my first daughter, I actually seen her being born. You know, they took the mirror to see. . . . But yep, and they're crazy 'bout this little black woman right here [pointing to herself]. They's crazy about her. I think sometimes now they think they're my mama, though, but we share everything. Everything. I tell them everything. I ask them everything I want to know, I ask them. . . . [My kids visit] about every Sunday. It's very, very rare that I don't see them three times out of a month. It's very rare. . . . My mama's been bringing them here ever since they was little, every Saturday. And when they started getting a little older, I told my mama, "Why don't you take them to the park, or ya'll just go out somewhere?" She says, "Lord, those children want to come up here to see you. That's why I'm bringing them up here to see you." And then when they got old enough to drive, she let them have the car and stuff, so I said, "Ya'll got a life other than being up here around me all the time. Not that I don't want ya'll up here around me, believe me I do, but it's not fair for me. I already did my damage. I messed up ya'll's life first, then I messed up my life." But I messed theirs up the worst, though, by not being there with them and for them. And I tell them, "Why don't ya'll just take a week off? Go to the movies this evening, or take your brother out and go out and get something to eat." And my little son, he say, "I don't want to go with them girls."

. . . When I get out of prison, I want to work with teenagers that's in trouble, like juveniles and stuff, and from first-hand experience, knowing what it's like, when I separated from my kids and the stuff that they went through. I think a child is everything, everything. I don't think you should even have a child that you're not willing to even say, okay, I'm gonna die for this child, you know. That might be a little strong, but that's how I feel about mines anyway. And I kick myself in the butt a whole lot of times and been on a lot of mental health from being in here knowing that I not just messed up my life, I messed up their life. . . . My younguns, I think they're victims. I know I'm the one that caused them to be a victim.

. . . I might have thought myself worser than a victim with my husband beating my ass all the time. I probably think I was worser than a victim then. Yeah, 'cause it went on for a long time before I was even fighting back. A long, long, time before I was fighting back. I mean, he'd come in about halfway drunk, he'd say, "Where the hell you been today?" And knowing I ain't been nowhere 'cause the car he got is a straight drive car . . . and I can't drive it. . . . His food is cooked, the house is cleaned up, and the younguns doing their homework, or when they were little, they're at the house and one of them might be laying down taking a nap, the other one might be in there looking at some kind of little stuff on TV or coloring in the coloring book. . . . Then he'd say, "Oh, what kind of damn shit is this right here?" What's fried chicken, macaroni and cheese, and cabbage, and fatback meat and hard biscuits? What is that? "Now what kind of damn shit is this?" Hell, and we were eating good on the salary that he was making any damn way, 'cause all his money he making, he get it, the first thing he did is to give his mama. . . . Then he didn't want me to work, 'cause I said the kids got to have this and I got to have this. "You ain't gonna be out there making people say I can't take care of ya'll." And here I go, black eye, busted lip, teeth missing, like to die. I did have a miscarriage behind one of the babies because I've been pregnant four times in my life but he beat the other one out of me. I was about two months pregnant with that one.

[But] I had the power to say that the cycle was gonna stop with me as far being abused by men. I said the cycle was gonna stop there. 'Cause when I finally did get away from him, it was a long time before I got involved with any other man. If I got involved with them, it was that they wanted to go to the movies, me and the kids went and he drove his car. I gave money for gas. He take us to the movies, he pay our way in and stuff, he buy the younguns some popcorn, or bought me something or other to eat, then a couple weeks later I go by and pick him up. I say, "Let's go to the movies," take them to the movie, do the same thing they did. I buy him what he want and stuff like that. And then I tell him, "I don't feel like I'm obligated to you now. And if I don't want to see you no more, then you can't make me see you, and you can't say, 'Well, I did this for you, and I did that for you,' 'cause you didn't do shit for me. You know, I do the same thing for you." And then you know, some of the time I'm gonna say I don't even want to be bothered. . . . It was just too much of a headache and a hassle and like a nightmare every time I thought about getting involved with somebody. . . . 'Cause I got scared to get in relationships. I got scared to go get beat. And I had got to the point, I said, "The next man that hit me, I'm gonna kill him." I said, "I been beat by the best and I'll be damned if I'm gonna be beat by the rest," that's what I said.

. . . My son—I love all my children—but he is the one that my heart really, really, really, really is for. I love them all, I love all three of them, but I love him, and I mean I love him. Because he's the most gentlest young man. He don't run around. He ain't been in no trouble. He don't even drink. He don't smoke. He go to work; he been working good jobs since about fourteen. He ain't fast like with girls. . . . And to look at him, and to think when he was small, I mean, me and him always used to be partners for whatever we did. . . . When we'd get movies at Phar-Mor, we'd get like some popcorn and we'd pop it and we'd have a little popcorn thing. I'd say, "Me and you are partners," and we'd see how many he could throw in my mouth, how many I could throw in his.

. . . But to look at him, and to think, too, that a man like to took this child away from me. . . . One night, he gave [my son] his bottle . . . and I was sitting there looking and something just went over me and I said [to myself], "You sure is a stupid bitch. That stupid black motherfucker right there liked to kill that little baby right there. You would have never even seen him. You wouldn't have never ever seen that baby right there." . . . I went in there and got the meat cleaver. He had done beat me so many times and kicked me with his old army boots and stuff, and then he's gonna have my baby. I mean, all sense of purpose just left. It wasn't his child. It was my child, my son. And I was sitting up there letting this murderer hold my baby. . . . So I got the meat cleaver and I was gonna cut his ass up with the meat cleaver in the bed that night. I hit him and called him, and I said, "You know you could have killed [son's name]? You remember that time you kicked me on the floor?" "Oh, I don't want to be talking about that damn shit." I said, "Yeah, but I want to talk about it." I said, "We wouldn't even be laying here in the bed right here now and hearing no baby cry if it were for you." And I just kept on egging it on. I got my ass beat that night, leave it to say, 'cause I was scared to hit him with the meat cleaver. I was scared.

But after so many times, I wasn't scared no more. One night I just started in calling. I didn't even try to wake him up. I said, "I'm gonna kill you, you black son of a bitch," and I had the meat cleaver and it come down. He was grabbing for it, and these fingers fell off in my bed, all three of them, and he went out that damn window, took the window stash and every bit of it. 'Cause I had took enough, took enough, took enough. And guess what? My brother had beat him up one time, the time he beat me up with [my son]. My brother beat him up, and guess what I'm doing? "Oh, Lord, [brother's name], don't hurt him!" I'm taking up for him! And my brother's beating his ass like he was beating me. 'Cause my brother said, "Fight me like you do my sister. Fight me." My brother was wearing his ass out and I'm sitting there hollering like a fool, "Leave him alone! Don't hurt him!" . . . He was hurting somebody that I loved. I was sick. I was sick about that man.

You know, I thought about that the other day, too. It says stuff in life—relationships—hurts, but you always get over them. And it's the truth, but at the time it's happening, you really don't think you ever will. You know, you can't breathe, and everything just takes the extra effort to do, little simple things. But when I started fighting him back, though, he kinda like started walking on thin paper around me. Everybody said, "She's crazy, she's mentally disturbed," and all that. I don't mind of being mentally disturbed but I knew I wasn't gonna be hit no more. I knew. I seen my mama go through it. You know, I had been through it.

. . . I've always raised my daughters don't put their hands on nobody's son if they can't get along with them. . . . Go get their mama or their dad and say, "Go get your son over there, 'cause I'm not going through that." The little boy [my daughter] married, I told him the same thing. I said, "I'm gonna tell you, the cycle stops with me. You're not gonna hit on her. If you don't like something she's doing, ya'll are grown enough to get in a relationship, you're grown enough to sit down and talk about how 'I don't like this or that you're doing,' or 'I think you should do this this way.' I mean, talk about it, and see if you can work around it." 'Cause nobody's got the same attitude, the same personality they do. That's the challenge in life with somebody else, knowing that I can be compatible with this person even though they got this, this going on, and I got this, this going on, you know. And I always told him, "If you ever hit her, I got a parole date, and when I get out of prison, you better be sure you don't be nowhere to be found because if you ever put your hands on her, it's gonna be hell to tell the captain when I come outta here, and I come out 2003, August the 26th, so you better get you some papers to go over damn seas or somewhere, 'cause that's not gonna work." And my son, I tell him the same thing. . . . And let me tell you what my daughter did. . . . She brought that boy's clothes home to that boy's mama, sure did, took that boy's stuff and told her, "Miss [X], I don't want your son no more." Said, "Here go his stuff, you can go get him, 'cause I tried to tell him to come off me but he ain't living with me no more." She sure did.

. . . [Women end up in prison] from violent abuse that started somewhere at home, and it's not always the husband that's always the abuser, either. Like some of them it's their fathers, or their uncles, or something like that. And I think there's just so much stuff that they take, and they just take it in, take it in, and they get to the point that they say they just refuse to take it anymore because they've already got to the last rung in the ladder. . . . I think they're saying that I've had enough and now why is this person doing it to me? And they want to strike back at all the ones that have built this rage up in them . . . whether it's husbands, uncles, or nephews, sometimes even the same-sex abuse. . . . And eight out of ten, if the children tell the mother about it, they don't want to believe it, and if they believe it, they want to deny it their own self that it's happening.

. . . Some people have even had the nerve to say, "Well, women are on vacation when they go to prison for a long time. And they should not ever get out. They don't have to worry about bills out here," and they say, "Oh, it's not easy in the free world." My sister's good for that. "It's not easy out here in the free world." I say, well damn, this is the whole world. This is one world right here. It's not easy in the world point blank period, whether it's free or whether it's confined. It's not easy either way. I tell people, "Let's trade places for just five hours, that's all I ask for. Not even a twenty-four-hour period. Just five hours." And you sit here and you wonder what your kids are doing. My baby done been in detention—she's nineteen now—from thirteen on up. She has been in detention, she has been in therapeutic foster care, she's been to mental health and all this, and it's my fault. Because when I was out there, it was me and my children. And everybody officer-wise know they don't mess with my younguns. On Sundays, I'm fixed up to the T. You may not believe it, but I be dressed to impress, because I want them out there to know that I'm all right. Even if I am down or crying on the inside, I don't want them to sit out there and look at my face and then know they're gonna go back home being upset. Because I've done enough to them by coming here and leaving them. And they didn't have no daddy, might as well just say. So, just see for just five hours, just see.

. . . [What's next for me is] letting my children grow up in my mind. That would be next. So that I know when I go home, I can't say, "Ok, let's everybody come in the room and let's watch videos" and do the little things we used to do when they was little kids, you know. I think that would be about the first and foremost thing that would be next. And back to Shaw [University] again, I'm gonna be so independent when I get out of prison. And it's education right here and a opening to further education, and all you have to do is get in the class and just try. And that's been the biggest thing, I'm gonna sell myself on saying that, 'cause I do want to be very independent. That's what I was before I came to prison, you know. I didn't think I needed to ask anybody for anything or do nothing for nobody or have nobody do nothing for me, 'cause all people did was talk about you if you did ask for help and stuff.

And that was kinda like a little fucked-up situation believing it like that, 'cause everybody in the world needs help. I don't care who you are. When I thought I was so invincible, well, I got out of this marriage through getting beat and I survived. He didn't kill me, you know, and I'd rather not get involved 'cause I don't want nothing from nobody, 'cause I don't want them to think that I owe them anything. . . . You think you're up on this ladder, even if you're down here on the lower rung. At one point with me—I can't say for nobody else—if somebody offered me a hand to come up on the ladder, I wouldn't have took the hand. I would have tried to do it myself, to get myself up on the ladder. Not because he had to reach down and pull me up there; I would have earned my steps, too. So when I got on the top, nobody couldn't say, "Well, I did this for you. You remember when you was down there on the number-two rung and I was up here at twelve and I pulled you up?"

. . . So learning to accept help [is another joy]. I'm not all the way there yet, but I'm learning. Somebody offer me a cigarette, I'll kinda like say, well, no, so I wouldn't have one. I'd say, "No, I don't want the cigarette." . . . I stopped drinking soda and drink water [now] 'cause I don't want nobody to say, "You remember two years ago when I gave you fifteen cent to buy this soda?" . . . [But now] I'm learning that I don't have to be all about, "I did it! I did it!" Or, "This is mines because I earned it," or, "I did it all by myself," you know. 'Cause it's a hard road when you try to do it all by yourself, and it's help out there standing on the sideline, like somebody cheering you on, you know, "[Audrey], I'm over here if you need some help." And I'd be thinking, I don't need your help, and I would be needing it, you know? Just for the sake of being able to say I did it all by myself. Phew!

And then, after the kids grow up, take care of my mama would be the next thing for me. And work my job, and that's how I'm gonna have to take care of her. 'Cause I don't think she should have to do nothing when I get out of prison. She really shouldn't have to do nothing anyway. She raised six kids. All of us are grown. She should be just sitting back now when she can't work, and everybody should be taking care of her like she did us. And she did a good job, very good job. Sure did. . . . I guess I can say another thing as far as my mom, I think I respect her a little bit more than I love her, because like I say, she raised all six of us by herself. And I seen her go through hell with my stepdaddy beating on her and stuff like that. And I don't agree with the stuff that she say sometimes. She wants to mumbling and grumbling about something that happened twenty-five years ago and I might be about two days old when that was going on. . . . But that's just my mom. I don't think it means anything. It's just her, and they went all over her when she was little. 'Cause that's one thing she never talked about when she was small. Only thing she said was, "When we was little, if we went over to somebody's house and we got in trouble, they'll beat us and then they'll take us home and then our mom and dad will beat us, too." . . . But she earned my respect that she did raise us and did a wonderful job and then to raise mines, too. So I owe her something, you know, and that's why I say, too, that when I get out, I want my mom to just sit down and not do nothing. And I think that's more like I could pay her back for when she do gets through grumbling under her breath and stuff.

Reading Narrative

"What fueled this fire for the fire
to come all the way over to here?"

I STARTED READING true crime books about two years ago in here, and I think the first one I read was *Small Sacrifices*.[1] That used to just fascinate me so much that a woman would kill her kids like that. I got kind of hooked on that book, and I just went all the way through Ann Rule's, and it's like *The Stranger Beside Me*,[2] Ted Bundy, and I read all of them. *Dead by Sunset*.[3] I've probably read about forty-two true crime books. . . . I think the true crime books do good, because they do that research, and you go all the way back through; it's like you was sitting in on the trial of what's going on. . . . And then it's like you get caught up in it, like a whirlwind, like you can actually see the action.

. . . You read the paper, and then you see the people that the paper [describes] when they get here in prison, and they're not anywhere like that newspaper said they are. I mean, it's all kinds of us in here. We killed grown-ups, they's killed kids, and all that. But the media makes it just sound like we're sane when we kill. But they don't say how much we've took and took and took and took before we got to this point. . . . It just makes it like you just get up one morning and say, "Okay, I'm gonna kill this person" and that's it, you know? They don't say in the paper well, this lady was at her own home when this lady ventured into her house. . . . The attorney just says, "Well, #1234, Audrey has killed [victim's name], and they was drunk." And that's it. They don't say that, okay, she called us two or three times, and we didn't go. They don't say that.

. . . They saw me in a different light, okay? I'm a single parent. When I leave my children, I leave them because I go to work. It's a verifiable thing that I go to work every day. It's a verifiable thing that my kids go across the street. It's a verifiable thing that I'm not trying to be involved with nobody, just me and the younguns, just me and them in that house trying to have something so that they can have something when they got grown, some place that they could stay without somebody saying, "Well, you're gonna get evicted. You got to get out." They didn't take none of that in perspective. I'm not saying it would have helped the crime any better or any worse. . . . But they just leave out the background that led the women up to do what they did. But the men always have that excuse, "When he was young, his mama used to make him wear a dress because she wanted a little girl," you know, and all this kind of stuff. And it's never any explanation for the woman. People say she was laying in the bed one night and the gun was under the pillow and she just thinks, "Well, okay, I'm gonna kill him." And he's been beating her and beating her, and she's been scared 'cause if she leaves, he's threatened to kill her if she does leave and she better not say anything about it 'cause he beat up her up bad.

. . . Lately, it really just started getting in the media now, about when women kill husbands that beat them. 'Cause a long time ago—and I went through it with my husband—if you call the policeman, they say, "Oh, that's your husband and we're not getting into the domestic squabble," you know. And it's like we're calling wolf all the time when we call them, but it's not really wolf; it's something really going on. But they get out there, it doesn't matter you have a black eye or your lip is busted and you're standing there crying, they want to think that, well the man had some justifiable reasons. . . . And this woman, she starts going, "Well, maybe if I can disappear, he'll love me better. Or maybe it's me. I'm always the one where it's something wrong." 'Cause the men make them believe that they're doing something wrong. . . . It hasn't never too much been in the media, though, about domestic violence, women that fight back. And even when you read it in the paper or you hear about a man beating his wife, it's not ironed out. All the wrinkles is not ironed out. Because I mean, okay, he beat her. Why did he beat her? Because *he* said that she was running around on him, or because *he* said he caught her in the bed with another man.

. . . Pretty much the [true crime] books I've read, the women kill for money more than for anything else. . . . But somewhere in the subconscious of your mind you think, "But it had to be something more than that." Because the way they portray a woman in the book as killing a man, it's like it's as simple as just breathing, you know. . . . When they write about the women, they don't say none of the stuff that she went through when she was growing up, or her mom did this, or her dad molested her. . . . Like *Precious Angels*,[4] when that lady viciously killed her two children . . . it don't say what that woman's parents might have did to her, or what her life was like before it got to this point. . . . They don't say what's going on in the household with her, or what went on with her when she was this age, and this age, that may have put her over here to this edge. . . . It just makes it seem like she's just a coldhearted bitch. She just gets up and just, okay, I'm gonna kill them.

. . . That's what I would like to see in true crime books talking about women. I'd like to know some of their backgrounds, what put them there, or what fueled this fire for the fire to come all the way over to here? . . . Every time that men kill, it's because something went wrong in his childhood. . . . Don't make no difference what man it is, they'll tell you something about his background that led him to be the kind of person that he was. His dad was having sex with him or sexually abusing him, so when he grows up, he thinks it's fine. It doesn't say that girls will go to their mama and tell them, "My daddy's doing this to me," and then the mama like slap them down. "You little lying slut!" Then they don't want to go back and tell them again that it's happening. They think it's all right that he's doing this to them 'cause they reached out for help and the only thing they got was their arms chopped off. . . . Background doesn't excuse anything. It really doesn't. [But] if you're not going through what nobody else is going through, walk in their shoes for a little while and see for yourself what is going on. . . . Please take a seat and ride in this car here for a while.

. . . Aileen Wuornos, that was the first I've ever heard of a woman being called a serial killer, because they said she was killing them on the interstate by Florida, killing mens. And I think they was kinda like at a awe, too, to think that a woman could kill men and just get away with it complete, and complete, and complete, you know, keep doing it. . . . I think I was more interested in reading that book, Aileen Wuornos, 'cause I just wanted to see could a woman be as vicious as a man, as far as how they committed their crimes and stuff. 'Cause at one particular time, it was like a woman's weapon was poison, but now it's guns and everything, pretty much what the mens is doing.

But *Dead Ends*[5] wasn't no good. It was too much of everybody writing it, putting it together, and it was plain to see she didn't have any input in it until at the end where she read her long list of stuff that she said. . . . When they gave her a chance to speak on what was going on with her, she should have took the opportunity then and told her story. Because they just left her looking like just a bitch. A villain that was just out with a gun slinging it around like a cowboy, just shooting people for no reason. . . . When I was reading about how she was just killing them just for nothing, I thought that somebody must not have been writing that book right. I think they just kinda, I thought maybe they might have had a grudge against her since she was a woman killing men.

. . . I mean, where are the people at that they talked to about knowing when Aileen was getting ready to go to be a killer? Where are the people at that they asked about what was going on? They didn't say nothing. . . . If she was prostituting and all this, what got to the point for her to start killing the rest of them? . . . It was none of that from the people's perspective. It wasn't anything about why her husband had beat her up. That's all it said, that it was just one time. And I don't think nobody just get hell in them from somebody beating on them one time.

Yeah, it is something left out that we're not hearing, or it's not a true story. 'Cause from being in the experience my own self, when my husband beat me up, I was terrified, scared to death. I wouldn't have left him for nothing in the world 'cause I knew he was gonna kill me, and that's what he said. And if he didn't tell me he was gonna kill me, he beat me one time, then I would have tried to be very submissive. "You do this!" I would have jumped and did it. But it wouldn't have put the hell in me to say, "Forget the men generation all together. I'm gonna get involved with this woman." . . . I don't know, it's a whole lot of stuff in the middle somewhere that just didn't come out in this book.

When she told them about how her husband had beat her, she left her husband and got involved with her girlfriend, I would have said how her husband abused her. 'Cause you can be abused without really being physically, you can be mentally. I would have said, okay, he verbally abused her, mentally or several times physically, and I would have told how that went on and what he would have said to her that would make her say, "Okay, damn the men." . . . I would have had something in there that say when her husband beat her, how did it make her feel. 'Cause I don't think one time could make nobody be as vicious and cold as she was. . . . It would have to be something that kept going, kept going, kept going . . . It had to be not just physical, and I think the rest of it was like mentally and emotionally abused; I think that's what she was going through. And she felt like she couldn't win the war physically.

. . . Now if they had went on with the story to say that her husband did her like this, did her like this, and he always said, "You sorry little slut, you ain't nothing but a whore anyway," or if she was out somewhere like at work, and he said, "You come your ass in from work, you gonna bring your ass here, and the only thing you're good for is to stay in the house and cook" and boom, slam her aside the wall and then have sex with her, then I could see, if that was on and on. But no, I think they did her a very bad injustice. Very bad. 'Cause it made me mad as hell with her! . . . Aileen Wuornos was a victim of the author. . . . They shouldn't even have wrote the book. They just wasted the paper.

10 Deven

—∿—

Life Narrative

"Society, it's a boys' club still"

I WAS BORN in Ohio, born and raised there. My mother, my father, my step-mother all raised me. My older sister, she's seven years older. So there's a big gap there, and even though they kind of pushed me off on her at times, I pretty much was an only child. Family life was very good. I enjoyed it. Did all the norms, I guess, if you want to label it as normal. You know, we visited the grandparents. Had the big holiday sit-down dinners. My mom was in insurance, and my dad was a banker. . . . My parents did divorce, so every other weekend I spent time with my father and my stepmother.

School was great. I really enjoyed grade school, junior high, high school. I absolutely enjoyed it. They kind of knew who I was from my sister, but then they got to draw their own conclusion once I entered their classes and stuff. I would have to say my favorite subject was English. Grammar, composition. I love to write letters. I frequently write home to family and friends. So I just really enjoyed that. I think that was one of my better subjects. Yeah, math was not a real good subject for me. Although I did like American history. I liked learning about, you know, what our forefathers did.

My number one joy in my life is my daughter. My number one. She is, oh my God! She is my blessed event. It took me a long time to get her. Other joys, every day is a joyous occasion. It's just what you do with the day. I mean, as long as you don't let any, if somebody's negative, and you don't let that rub off on you, then the day shall remain positive.

In regards to [relationships that have been important], I would say all of my parents. I mean, they have great business ethics, and I think as I got older, I bonded better, and I have an absolutely wonderful relationship with all my parents. My boss, who I've worked for for five years. She's from China. And women in China only get to go to school for up until fourth grade, and then she's self-taught. And I guess that just inspired me. And she taught me so much about the business world. I'm in property management, and I just, I absolutely love her. She's just awesome, and she's an amazing lady. My best friend, who passed away, . . . turned out to be my neighbor at one point in time, and then we ended up working together at a restaurant. And that was the greatest experience. I mean, I just really enjoyed the camaraderie.

Violence has been a big part of my life. Domestic abuse. Emotional. Physical, financial, mental. I don't know, I got like prince charming, and then two weeks later, they'd turn into Satan himself. For lack of better terms, that's just how it went. So I rode that merry-go-round ride with them, the ups and downs. And you know, "Oh, I can change them and this'll get better," but we all know how that works [laughing]. There were six different men in my life [laughing], and unfortunately, when I'd break up with one, it seemed like the one that I had beforehand would call me back. I've been on this revolving circle with the same six for like oh, a very long time, but now my daughter's father, we've been together for six years, and we rode that emotional ride for a minute there, too. I would have to say most of that was due to our drug abuse, and how we beat ourselves up, and then we would take the aggression out on each other.

I guess I didn't really know myself, but of course, I would put it on the back burner, you know, and I made these men my world, so to speak. But today, my daughter's my number one priority. Everything else falls to the side. I had ten miscarriages, and I got shot when I was seven months pregnant with her, so God truly blessed me with this little angel. She is my miracle, and she is my most precious gift from God. So, just everything that I've been through with men, I'm just not real men oriented. You know, I guess I grew up. Your parents are always saying, "Grow up, grow up." So I wouldn't want to be anyplace else. Prison has been a very wonderful learning experience for me, and I think I'm getting all I can get out of it.

. . . It's been really rough because I have missed all of [my daughter's] first moments. . . . I just have to remember I'm powerless and I have no control over that. And I just have to deal with it. . . . But you know, I'm grateful that my mother has temporary custody of her. Her father's still part of her life, and she's enjoying her grandparents, and I think that's wonderful because I enjoyed my grandparents. I want her to get the best she can out of the grandparent experience because unfortunately, my parents are up there in age, and I'm not sure how much longer they're going to be here. I pray forever, but that's fictional. I did the domestic violence group [in prison]. I have been in and out of these relations for a long, long time, and . . . they're just kind of like, suck up and realize this man is no good. Let's move on. And you know, even when I came to prison, my mom said like three of my ex's have called, and I said, "When they call on the phone, ask them, 'Well, uh, why did you break up with her in the first place?' If you didn't want me then, why the hell do you want me now and what are you doing in your life? You know, give them my address. If they feel that compelled and love me that much, then they'll write me, and if they don't, well then I know where they're at."

I was kind of a '70s kid. You know, I grew up with marijuana, but that was because of my sister. She was very experimental, and like I said, we were latchkey kids. Mom and dad were business oriented, and we were at home after school, and trying to fit in with my sister and her group of friends, so I chose to do what they were doing. And then as I got older, I still continued marijuana use on and off. My biggest downfall was the cocaine and crack. Yeah, that just wiped me out. Miserably so.

I've done NA, AA on the outside world before this, oh yeah. I've done many, many programs pertaining to drug addiction. I know I'm an addict. And I know that it's something that I don't care to do now. My daughter, it all boils down to my daughter. You know, God blessed me with her, and I just can't, there's nothing that would drag me away.

When I came to prison, I had just had the baby, and my probation officer gave me a parole violation while I was giving birth. This case is from 2002. They gave me three years; well, they gave me six months in a rehab so I went and did that. It was ninety days in, ninety days out. . . . I remained going to my meetings, and I was doing really awesome. And then [Ted, my baby's father] and I, we rented a house together. Well, then I got pregnant. And when I went to see my [parole officer], he's like, "Well, if you just pay off these court fines, you can go ahead and go." . . . In my mind, I was just like, well, all you're worried is about is money. I'm going to give what I can, and then I never reported. Well, then I got shot, and because I hadn't been going to see him, he [gave me a parole violation] then. . . . Well, then that was like another thirty days, and then I was giving birth to my daughter, and my probation officer, I was supposed to see him that Monday, but I was at the hospital. I called and [Ted] had called and left messages, but he said that we didn't. So therefore, he [parole violated] me.

[Ted], he was really a good dad. Very supportive. I mean, he was our bread-winner, and I stayed at home with the baby all day. Well, being a first-time mom, I was like fanatic. Everything had to be perfect. Laundry all had to be done. Dogs had to be taken care of. You know, I was working myself to death. So by the time [Ted] would get home at night, you know, I didn't have any adult companionship, and I really needed that. But I didn't use the tools that I knew. You know, I didn't reach out to anybody. I wanted them to come to me. I guess I was really absorbed with [my daughter]. But first-time moms, I don't know if you have kids, but I was very consumed with her. And then [Ted] continued to use the whole time we were together, like marijuana, drinking, and then one night he came home, and he was just literally drunk, and it pissed me off, and I guess as a way of retaliating against him, I was like, "Well, let's get crack." And then I dropped dirty [urine], and I'm here.

I think women end up in prison because of the men in their life. I really do. I've been in quite a few groups, and you know, I have to say that society, it's a boys' club still. It's still the boys' club. Men are supreme. I don't care if there's ERA or not. Because we all know women are treated very differently, you know, and if you have a different ethnic origin, then you're really treated differently. I see it all the way around the board. I spent twenty years in corporate America. And I've heard so many women say to me, "Well, I'm trying to please him." And I can relate to that because, you know, you want to have that. I think society gives us this false picture of what life is really like. It's no more June Cleaver than *Brady Bunch* and whatever else. It's just not that way. And I think women don't really, from a young age, don't really get the full effect from their family as to what their self-worth is, and I really think that needs to be instilled in them so they don't go out and try to find this man [and think], "Oh well, I will change you." No, you won't. Reality says you're not going to change them. Let 'em go, 'cause if they love you, they're going to want to do it themselves.

Maybe in the younger years, like elementary, we should start telling girls about their self-worth and their self-value. Somehow these little girls need to know that they're not plastic model Barbie dolls, that they're living, breathing, human beings and they can do anything they want as long as they're willing to work hard for it and achieve that. I mean, if you want to be the president, then by all means do what you gotta do and be the president, and don't let society knock you down. You know, buck the system if you have to. I feel too many people conform to society's ways and society's rules. I mean, granted, there are laws we have to follow, and yes, we should follow them, but in speaking about the female, though, I really feel that nobody tells these little girls what their self-worth is. . . . When you come up with your own views and own ideas and if they don't blend into society, then you're kind of a social outcast.

. . . I've got twenty years in corporate America. I have a awesome resume, you know. Unfortunately, I have two felonies. So I want to go home and be a mom. And do what I gotta do for [my daughter]. And I really want to go to college. I would like to get into the medical background. I'm thinking maybe transcriptionist or medical billing coder type person. I think that would be a better profession for me 'cause a lot of that stuff I can do out of my home. So I'm thinking, get a job in the hospital or private practice. . . . I'm going to be a single parent, so I want to make sure that she's very well provided for. I'm thinking the medical background 'cause of the benefits, and I know they will cover myself and her. . . . The halfway house that I'm going to go to, I really want to go and get all I can out of their program because being a first-time mom, I know you can't get it right or perfect or anything 'cause that just doesn't even exist, but I just want to know that I'm giving her all that I've got for being a kid and having a good life. I want her to never end up here. You know, that is just my ultimate goal. And that she is a very well-rounded individual.

. . . Back in the day, [people] would want to raise barns together, you know. If you had to go to work, and the neighbor lady didn't work, "Well, bring your kids over and I'll baby-sit them." That kind of daily "build barns together" has gone by the wayside. Nowadays, you want to run over, slip on your neighbor's lawn, and sue 'em to death, you know. Nowadays, you don't even know who your neighbor is, and God forbid, they'd be a sexual predator and here you have a little one. . . . People aren't willing to be open-minded and to see things from the other side, you know, maybe do a little role reversal here. What if you were in that person's shoes? What would you have done? And quit being so quick to condemn somebody. Help build them up so they can reenter society or be something better than what they are. . . . Have you ever watched *Star Trek,* where they have like societies within a society? There's a big community out around us, and it's like we don't even exist. . . . I really think other people need to realize that just because we are in prison, we are still human beings. We are not second-class citizens. I put my pants on the same way you do.

—m—

Reading Narrative

"I need to know what's gonna happen next!"

I LOVE READING. I've always loved reading. Like, today when it's raining, I like very much to sit down, read a book, read a magazine. . . . I read a book a week. My favorite place to read is on my bunk. Door shut. Got my own little secluded place. Quiet.

My parents weren't big readers. So I'm so grateful that my teachers kind of pushed me into the reading thing. . . . And being a tutor here, I know there's a lot of women that do not know how to read. And I would just be devastated if I didn't know how to read and could not know this information. You know, they say knowledge is power.

School got me involved in reading, but my sister, when I was young, got me into V. C. Andrews, that whole *Flowers in the Attic* series.[1] And I never really realized what a whole 'nother world was out there within the reading. I'm in awe of the reading materials that are available. And I'm kind of mad at myself that as a child, I didn't frequent my library more. I read V. C. Andrews and John Saul. He's kind of like a Stephen King writer. I was more reading fictional. Some biographies here and there. . . . And then being pregnant, I swear I think I read every child's development book that there was out there. You know, *The Birth Book*[2] was just absolutely amazing. *Parenting Magazine*, I read it from front to back, fine print, the whole nine yards [laughing].

[Before I came to prison,] I read because it was relaxing, kind of like watching a movie but only in your mind. I really enjoyed it. It was at home. I had a fireplace on. You know, when it snows, our back of our home is nothing but glass. We look like we live in a snow globe. So to lay in front of a fireplace with the dogs and read a good book, I mean I just loved it.

Now I still read for relaxation. Back then, I guess they were books recommended from girlfriends that I went to high school with and stuff like that. So I thought, okay, let me check it out and see what the hubbub's about. You know, and then we did our own little book club over, "Oh, did you get to this part yet?" But today, the books are learning. I learn more from them. The books that I'm reading, I get a lot more out of them, but I still find it very relaxing. Very calming, kinda take me out of this place.

. . . The [main prison] library is small as ever. . . . The only time I really go to the library is to read the [local newspaper] just to catch up on the news back at home, or if I have a speech that I got to do for Toastmasters, then I go and check into that. But other than that I just, I don't know. Too much hubbub. They use the library for all the wrong reasons. Like it's a meeting place, and you know, just drama. Drama, drama, drama. You got seven hundred women crammed into some not really great atmosphere here, and I'd just rather stay where I'm comfortable. I mean, they say that the COs[3] are here for my safety and security. I keep myself safe. I keep myself secure by not subjecting myself to the drama that goes on in this place. It's girl on girl stuff in the library. Girlfriends, relationships, very loud. The library is supposed to be quiet. But not everybody's there to enrich their minds. . . . When I was writing my speech, I got kicked out of the library at least seven times due to other things going on in there and COs not liking what's going on in there. And unfortunately, even though you're being quiet and doing what you came there for, they're not going to single out one person. It's gonna be the whole group.

. . . Everybody I know is always looking for a James Patterson book, and then they have something called Triple Crown Publications that, I believe these people are in prison writing these novels, and somebody's printing them. But I've heard about these books, and these books should not be in here. They're talking about gangsters, sexual altercations between men and women like threesomes, foursomes, being gay, sodomizing, stuff like that. . . . Why would you want to read trash like that when, you know, society is going down that path already? I just really don't feel that those are good books for prison. There's a lot of people that are just really craving those books and will read them in a day and want the new one. I want something that's going to broaden my horizons. They can relate to it because that's what they were doing. So I guess my thing is that if you're going to read what you already done, aren't you going to go out and do what you already did?

. . . I like to sit in the spiritual library. The lady that runs it, she's very spiritual-based. It's a very calming, very relaxing atmosphere. I talk to her a lot about, you know, if I come questioning or anything like that. She's a beautiful person, very spiritual and I just really enjoy her conversations.

. . . Today, I read all religious books, spiritual: Joyce Meyer, Gloria Copeland, Larry Crabb. *When God Whispers Your Name*,[4] *The Purpose Driven Life*.[5] My stepmother suggested *The Purpose Driven Life* so I automatically got it, read it, loved it, very mind opening. It's very, very uplifting stuff. And Joyce Meyer is very self-help and spiritual-based as well. I feel just very compelled to read that. Kay Arthur, hers are spiritual, too. I read *Our Covenant God*.[6] Gloria Copeland's *God's Will for You*.[7] Joyce Rupp's *Dear Heart, Come Home*.[8] Joyce Meyer's *Me And My Big Mouth*[9] 'cause my attorney said, "Well, if you would have kept your big mouth shut, you wouldn't be here." So I felt the title was fitting. It's absolutely wonderful. I've read a ton of Joyce Meyer's books.

I was in a program at [another prison] before I got here, and it was called Tapestry, which is behavior modification, drug rehabilitation. And they had their own separate library within the building, and they had a religious section. . . . And one day I was reading the Bible, and I was praying, and I wanted something to read. I wanted a book besides the Bible, and I walked out, and I got this book, and it was called *The Scarlet Letter*.[10] And I thought it was based on the movie. It wasn't. It was based on biblical times when King Herod was king. . . . So then I got more into the Bible. Got more into praying. And the lady that showed up next to me came up with the book by Stormie Omartian called *The Power of a Praying Woman*.[11] So I can only assume that these were all books that God kind of put in my path because these are probably not books that I would have sought out on my own, you know. So I went from *The Scarlet Letter* to *The Power of a Praying Woman* to *Our Covenant God* to [Max Lucado]'s *When God Whispers Your Name* to Gloria Copeland's *God's Will For You*. All sorts of Kenneth and Gloria Copeland books, and I just kept on that path, and I've learned a lot from all the books.

I decided to do all spiritual books because I felt that I needed to get more in contact with my higher power, and I like the positivity. I like the self-help, and it really helps me stay positive in a negative environment. It helps me to deal with a lot of other issues that this place here just doesn't have the manpower to help touch on. Like anger, like pettiness. I have never seen seven hundred women that are more petty. You know, instead of fighting and trying to stab each other in the back, we should be bonding together and doing what we need to do to help each other out and to, you know, feel our self-value and our self-worth. There's favoritism for certain ethnic origins here, and I'd just as soon be blinded to it and stay in the book where there's positivity and stuff like that than interact and deal with the drama that goes on around me.

. . . *When God Whispers Your Name,* wow! It was just an amazing, amazing book! [Max Lucado] is telling you about experiences that he went through. . . . This one story was about him being on a flight, and there was some turbulence, and he started to get a little nervous as to what was going on. But for some reason the pilot or whomever got on the loud speaker and said not to worry. You know, we're in God's hands. And he said he just remembered feeling all calm. The plane landed and it was all good. And I guess for the days that I get all wiggy or get all upset, this is all part of His plan. And I just gotta go in the direction that He needs me in. It's very relaxing. I mean, *When God Whispers Your Name* is all about how God speaks to you through the other people, places, events, books, and stuff like that. You know, I don't go walk into the religious library and reach for a book. I'll look and for some reason the title jumps out to me, and then I reach for it. So I keenly assume that that is God trying to tell me, "There's something in there that I want you to see." So that's when I grab the book. That's how I found all of those books.

. . . I suggest a lot of the books that I read to other ladies that I know that are more spiritual or stuff. Or if somebody's feeling down and out, I offer them something that's going to be uplifting to them. . . . They've come back to me and said, "God, Deven, that was great. I really needed that boost." I really think they just boost you. They open your mind to things that, you know, we kind of have tunnel vision. And then this kinda opens your brain up; you're going, oh wow, let's look at myself. You know, it's more of a self-look thing, and for me,

I could see how I was, or disturbed thinking patterns and see the way I think now. . . . It opens my mind as to a new way to look at things, look at situations. See how I handled them in the past. What can I do to maybe improve so there's more of a positive outcome than a negative one. . . . Kay Arthur and Gloria Copeland were the ones that did it for me. And Joyce Meyer. I mean, all of their books have just been very inspiring, to take a look at you, take a look at society, other people around you. Because I was highly judgmental and very opinionated. You know, you get set in those ways, and I was very very much a "that's the way it's gonna roll" type person. And now today I'm able to see the other side, so to speak, and I feel that I'm more open-minded. I'm not so critical and judgmental of other people these days.

. . . I've read all of Stephen King's books, and they're fictional. Yes, it lets me escape from here, but I guess I've escaped my whole life, so let's get down to reality. . . . I have an active imagination myself, so I could write a book myself that's imaginative. I want real. I want sustenance. I want to feel like I've learned something from what I read. . . . You never know what I might get out of a book. Maybe there's a sentence in there that I need to see, that I needed to read. And maybe I'll have some wonderful epiphany about it. . . . When I was out in the real world not doing the right thing, I kind of let my brain cells go dormant, and I had things that I was thinking about and wanted to do but just wouldn't get off the couch and do it. Here I have put every effort into doing those things, and the books just kind of reaffirm what I'm doing for me. They kind of help me stay on that path, and it also opens my mind and my eyes to other areas as to well, you know, maybe we should try it this way today. They say try something for thirty days and it may become a habit, and it may not. But it's up to you.

. . . I think everything that I'm reading is something that is helping me to empower myself to get to the place that I want to be in life. . . . Every book kind of stays with me. Sometimes like a little slogan, a catch phrase. Maybe a story that somebody had told in the book that I could relate to. And then maybe applying what [I read], and then I'll see how the results are for myself. . . . I like the fact that [self-help] books make you think, because this is a very dormant place, and you can just lay here, you know, with the life sucked out of you, or you can seek life. And today I'm seeking life and what it has to offer and how I can make the best of it.

[Joyce Meyer's] *Battlefield of the Mind*, oh my God! Absolutely awesome book! . . . It's inspirational. It's uplifting. It gives you another way to look at things and look at people, look at society, and it opens your mind to a differ-ent way of viewing people, places, things. Like we could look at a tree, and it's green. The leaves are green, and it's brown, but it doesn't have to be that color. It can be red. It can be purple. It can be anything that we want it to be. And just because through all these ages everybody said the leaves are green, and the trunk is brown, and that's the way it should remain, with reading these books, they kind of open your mind to see that it doesn't have to just be green and brown. It can be yellow, pink, purple. I mean, it can be anything, anything that you want it to be.

Everybody thinks, oh, you're a bad person, you know, you get a stigma that kind of goes with being incarcerated, and I'm just not that person. And for me to come through the gate and have you treat me like a second-class citizen, that I'm a lower life form, you don't know me, and who are you to judge me? And who are you to treat me like that? They kind of just group you. You're incarcerated. You're a bad person. Blah, blah, blah. Done deal. And just from reading *Battlefield of the Mind,* when I saw somebody that was dirty and filthy, I thought they were a bum. But it doesn't mean that they're a bum. It's how they prefer to live their life, and so instead of labeling them as a bum, and just rolling with society in the everyday, normal thinking, I've opened my mind to realize that just because there's that label or stereotype, that's not who they really are.

. . . Joyce Meyer writes about her life, and you know, her spiritual quest to find the God of her understanding, and what God is to her. And I guess for me this whole journey has been all about the spiritual journey and me getting to understand the God of my understanding. And with the words that she's written, the scriptures that she's quoted, I've been able to internalize them, and it's helped me to really sit back and look. You know, kind of look and watch people, watch mannerisms, . . . be more of an active listener and listen to exactly what they're saying . . . to help me get a better idea of who a person really is instead of just seeing them at face value.

When I walk out this door, there's not going to be any big grand parade when I go home. "Oh yeah, Deven's back in town," or anything like that. I just want to go home and pick up my life where I left off. And not everybody's going to be willing to [let me] do that. So I had to come to some understanding about that. All the spiritual books give me new hope, new ways of looking at things, and help me be a little more accepting of others and the situations they're going through. . . . There's a bigger picture to look at. And if you open your mind and open your eyes, you'll see all the different variations of the picture. You know how they create DVDs now, and you got three alternate endings? Life can go like that, you know, as you look at the big picture and the choices and realize, well, before you make these choices, this could happen, that could happen, or this could happen, and if you weigh out all those options, then I think you make better choices. And that's where I'm at in life, and I'm trying to make better choices.

Through the books, through the spiritual readings, through God, I've gotten in touch with a lot more of my inner self and knowing who I am and what I need to do for me. And what I need to do about others around me. . . . Reading the books helps me to put my thoughts and my feelings together to explain it more to others. I look forward to the next chapter only to see what else that I can get out of it, and you know, maybe experiment with, see how well it works for me. Is it going to be something that I need to do for thirty days? Maybe it'll become a habit. Maybe it's something that I need to do periodically. . . . I just can't put down my spiritual books! I need to know what's gonna happen next! It's like watching a good movie, and they want to break for a commercial, and you're about ready to flip out. No!!!

. . . Joyce Meyer and Gloria Copeland are two of my favorites. . . . And I've read them describe [the same passage] from different perceptions. So I can take a little bit from this one, a little bit from that one, put my own ideas in, and it makes more sense to me. . . . I have moments that I just wasn't comfortable with their perception of the whole thing. I know there was one time in Gloria Copeland's book that I thought, "No, I'm not going to try that." . . . In one of the books, it said if you're in a good Christian marriage, then the book of Titus in the Bible is something that the woman should read because in that there's the full description how the woman is supposed to be with the man. If the man's the head of the house and you're letting him do those things, then you should be submissive. But now if he's beating your butt, no, no. I agree with it if you're living a good Christian life and that's the kind of man that you find. But now all the men I find, hell no [laughing]! Hell no! I've been way too submissive [laughing]. I would like to have that relationship, very much so, but no [laughing]. I have yet to have it. . . . I've always been outspoken, so I guess maybe this time around, I would like to be more submissive, but not with somebody who's going to whop me down. I want somebody that's going to be a good companion, good partner, a give-and-take situation. It's not me always giving and them taking. It's 50/50 or maybe 80/20. Maybe he's going to do more for me than I ever thought. He's the breadwinner, the grass cutter, the window cleaner, the fix-it man. Good with the kids, good with me. Complimenting of myself, the house, the kids. Good lines of communication. Somebody that doesn't try to dominate me. Equal.

. . . I see a lot of ladies reading *Chicken Soup for the Prisoner's Soul*[12] . . . and I was really excited to get my hands on it. . . . The stories are just amazing. I just found a lot of inspiration from them. Being in prison myself, I can relate to what they're going through. I used one of the poems to send home to my mom and dad about not getting mail in a timely manner [laughing]. So I'm sure they'll be thrilled with that! I told them that they should go read the book. My stepmom's an avid reader, and yesterday she came for a visit, her and my mom and my daughter, and I just told them they should check into this book, and then they could maybe understand exactly where I'm at. And I told them it's not just prisoners writing. It's ex-inmates, it's people that work within the institution and stuff like that, and it will maybe give them a better idea of what we have to deal with on a daily basis here.

See, me being a first-time mom, I like that there was this guy who had a really good relationship with his son, and then he had a very long prison term. And the letter that he wrote to his son, he just kept putting off sending it to him. And you know, there were so many things that he wanted to say to him, and then he ended up being killed in a tractor accident, and so it just kinda, my daughter's only eighteen months old. Like I said, I've been through hell and high water just to have her. And it just made me realize how precious she is. . . . I write her on a weekly basis, and sometimes there's some weeks that I wonder why do I write her 'cause she's only eighteen months old. But then I get back to reading *Chicken Soup*, and that kind of helps me realize that the more I reach out, the more of a bonding situation we're having. So, I want to make sure that we keep that bond. I'm sure my mom's keeping the letters, but . . . I don't want [my daughter] to get that, "Oh well, if mom did it, then it's okay for me to do it." There's too much negativity already out there in the world, and I really want to keep it a positive flow.

This has been a really great spiritual journey for me as well as a very life learning experience. . . . Somewhere along the line, I guess I grew up, you know. And it's kind of sad to label it in that terms but I really did, just watching other people, and not being so judgmental and critical. I know the changes within myself 'cause I was very opinionated and critical of others, and then I realized if there's something I don't like about that person, I need to take a look inward. And it's really neat that some of the stories are based upon interactions with other people, and I guess so now when I go and I talk to people, I tend to be even more of an active listener. Because you know, if there's something there that I need to get, I want to make sure I get it, and I don't miss it. You know, 'cause definitely I've missed a lot of that [laughing]!

And just the whole change thing, there's a lot of stories that talk about change. There's a whole chapter on change. And you know, I really didn't think that people do change. Yeah, they do for, what, maybe a year or two, and then they just fall right back into that rut. But today, I see change in a different light. That if you really need to, it's all within you. And I like the fact that I know I have changed. And the people that are around me have seen the change within me, and a lot of people comment on that. And that makes me feel good knowing that other people see it 'cause, nine times out of ten, you're not the first one to see it.

The stories taught me in a way to kind of keep my eyes open. I guess for a lot of years, I walked around with blinders on. And you know, you grow up with your parents and your family, and I think a lot of that rubs off on you, and I realized how much I was like my family. I'm not saying that that's all bad, but there's other aspects that I needed to go and venture out and try myself, but because I was so much like them, I just didn't want to put that foot forward to do it. And now, after reading some of the stories, I had just found that I can't let anything hold me back. If I'm gonna go a different direction, and live in another state or something like that, I've just got to let them go, and they're just gonna have to be happy for me. And if they're not, then that's something they got to deal with 'cause I can't make everybody happy.

Growing up in my family, I'm the backbone. I'm the smoother-over. I'm the one that knows everybody's itineraries and schedules, and I made sure that whatever I did for Dad, I did for Mom. Whatever I did for Mom, I did for Dad. I was always helping my sister. She's been in and out of a thousand rehabs along with the county jail like a revolving door, and so I've always tried to keep my parents, "Oh it's gonna be okay. We'll do this. We're gonna do this." And then when she gets out, I'm trying to be supportive of her and then she runs off on me [laughing]. And my parents were very judgmental about and very critical of other people, and I got a lot of that. And if it wasn't done their way, then just hit the highway. Today, when I sit back and read some of those stories and I think about past relationships that I've had, be it a friend, be it a boyfriend, I can see where I was very critical and not listening to their needs or not listening just to the general overview 'cause I wanted it my way.

. . . [I participated in a] really interesting group. It was Faith-based Domestic Violence. It was based on a book called *Refuge from Abuse*.[13] And the two ladies that wrote it were Christian, and it showed how Christian women could deal with abuse. Like how the cycle starts and where to go afterwards. You know, you find a confidante within the church, and check out your church background. Do they have programs within the church? Does your community offer programs? What's your pastor like? If you go tell him things that are happening, is he going to provide you with a safe house? Is he gonna help you out? You know, it tells you basically how to build a support group.

If you're ready to go and get out, you know, and you're trying to build up a plan, make a plan, make sure you've got the right people involved. It was only like a ten-week course, so we met once a week, and it was really neat. Chaplain [X] was the advisor of the group, the facilitator. And we would read the chapters, and then we would go and get our outlines about the chapters. I would meet with her on a one-on-one basis, and I would read the chapter and give her my own outline about it.

. . . I love to hear other people's views. You know, anything to broaden my mind. The way I'm thinking is not the way you're thinking. So they might open my eyes to, we could read the same sentence, but you could get something totally different out of it than what I could get. And I really like that aspect because everything's not black and white. There is a gray area. And I like being able to see that, you know, what did you get out of this sentence? And maybe I didn't get that. I like to know other women's opinions.

. . . That Toni Morrison, I have not read any of those books, and I would absolutely love to read that. All the ladies in the group pretty much knew a lot about her. I kinda felt like an outsider because I didn't open my mind to going that way. So I mean, I very much want to read that. I want to go check one out [laughing].

[After reading Toni Morrison's *The Bluest Eye*]: I absolutely loved how she writes. I mean, the description is just amazing. It puts you right there. I was shocked at the ending, but then I guess I could relate to it. 'Cause I think as little kids, we always wanted to be different than what we really were. . . . What she was describing was a time of depression. You know, a time when people just put stuff way back on the backburner and nobody faced what was really going on. And I guess, you know, in that area I could relate to that because I was the type of person that if something was going on, I'd rather shove it on the backburner and keep smiling . . . because it wasn't for you to know. It wasn't for anybody else to know. It was my own personal business, and I'll deal with it accordingly. So, I could really relate to that portion of it.

. . . I really felt sorry for the mom, and I guess I really felt sorry for [the daughter, Pecola] because nobody was really tending to these kids. It was just fend for yourself kind of stuff. And I was a little shocked, a little dismayed from just the lack of interaction between parent and child. It was more, "You do as I say and be quiet." . . . It was a learning experience, I guess. You know, you need to pay attention to your children. You need to pay attention to the world around you. I mean, to be aware is to be alive.

The part where she was raped, I was raped, and I kind of could feel her pain all over again. . . . I think that's good because it's not something I need to carry with me. It's something I need to let go of. . . . I have a lot of anger, a lot of revenge. Like, if I would have saw him again, I could have easily killed him and had no remorse. I would have thought, "You deserve this, buddy." . . . From day one of getting here, all the books that I've read, and the things that I went through in Tapestry, help with our distorted thinking patterns and get[ting] a clearer perception of our thinking. It has really opened my eyes to see that I was very negative, and I just didn't want to see the part that I was playing in things.

. . . But in the times that they were growing up, that is another era that I just really didn't know about. Really another class of people that I didn't know about. . . . I'm living my life. I can live it in a book, yeah, but why? I want to experience new and different things. . . . In the back of [*The Bluest Eye*], it explained more about being black in that era. How, you know, you just really didn't even exist. And the kids really didn't even exist. I mean, it was really, it was something to read, and then to read about how the mom went and worked for a white family, and then when the pie got spilled and the kids were sent out, and she coddled the little white girl but couldn't even hug her own kids. I mean, me being a new mom, that's all I want to do is hug my baby. You know, so it was amazing. And it kind of gave [Morrison's] perspective of why she wrote it, and the way she wanted to write it. She wanted to be descriptive, but she wanted to put it in a language that was spoken back then, so that was neat.

. . . I read Joan Baez's [auto]biography,[14] and that was really neat. I guess reading that [auto]biography kind of led me into all the other self-help books in a roundabout way. . . . In Tapestry, you have to find [a book about] a woman of inspiration and read it. . . . Other women read about Oprah, Hillary Rodham Clinton, Whoopi Goldberg, Barbara Bush, Laura Bush, Marcy Kaptur. She's one of our Democratic representatives for the state of Ohio. . . . We had to choose from books that were there. If you had a family member at home that was computer literate, they could get you something off the computer and send it into you, but then you had to go through whatever mail regulations they had there 'cause God forbid you have something that they don't want you to have! . . . I was looking through this small bookshelf that we had in one of the classes, and it was so amazing that this book just kind of popped out to me.

. . . [Baez] was a very amazing woman. You know, she fights for a lot of big causes, and I just thought it was very inspirational. I had to give a twenty-minute speech on her. And just hearing about her parents, her parents were alcoholics . . . but they had standards for her, and they wanted her to be raised this way. And she kind of was bucking their system. It was really neat to see, you know, she told about the chaos that went on in her family. And then how she met Bob Dylan, how she got into singing. Next thing you know, she's doing concerts. Well, then all of a sudden, she got involved with Amnesty International. And then she opened up another foundation of her own. . . . I learned from her not to be a people pleaser. She didn't please [her parents]. She did what she wanted, what made her happy, and that's what I got from that.

. . . I like to read about men, too. I mean, look at the guy that made UPS. He was a black male who was not raised in a great neighborhood, lacked education, but decided to get out of there. I think he ran away from home and lived with another family. And got an education, and now look: he owns a multimillion-dollar company because he stuck with what he believed in. I read a magazine article about him. I think there's a lot of men out there, too, [whose] stories are wonderful.

I would like to see more biographies [in the prison library]. I think there's a lot of people out there . . . that have maybe been in a dark place and have found the light and now are living these wonderful lives. Needless to say, that's not how it always goes, but I really believe that somehow one person's words can affect another one to either make a right or a left. And I think, you know, if they make that right, it's gonna be the most beneficial part of their lives. And in biographies, you can relate to the person as to maybe if they were an alcoholic, drug addict; even if they weren't those things, maybe they were in a domestic violence situation. Maybe they were the abuser or they were the abused. Maybe it was back in the past, kids' issues, you know. Parent issues, growing up with alcoholic parents. Because I feel that society is kinda—that word dysfunctional, I just don't like it. I think it's a label, and I think it's a cop out. . . . I think some of [the authors], if they would dig just a little deeper, maybe it was something that they did or something that happened to them would [resonate] with another person that's reading this book, and it might open their eyes to realize, "I don't have to let this bother me anymore." Or, "I don't have to live like this anymore, and let's go on."

Maybe the library could add some more political stuff. . . . I think there's a lot [of women] that lack the knowledge of how the government really works, how voting works, stuff like that. And I think we, as women, need to em-power ourselves with that information so we can go out there and make the changes that need to be made in this world. [But if you said that in prison], they'd throw you in the hole[15] thinking you were trying to overthrow their little mastermind of a compound, which wouldn't be too hard seeing that [the correctional officers] just have GEDs and are some high-priced babysitters. Talking about political things is called inciting a riot. There's a lot you can't say. You can't say that we will have a hunger strike. You can't say that I'm gonna make up a petition. Oh, oh, no. Oh, no. That will not work. And basically your political view of, well, basically your views here mean crap to any- and everyone.

. . . There's so many things that need to change. We're paying $30,000 a year to house an inmate and only $10,000 for a child in our public school system? What is *wrong* with that?! You know, maybe if you would have gave them the education or got them hooked up in some type of work program, they wouldn't have had to come here because they would have been making the money; they would have been able to support their family. . . . Instead, you're gonna pay this place $30,000 a year to have some overpriced babysitter sit there and tell me when I can eat, sleep, and do whatever and disrespect me like I'm a piece of garbage, but yet we're not gonna give our kids a chance. I mean, I'm so amazed.

The minute I became a tutor here, I just never realized how many people were illiterate. And so I did my second speech for Toastmasters in regards to education. And then when I was doing it, you know, there weren't any books here to look up except an encyclopedia. And then by the grace of God, *Prime Time* had this wonderful thing on . . . about how we cheat our American children, and it told all about public school systems, your local school systems, the school systems abroad. . . . As parents, do we think about that stuff? No, we just have our kid to be able to say their ABCs, go to school, get a diploma, and get a good job. But they're not going to be able to get those things if we're not giving the school system the money to work with. So I just put that information out there to the ladies to maybe kind of open their minds, and you know, maybe they got kids that are going to school.

. . . [When I leave prison,] I think my reading horizon is going to be based on what my daughter wants to read. Seeing that she'll probably be like two, and I'm going to be trying to go to work, college, and take care of her, if I have an afternoon to read to myself . . . my biggest thing will probably be parenting magazines, *Woman's Day,* and any books that are based on child development. I'm a first-time mom. I just want make sure I mold her in every way, shape, and form.

11 Solo

—ᴍ—

Life Narrative

"That's a soul that you're stepping on"

I WAS BORN in Mississippi. My maternal grandparents raised me until I was six. And then they boarded me on a train. So at the age of six, I was on a train by myself. That's a very vivid memory. It's a good memory. And I arrived in Chicago, Illinois, with my great maternal aunt, whose name is [Solo]. I'm named after her. I stayed there one year, so at the age of seven, I was boarded on the train again by myself to go to Cleveland, where I remained ever since. My two brothers were with my mother in Cleveland. I had saw them whenever they would visit Mississippi, so I did know when they were born and different things like that. But I hadn't actually lived with them until I was seven years old, close to eight. [Then I] stayed with my mother until she passed away.

When I was in Mississippi, I remember vaguely getting on a big yellow bus, going to school. School, of course, was segregated. I remember the bus picking me up and all the dust that would come up with the tires, and my grandmother would have me with these pretty little dresses. She had been a domestic for the same family until she passed, so I had grew up with a little girl and her hand-me-downs were my clothes. Of course, I had really nice clothes. And I remember I didn't want my dresses—which my grandmother used to starch and iron like she did the family's daughter's dresses, and I had a lot of petticoats—I didn't want the dust getting under my petticoats. And I used to cry that they were going to get me dirty. And I had little parasols with the ruffles. . . . And I was teased because I had nice clothes. I don't remember too much about school other than that there were no white kids. I only saw them when I went to the family where my grandmother worked. The girl and I, we played together. I remember her father had built this playhouse in the back, and we could go in and out of this playhouse.

. . . When I got to Cleveland, it was in the winter, and my grandmother who was sending me boxes of clothes didn't have any coats for me 'cause it wasn't snowing in Mississippi, and I remember she had ordered me something out of a catalogue and that was my first time getting a Sears and Roebuck catalogue 'cause she sent it to me for me to see the pictures. And she had sent me a little red coat with a red muffler that hung around and you could put your hands in. I thought it was the cutest thing. And I remember thinking, if I wear these clothes to this new school in this new city, will I get picked on like I did on the big yellow bus?

Well, there was no yellow bus. I had to walk to school, and I was living on [X and Y] streets, which was a very really poor area. And all up and down [X] street at that time, all the businesses were owned by Jewish people. And I remember going to school having to go past these stores. And it seemed like everybody knew everybody's kids. So whenever I would stop and linger around—because I really was afraid to go 'cause I was going to get picked on—this Jewish lady named Ms. [X] would always call me by my name and tell me, "You better get to school, [Solo], or I'm going to tell your mother." So there was a stark reality of white and black in my childhood, but I didn't feel it in the sense of racism because they all helped me. They were all sort of supporting me.

And my only issue really was that I was being called "country" because I was from the South. Maybe I talked different. I'm not sure what I did different, but I quickly knew that I wanted to fit in, really bad. . . . I was picked on. I'd be happy to get the clothes because they came from my grandmother and they were nice. But then when I would go outside, the kids who didn't have, they resented me, and they would pick on me, so I didn't want that. But I wanted to be different at the same time. To this day I can't really explain it, but I know it was a root of my criminality. I just cannot articulate it. I wanted to be different, but I wanted to be accepted. The things that the kids that I grew up around did, I never could excel in that. I never could excel in sports. I never could cuss real good 'cause there's an art to calling your momma names and I couldn't never do it right. So I was teased for that, and then I always had some kind of different way of talking that they would make fun of. I physically developed later. So just a whole lot of stuff.

And then I had been watching my mother's humiliation too. At that time, the welfare system was not like it is now. They actually came and invaded your home. And you couldn't have things. Like the mother couldn't have a TV and you couldn't have toasters and wasn't supposed to have phones, and pretty much the state actually took care of you. And we had surplus food, and they pretty much controlled our lives. So if you ventured out of that, you had to hide stuff when they come over. And the princess phone had just come out, and you could unplug it and take it upstairs. And people upstairs would bring theirs down. There was all this covert stuff when the welfare wasn't coming. And again, they were white. And they always wore black. It felt like it was a stark world. It was a black world and a white world, seemed like. And my mother having had work and then couldn't work, she was in debt with Ms. [X] and it's like it never ended. . . . And it was almost like the people in the store knew everything about my mother, including when she had her period. And I was feeling some kind of shame for my mother, but I didn't know why.

. . . And I remember at the age of ten trying so hard to still fit in that I started lying. I started fabricating stories. Everybody was poor, but it was things going on in my head that were different than everybody else's head. The Sears and Roebuck catalogue that my grandmother had sent me at the age of seven became my template for everything I thought was good.[1] So I would get these catalogues, and at that time they used to mail them to people, and I would steal them off their porch [laughing]. I'm seeing it, and I would come home, and I would cut families out. Of course, all the families were white, and I would cut out furniture, and I would put it in sections, and I would play like that for hours and hours. By myself. And I would change it around. I would get the Kenmore washers. I would get a daddy 'cause there was no father figure in the house, and everything came out of this catalogue. My mother had four [children]. It was me, my two brothers, and then we had a little girl, little sister. And I was responsible for keeping my sister, but I would be so occupied with this fantasy world that sometimes I neglected to dry her, and she would get a diaper rash or I would hear her crying, but I would purposely ignore it. And I didn't really study the way I should have like for homework because I was in this fantasy. So I didn't excel well in elementary school. And they were always calling my mother to the school because of this. I didn't know the answers, and I was always having to write "I will study" or something a hundred times. Then I would always go back to that catalogue and I would save my little families in this little shoebox and dare my brothers to touch it. This was sacred to me.

My grandmother was still sending me clothes but not as many and not as often, so pretty soon I did start to look like everybody else. The clothes didn't single me out anymore. So to compensate for not having the nicer things that I used to pretend was from my sister, I used to pretend I had a sister down South. My sister's going to send me clothes. So the little white girl that was really my age—and I can't remember her name now, really I can't. I remember the family's name, but I can't remember her name—I would pretend she was my sister.

So I guess around the sixth grade, it became apparent to me that we were really poor. And so my fantasy world then became a reality in terms of lying. I had already been lying about a sister I didn't have. I wasn't doing well in school. I wasn't reading. And there was a library over on [X] Street. [X] Street at that time was the same Jewish people who owned all the businesses. They lived there. Big beautiful homes. So what I started doing was venturing further into their area by myself, and I would go up and knock on their doors, and I would say I need some money to go to the YMCA. And they would give it to me. So this became my pastime. And whenever they would open their doors, I could take a peek in and it was always beautiful furniture and of course, color TVs and drapes and carpet, things that I had saw in the Sears catalogue, but we didn't have. So I wanted to get closer to this world.

So what I did, I went into the library, and they said, "Well, you need a library card." And I said, "Okay." And I remember filling out the card, and I got the card because I just wanted to be in that environment, this little ol' black girl living in that library. I remember that. I was always aware of that, not in the sense of I'm black, but nobody looks like me. That's how I knew it. And I didn't feel uncomfortable because I'm a child, and obviously, I must have been likeable because no one ever hurt me or called me the "N" word. That never happened to me as a kid. Matter of fact, they were nice to me. And that made me want to stay closer. But the irony of it is this fantasy led me to reading because now I had something that would make me unique again when I went back to my poor environment 'cause I can read.

. . . It was so much happening to me at that age, and the only time I was able to escape was in books. So, reading stories like *Jack and the Beanstalk*. The nursery rhymes was my number one book, of course, but then I would venture and try to read other books. And I remember reading a story about a little prince who comes with his poor little twin and they switch places. Maybe it's *The Prince and the Pauper*.[2] Anyway, the little poor boy switches places, and this was a pretty big book for me to read 'cause there was a lot of pages. And I would read, and the more I would read, of course, I would come home and share with my brothers. My sister was still a baby. And I would get them caught up in my world 'cause they would sit and listen to me read, and that made me feel special 'cause I could read. Well, doing this helped me to get better in school. So when my graduation came, to my surprise, my teacher had nice things to say about me.

So from there we moved, and of course, the riots had came about, and the climate was different. And they had burned down most of the Jewish establishments and then there was nothing there. So instead of this vibrant neighborhood where people were buying and selling, you had all these burnt-down buildings, and you smelled the decay and the rats and burnt and charred, that's the environment I had for junior high. And at this time we were living on [X] and . . . they burned all of [X] Street down 'cause that was all Jewish. . . . The black nationalists were there, and I had to encounter them on my way to school. The first day my mother took me to school because they were recruiting young kids.

. . . And I'm feeling the difference in my mom now than when I was little. I'm sensing a pride in my mother. She watched the news every night because of Martin Luther King and the civil rights [movement] and things that were going on in the South, and she was conscious of it, and she wanted us to see it. So we were forced to watch it, and she would explain it to us. So I saw racial pride in my mother at that time and a defiance. She really resented that they had burnt down everything. The nationalists, the riots, the angry people who had no plan. Just burn it up. They had no plan. Because what they did, they took away something and replaced it with nothing. And [X] Street to this day is still nothing, but instead of her saying, "I'm glad that you took away this oppressive Jewish businesswoman" who for real would keep my mother in debt—I know that now, 'cause they were forever overcharging her—she was angry that it was gone, because see, there were jobs with this. There was credit with this. There was unity, and they took that away, the nationalists and the [Black] Panthers and that whole climate took that away and replaced it with nothing.

So here I am in junior high not really feeling different as I did as a kid. Nobody's really noticing me. My grandmother has long since stopped sending the clothes. . . . And all I have is the books. So now the books I'm reading are books about Marcus Garvey.[3] We had an African American teacher who first introduced us to black history, and that was not a given topic in the '60s, and he was always being called up to the principal's office because he was very radical. I mean, this man had an Afro before Afros was popular. And he had this big beard . . . and he was always spouting off about rights and slavery and stuff. And they was always calling him in, telling him to talk it down.

In my school at that time, it was still all black [students]. Desegregation was happening, but I think they did the elementary schools first 'cause I didn't encounter interracial until I got to [X] High School, but there were white teachers. And that was becoming an issue for me. . . . The nationalists would march up and down the street as though they were protecting something, but there's nothing to protect. It's burnt down. . . . They were this huge force, dressed in black and the berets and they had the flag, and they may have even had weapons. I don't know, but it was like this huge sea of them marching up and down the streets shouting out, "Freedom from the fascists!" and "Freedom!" And I have to cross the street to get to school, and they're trying to tell me, "Don't get the white man's education," but you have nothing on me. So I was angry, and I wanted them gone. And my mother had already walked me to school the first day to let them know, "This one you will not get." And she had told me, "If you even stop and listen to them . . .," and I was terrified of my mother, far more so than them. So I never heard their indoctrinations. . . . See, I had read about Huey Newton, Eldridge Cleaver, Angela Davis,[4] Jackson's *Soledad Brother*,[5] the whole nine yards. In my way of thinking—because I'm living where you're not, and I'm seeing the decay—I'm thinking you don't even have a plan. So I always knew to join that was nothing. You're not going anywhere.

So now I'm in school, and my whole world is consumed with black history. I want to know everything. I started reading books, very upsetting books. Have you ever read the books *Mandingo* and *Master of Falconhurst*?[6] They were about slave people. They were fictional. They were extremely popular. And it was always a illicit love affair in it and a whole bunch of abuse in it. . . . I started reading James Baldwin's books. I hadn't met Toni Morrison yet. Alice Walker was there. I think she must have been very young at that time because she was writing about her marriage and down in Mississippi. . . . And I was reading Langston Hughes. That's where my world went at that point. And I was just trying to get through junior high. And so I did. Nothing really traumatic happened, to be honest. No. We were still poor, but I think I had kinda accepted it, and I had little odd jobs to compensate for that. When I got to high school, that's where integration started, and white kids were being bused in. And I think my world at that point got fused with boys. Boys became paramount, and of course, I got pregnant and I didn't graduate.

And the seed that I had planted when I was ten, when I was going to those homes trying to make my home like Sears and Roebuck, led me to commit crimes later on the pretense that I have a baby now, and I got to take care of my baby. So at that time, once you turned eighteen, you could get on welfare, and of course, you could get subsidized housing. So I got that. So I'm living in the projects. . . . I was a payroll clerk out at [X], and with my creative imagination, I thought, well, I'll just write myself two checks. Didn't play it out. Didn't know that the checks are going to come back and so I got caught, but not before I got about $500. And they didn't arrest me. They didn't make me pay it back. They fired me. But he sat me down and told me, he said, "If this is the life you're about to choose, you're going to end up in prison." I didn't believe that. I'm just nineteen. And I wasn't going to the library anymore, and I wasn't reading books. Pretty much didn't have time. And it's like the streets just sucked me up. Everything about the streets sucked me up. . . . It was around the '70s, and all you heard was, "You can get money. You can get money. You can get money." It was all about illegal money. And my world had just spun out of control. I never gravitated toward the drugs, but I got deeper and deeper into crime. And I did go to prison. And pretty much that's how it went.

. . . When I very first went [to prison], my mother, of course, was alive, and it was humiliating 'cause I had hurt her so bad. And I felt every day of it. The second time I went, my mother had already passed away. My mother didn't even live to be fifty. And I had become so entrenched in it to where it was like a playtime. I continued my criminal activity in prison. As a result, I spent a lot of time in solitary confinement from violating the rules. My entire criminal record is financial stuff. And I just defied authority. I was going to do it my way no matter what, and of course, I had kids, but I still wasn't thinking about that.

. . . [Solitary confinement] is terrible. That is terrible. You're in a grave. You can't do anything. Everything's brought to you and you're in a room all day, except to come out of the showers. So when I would come out, I would entertain myself by singing, doing little mock concerts. And then when I was in the room, I would develop a routine. Like I have a lot of hair under here, so I would take my hair down and take all day to braid it on purpose. Stretch the hours out. Then I might write. And I would clean the floor. And I would look out the window. And then I'd devote a whole day to just reading. I was a Christian then, trying to be. So I would read the whole Bible. I would break it down into sections. You're in a grave and you're trying to live. That's how to best describe it: trying to live in a grave. You're trying to live 'cause you're not dead yet, but nobody hears you when you call out, "Hey, I'm alive!"

. . . I was in solitary confinement [when my brother was murdered], and I remember the chaplain coming back. And no one wanted to hear the chaplain call their name because you already know it's bad news. . . . I remember when I got in there, they said it was my brother. You're so restrained, so I couldn't do nothing. So I cried when I got back in my cell. And I had two more months to do in the hole so I couldn't even call my family or anything. My sister sent me a news article and I remember praying—my brother was such a good, spirited guy—that whatever had happened to him that we would find out, that the good that he did in the world would bring back the good news of how it happened, and why it happened. . . . And maybe six months later, my sister wrote me and told me that the guy that did it surrendered. . . . My brother basically was a victim of his lifestyle, because he had gotten addicted to drugs. He was out there, and guns were part of his world. But I remember him always like he was. He just had such a vibrant personality, even with nothing. "You want half of what I've got? I have nothing but you can have half of it, though" [laughing]. That was my brother. . . . He loved me. I was his big sister. I had him for the time that I had him. That's about it.

. . . Nine months [was the longest stretch that I did in solitary.] I kept going back. I was angry. I was angry at all staff. That's when I first met Warden [X] and she was the first nurturer. She came back to see me and I thought she was going to let me out, and she didn't. She said, "No I'm not here to let you out. I'm here to let you know that you have too much potential to keep wasting it like this." That's when I started getting myself together.

. . . [This time,] I graduated from college while in prison. I got my GED while in prison. I now work as a law clerk in prison. I have been extremely successful in winning cases. I became Muslim in prison. I've learned Arabic in prison. I've learned to read the Qur'an in prison, and I have learned how to put things together where I have my own program here in prison. I have a program called Act Up, and it became a DRC[7] Reentry program, so that means central office has approved it for this institution. They ultimately want to implement it for the male institution, so it's a possibility I could get a job out of this thing if I do it right. . . . It's a character-building program. It lasts eight weeks. We graduate, the whole nine yards. I just had a fundraiser . . . and I'm pretty much trusted, for lack of a better word. I'm in charge of twenty women every Saturday for eight weeks and the recidivism rate is only one [woman] has come back in two years. And they do change, and I'm pretty damn proud of that because I could have went other ways in prison, but I didn't.

. . . I know that we all play roles. I'm just tired of playing the role of a inmate. So how do I change that? I make a transition. Everything we do in Act Up is theatrical dialogue. I get center stage. I look around. I make a decision. Stage right, stage left, whatever. I decide to make a character embodiment. I transition from who I am to being what I want to be. How do I do that? I have to get rid of the negative character traits and incorporate positive character traits through whatever means possible, through conversations, reading, television, whatever. And then I work on it like I do a script. So I learn a new script, and it becomes memorized. And then I perform. And then as a result, I change.

I've been very fortunate that Mental Health is assisting me now [with Act Up]. I have some [local] professors that come in and assist me. I have evangelists who come in. And then me. I'm the main one. I do like a fifteen-minute monologue, basically. And I'm like in your face. I play the role of a very aggressive motivator. And I'm very dramatic with the women. And because I'm one of them, I know what they need. I know when to back up. I know when to proceed. And then I give them a small script, like six, seven, eight, nine sentences. And the first thing they do is get a piece of [a] Shakespeare sonnet. . . . I break them into small groups, because women tend to bond faster. . . . And they have to memorize this and create a way that's fun to present it. Because nobody wants to change when it's hard, but if you can show me where it's easy, I'll benefit. So they come back and that's their first time, and they present that. And they're so creative.

. . . I have a really good team. We call it our Act Up navigate team, is what we call it. I have a unit manager, she's on board. I have a doctor from Mental Health. We have a CO.[8] We have a professional from [a local university]. We have an evangelist from outside; she's a minister. And Dr. [X] from [another local university]. . . . They each come in for like a forty-five minute guest speaker role. . . . Dr. [X] always talks on body language. And then we do little interactive drills. Like I'll say, "How am I feeling now?" and see if they can read it. Because body language is very important, and then I give them assignments like watch the news or watch some program and tell me how you perceive that person. The two anchors, do they like each other? Can you feel that? You can see it in the body language. What's going on with them? And then they come back and they report, stuff like that.

Then around the fifth week, I'd give them the monologue, and I'd say, "Now the first step, you've already conquered that. You know you can memorize 'cause you just did it with Shakespeare. Okay, so now you have these characters, and they're various characters." Some I've gotten out of a thespian book. Some I make up. And so they have to memorize these. And then they practice basically the remainder of the week on these scripts. And then they do what's called an audition, and we have outside guests come in, and we have several alumni sit in. And they come in by themselves. Because in real life, when you change, you're going to step out by yourself. So you have to be able to take constructive criticism, knowing that you gave it your best, and be critiqued. So they're critiqued on believability, projection. A lot of these women don't really project when they speak 'cause they've been beat down or whatever. It's always six judges 'cause the highest score is thirty, with five points being the highest in each category. So four inmates and two staff or two guests come in and evaluate the auditions.

And what has happened is that the women's self-esteem has been raised so high that they want to do it, and they are creative. And normally only one person gets thirty. But this time I had four! So it's a great thing. And from that group that went home, only one woman has returned to prison. . . . It's the group that changes the women. Nobody is the same afterwards. I've seen them go from being shy, insecure, scared, feeling like a failure to getting your GED, enrolled in [college courses], completing the horticulture course, getting in the choir, becoming dancers, acting in my plays. And what it has done for my life, it has allowed me to see that even as tarnished as I am, people—even . . . professors—will deal with me or communicate with me if I have a focus. And I didn't think that before.

. . . [Before I came to prison,] I was working for a woman who had her own leadership development firm. . . . The first time she sent me on assignment, it was at the headquarters for [a prominent company]. And my job was to do a three-day seminar at this resort. So everything is out of my league. And I get in there and this is chemical engineers, again out of my league. And I shrunk. I thought I could do it. She just kept saying, "They're just people." They're not just people. They're like super-smart people, and I'm playing these games with them that I know work, but they're like so smart until it's not working, and I'm trying to get them to understand that they have to allow the kid in them to come out in order to be creative because they were trying to develop a new [product for children]. . . . I lost control of the group. . . . So needless to say, that was a bad experience for me and when I came back, I just didn't feel like I fit in that world. So [my boss] gave me the [X] Schools assignment. My job was to meet with her and discuss what we could do to help the schoolkids' academic scores go up. And again, I felt overwhelmed because these people are very smart. And here I am an ex-felon. So it didn't take long before I reversed back to my criminal ways where I felt in control, where I felt I fit.

. . . Ironically, now my world has turned back to the experience I had gotten from working with her. . . . I learned a lot from her, a great deal more than I thought because when I step up in Act Up, really I'm imitating her. . . . She got results, you know, 'cause she allowed [clients to understand that] you can retain your intelligence, but you can also be a kid, and you can learn to create and play. That's what I learned from her.

. . . I have been in relationships where I've had like black eyes. I've never been severely beaten. I don't think I would tolerate that, pretty sure I wouldn't. But I did tolerate some domestic violence with my children's father, who is now deceased. I was young. He was young. We were kind of like trying to work that out. I pretty much provoked a lot of it. He wasn't per se a violent man, but I would push buttons. . . . I was raped twice by strangers. . . . I was raped once on the street, taken behind a house. . . . The other time I was at someone's house, a friend of mine, and the insurance man came over and raped me. The insurance man was a friend of his. . . . I didn't even think to tell his job or anything. I don't know why I didn't think to do it. Maybe I thought no one would believe me because he kept saying that: "You're nobody. I'm everything." . . . And strangely enough, when I hear on television and I see in movies women who are so traumatized when they go through all of that, I wonder, am I wrong or are they wrong? . . . I see all that they go through, and they don't ever want to have a relationship again, and I'm thinking, but it happened to me, and I didn't get stuck in it. I just don't get it. I don't know if maybe something's wrong with me. Why didn't you care enough about you, [Solo], to report it and go through the process in court?

. . . The majority of [women] come [to prison] because they have allowed themselves to be victims. And then they got comfortable in that role. "I'm a victim of my environment. I'm a victim of my relationships. I'm a victim of my lack of education. I'm a victim of the skin that I was cased in. I'm a victim of my sex." I hear it being their legal advocate. Like I'll say, "When were you incarcerated on this case?" "Oh, I don't remember." [I say,] "This is too profound for you not to know the date the police came and arrested you. It's too traumatic. How could you not know? . . . The reason you don't know it is you want to stay a victim and you want me to enable you and I refuse to do that." Then they say, "Well, you know, I was on crack." I say, "Okay, so now you have to replenish your brain cells. Have a seat. Think about it. Do you want me to help you? Then you give me something to work with." . . . I'm not going to let them be a victim. Either you stand up and be a woman with me or you go to the next clerk. You're just not going to do it with me.

Because I think the majority of the women come in, and it's easier to say, "Well, my man this or my man that." When I do their judicials,[9] I tell them, "The judge only wants to hear three things. . . . The first thing I want to hear is admit responsibility. . . . The second thing, show some remorse. Who was hurt besides you?" And a lot of times they'll think because maybe they didn't actually physically hurt someone, that no one was hurt. Then I say, "Well, let's think about this. Who is taking care of you now?" "My mother." "She was hurt. If you took a check and you wrote it and you cashed it at a bank, you hurt customers. At some point somebody else had to pay for that bad check. So apologize to those customers. Apologize to that banking institution and apologize to your parents. Show some remorse. Let the judge know that you have sat in prison and thought about, God, I did hurt people. The third thing, give me a plan. You want out of prison. What are you going to do if I let you out?" . . . And usually when I push them enough, they'll start digging deep. . . . Now when they come to me, they're prepared. Word gets out. "Go to her, and have your stuff together."

. . . [To keep women from coming to prison,] they have to be empowered, like I was. Someone like Warden [X] has to stop and say to them, "You have too much potential to just keep wasting it." Someone like my boss has to say to me, you know, "Use your natural talents." Someone like Dr. [X] from [the local university] has to come over and say to them like she said to me, "I believe in you." They have to be empowered. It has to start when they're kids. . . . It's too easy for parents to let their kids go. I call it the second form of slavery, you know, especially for African Americans.[10] At some point in our history, our kids were snatched from us. They fought tooth and nail to try to get that which they have brought into the world back. It's too easy now to just let Children's Services have your kids. . . . You have to go to the schools. Maybe you go to the elementary schools, 'cause whether you want to face it or not, they have sex. And you got to let them know: don't just teach safe sex or abstinence. Teach nurturing. So that if you're going to have this baby, love this baby. Teach them to love themselves as little bitty kids. Don't let a little child like I was in the seventh grade with my hand up all the time, all the time trying to learn French 'cause I love the way it sounds, and the teacher instead ignoring me and then finally telling me I didn't look right. Don't let someone crush a child's self-esteem like that.

With my kids, because of my choices, I was away in prison, and I'm sure, no doubt in my mind, somebody crushed their self-esteem. Somebody stepped on my babies' life. I know they did because I can tell by the way they believe or don't believe in themselves, and I'm their only hero. That's why I got to get it right this time. But it has to start with nurturing. I don't know what it's like in a suburban family. I mean, I'm hearing more and more that there's not a lot of differences. It's just more affluence, but as a nation, I would just say that we just got to start going back to nurturing. . . . Fathers need to know what it is to nurture. That can't just be assigned to the female sex. Any human being needs to be nurtured, needs to know that they're cared about in every area. I care about you psychologically, emotionally, physically, spiritually.

They need to know that, and then we'll have a more sensitive society 'cause we'll care more about each other because we have been talked to from a baby. You know, don't just take care of my needs, my physical needs. Take care of *me*! Let me know that I matter. And that's got to start . . . very, very young because it's hard to nurture someone when they get to my age if they've allowed themselves to become extremely hardened 'cause of their conditions. It's hard to get in there! Because there's a trust issue and so much damage.

Like, look at me. I'm a wreck now, you know, from something that happened in the seventh grade. My God! You think it's gone and then as soon as you say it out loud, the words hit you again. I see her! I can hear her! [pause] And I didn't even know how to handle that as a kid. I didn't even know how to handle that insult. I didn't know where to go with that. And then I had to come back to her class, and I just shrunk. I didn't raise my hand again. I hoped that she wouldn't see me. I wanted to disappear. I just didn't know what to do. How am I going to tell my mother the teacher called me unattractive? . . . Who's going to reprimand her for what she said to me, and how is she going to know all the damage that she caused by just that one statement [crying]? Oh my god. I just can't get past it [crying]. . . . I know that there was some kind of reverse racism because she was biracial, you know, so she was bringing some of that in it, too. . . . I don't know what it's going to take for that hole to heal up. Maybe it's going to take me raising my hand somewhere where beautiful people are, and they call on me [laughing]. Maybe that's it. That one has got to go. It's vicious. My god, that's too old.

. . . I've never been able to write a book about my life 'cause I've been stuck in the seventh grade. . . . When I read about other women's lives, I usually [skip] to where I am right now. Like when I read *The Color Purple*[11] . . . I identify more with the adult Celie. . . . When I read Oprah's book about her life, I get past that part about being a little kid real quick. I jump over that and I get to the adult person and I marvel at what she's doing now. . . . Princess Diana's childhood, I jump over that and I get to the woman now. I read it, but I don't retain it. . . . And I find that I do that in autobiographies or just articles, where a person starts out telling you about how they were as a kid. So I know that's a block for me. I'm thinking now that it's not about "can't" anymore. I'm thinking that I just won't. I don't know why I'm doing this. Maybe I'm selfish in holding onto that. But I think I'll be able to free the little kid once I'm somewhere in a room with beautiful people, and I raise my hand and it's okay.

. . . I believe right now that that's the only thing that I'm not free from, because I'm no longer enslaved or imprisoned by the changes, the physical abuse, the prison, the covering of my hair, the getting older, none of that stuff has locked me down. But there's a key that hasn't been opened yet to let that kid out who just wanted to be recognized. . . . [When something like that happens,] you go home, and you look in the mirror, and you tell yourself what you just heard, and then you just start letting other people beat up on you, and then that's what leads to the whole getting enslaved, becoming imprisoned to all this other stuff, the domestic violence, the whole nine yards. . . . When I have these emotional doubts, I'm not able to sit back and say, "You know what? I got to let the little kid heal. I've got to nurture her. I've got to love her." Because I want to move so far away from her and stand near the adult person 'cause the adult survived it. The adult is strong. . . . But the little kid gets in the way. If I'm in a room where I could make a contribution, the little kid'll get scared. If people are around me and they have a great command of the vocabulary, and I hear a word I don't know what it means, the little kid pops up. And if I'm asked something, and it's a little beyond my reach, the little kid is afraid to say, "I don't know." . . . So the little kid is a problem! And she won't go away until the woman frees her.

We have to nurture, and we have to say kinder things to people. We have to realize that that's a soul that you're stepping on, you know, and by me being Muslim, I understand more now that I need to protect the soul. The body, it's going to do what it's going to do, and it's going to decay. But the soul is too good for me to have lived as bad as I have and then condemn it to hell when all I have to do is ask for forgiveness because God is all-merciful. And so with a God that's all-merciful, I have to do my part to preserve my soul. And then *you* have a soul. So I can't just damage your soul just because I'm in the world and I've got a mouth to say stuff. Because when I damage your soul, it blackens my soul, and then that's more cleaning that God has to do to clean me up because of things I said to an innocent soul. And if we look at people like that instead of looking at she's white, she's Spanish, she's fat, she's this, if we look at them as souls the way God looks at us, I think we'd be able to nurture more.

. . . The staff that work with me in this program, they nurture me, you know. They tell me things that inspire me. They tell me things that I don't see about myself. They tell me, "Good job." They tell me, "You're good at that." . . . Yeah, I've been nurtured here. And maybe that's why I'm done because I got it, you know. I kept coming back until I got it. . . . [The prison staff] used to be the enemies, you know; it was always a battle. But now I've received quite a bit of nurturing here.

. . . In five months, God willing, I have to step outside these gates, and I'm stepping into a Islamic world 'cause I wasn't Muslim before, so I've got to find that community and be accepted. And then I have to reenter my adult children's lives with their children. And I have to try to develop this entrepreneur mind that's busting out of my head. And I also have to work [laughing]. . . . So what's next is, how am I going to balance all these things that I do while I'm in here as opposed to what I have to do out there, 'cause I'm not going to have that kind of time? . . . So basically, what I am going to do is try to manage my time. Continue to meet inspiring people. And even that's going to be a problem because my mode of transportation in here is my feet. . . . And then my faith. . . . I'm going to have to adhere to all the tenets of Islam, you know. How am I going to be perceived? Even my family, how are they going to feel about me, you know, all covered up? And how are people in the work place going to perceive me with all this going on in the media?

So mainly I'm going to have to manage my time and work on staying focused and staying in character. Like I tell them in Act Up, stay in character. No matter what people say outside, stay in character. No matter if somebody calls your name, stay in character. . . . What is my character right now? That's a good question. 'Cause I'm in this transition. I want to say so bad "entrepreneur," but I know that's not real. About the only one that's really real is "woman" 'cause I can be that even without being "mother." 'Cause my kids are adults now. . . . I can play the role of woman really well now 'cause I know that's what I am.

—ᘒ—

Reading Narrative

"Freedom for me was an evolution, not a revolution"

[HERE IN PRISON,] we can get a lot of fiction, but we can't get anything that they deem would incite us to rise up against them . . . or become conscious of the fact that you may be infringing on my rights. Any type of book that would give us a sense of knowing that they're wrong, they won't let us read that. They'll censor magazines if it gives that indication. But they lull us to sleep with romance! I'm telling you, four shelves of romance! Danielle Steel has a whole big huge section, and then they give us science fiction. And they'll give us a few *Newsweeks* or whatever, but you're not going to get any type of, like, *The Nation*. They won't let us have that. And no revolutionary-type biographies of, say, Castro or stuff like that, or anything that will cause you to get passionate and want to rise up. That's not happening.

It's books mainly to entertain. You get a lot of African American stuff dealing with fictional stuff. So you'll see women, they'll be over in the corner reading that, and they're not going to leave that corner. They don't have to worry about them [saying], "Come on, let's riot." . . . Basically, they give us books or will allow us to even order books that will either give the play to our fantasy of creating a business, or being a entrepreneur, or falling in love, or solving some kind of mystery, or knitting, stuff like that. We have a whole section of books over there on starting your own business.

The reason I say that they play to the fantasy is because it's not a realistic approach. These books are designed for people who have the capital and the wherewithal to go do it. We're in here. We're a whole 'nother segment. Then they got books that tell you how to write a cover letter and a résumé, but in reality, it's never going to be that. It's gonna be who you know that knows somebody, because as soon as you walk in with your beautiful little résumé and cover letter, there's the image of you being an ex-offender. I've tried it, and that's not how I got my job. . . . Those girls will get those books, and they'll sit in there, and they'll draft out business plans and all that stuff, and they'll be really, really excited about it. And you go home, and it's not gonna happen. No one's gonna loan you money. You haven't even worked for the last seven, eight, nine years. What kind of credibility do you have?

. . . [Useful books would be] the books that are designed to tell ex-offenders or people leaving where to go to these county, state, and federally funded places that are getting incentives for hiring us. Don't tell me I can go down here to the Marriott 'cause I already know all they're going to hire me to do is clean a room. Send me to a place that's getting a tax abatement for hiring me. Tell me that part. Don't keep me asleep to that part. But they keep that out of here because they don't want you to know this company gets a tax break. So tell the truth and put in there the realistic positions you can really get. It doesn't matter if you come out of school with a master's. You're gonna have to first get rid of that, wash that ex-offender stuff off. Tell the truth, and tell me that what I need to learn is social interaction skills. Because I'm going to have to meet someone who knows someone to get me somewhere. So they need to have more books on that, on how to communicate with people, how to make good impressions. They need to have more books on how to survive the first six months 'cause that's the hardest. . . . How to let your pride down. I mean, I sleep in a little two by four, but when I go home, I don't want to sleep in a shelter! . . . All of a sudden you go home with these grandiose ideas. We want more. Well, you can't afford more, so just go from one little shelter to another shelter until you're able to get you an apartment.

They need to have a book on what to expect when you get out for real, and that's what I want to do with Act Up. . . . I'm not saying don't teach me how to write a résumé, but just let me know that for real this is not it. There's going to be what I say to the person when I meet them. How to walk into a place and impress somebody that "hey, I've got some baggage, but I know I'm a good employee and I'm willing to do it. Bottom line, you want productivity. I'm gonna make that happen. You give me a chance. You don't have nothing to lose. I'm gonna show up and no, my crime didn't have anything to do with what you do. . . . Give me a chance. And you can get a little money from it, and if you don't know how, I'll tell you. They got abatements for you. Hire me, and let me be the first token. Doesn't nobody have to know."

And they need to have realistic books on that because everything that we have over there, they call it "Reentry," but it's really not. I've seen the turn-over. And I'm one of the ones who they didn't expect to come back but I did, because I've gone to college, got a degree, can articulate in some situations. But I had other issues. So we need to have books dealing with those issues. 'Cause you pack all these people into this compound and you don't have the staff nor the time nor the resources, including money, to really deal with why are you an inmate. . . . And it's just like, if you have a drug offense, you can't get a Pell grant. Well, don't you think I need it? Let me get it! Can I go to college please? But if you have any drug offense, whether it's drug abuse, or it's drug trafficking, or trafficking and paraphernalia, you cannot get a federal Pell grant. . . . You leave me no choice but to start drugs again and hope I don't get caught. 'Cause you won't let me go to school. It's crazy! And in ten years, they're going to regret these decisions. . . . You gotta nurture a society, you can't continue to punish it and punish it and punish it 'cause you cannot beat the sin out. You have to nurture the sin out. . . . You just want to beat me, beat me, beat me, punish me, punish me, punish me. And then expect me to come out of prison reformed. At some point I'm just going to become what you expect me to. I'm gonna become that monster.

. . . For me, reading is not to escape. It's more to understand me, like I read a lot of philosophy, a lot of psychology. Right now I'm reading Islamic philosophies and a book called *The 48 Laws of Power*.[12] I just got finished reading *The Prince* by Machiavelli.[13] I didn't read it because I wanted to know any military strategy. I read it because here was a man who influenced Italy, who pretty much turned the whole system around because he felt that he could change it. And he did, and he wasn't this great somebody. But the irony is that what Machiavelli did, we're doing now. We've adopted the same principles. Because President [George W.] Bush, there's no doubt in my mind he has a

Machiavellian attitude because he really believes that he is the commander in chief of everything, of the universe, you know. . . . And he doesn't care if he has to lie. He doesn't care and doesn't respect anything. I am the American president! . . . And that's what Machiavelli was. Machiavelli said pretty much by any means necessary.

And then I read Dante's *Inferno*,[14] to have an imagination of what hell would be like and all these different levels, you know. I find that interesting. And then I also find books on self-help. I'll pick them up, like a little psychology. I'll read that. I'm not too big on romance books. . . . It's always the woman waiting on some man to come and rescue her, and she run off in the sunset. I don't care how you dress it up. That's how it is. And it's too fairytale, you know. I don't care how intriguing Danielle Steel try to make it; in the end result, the woman is waiting on the man to come and save her. . . . I'm not too big on fiction, but if I do read it, it's got to be mystery. It's got to be something to hold my attention. I have to be trying to figure out the end result because I will always—it's my DNA—I need to be in control of something. I'm a controller. So I need to have some idea of how this is going to end. I don't want to be like, wow, I didn't expect it. I want to at least be like, yeah, I knew it. I kinda figured that. . . . And I like autobiographies if you catch my attention. Like I read Oprah's book, and I read some stuff about Princess Diana.

. . . I read the book about the Delany sisters.[15] They were interesting to read. I enjoyed that because that was real. I mean, to have lived as long as they did and as well as they did. . . . [Their father] was accepted as the minister in this school, which afforded the Delany sisters—there were the two sisters and their brother—afforded them an opportunity for a very good education. . . . And the mother taught the Delany sisters independence. They can make their own soap. They could sew their own clothes, and they never got married because neither of them ever met a man that equaled their father. And one was the first black dentist in New York, and one was a teacher. . . . I just found them to be interesting because they didn't really speak of racism in the sense that you would think it would have been. They kind of like used it to their benefit. Like their father told them, "You are who you are. But it shouldn't stop you," you know. And then they had the example of their father, who was very dark complected, but it didn't seem to bother him. And he was able to get a lot done, and then their mom was very fair, and she knew a lot of stuff: how to make hats and dresses, and she knew how to do teas, and so they had those cultures mixed together.

. . . But mainly, [I read] philosophy. I like the Greek philosophers. . . . I had taken a course on women's philosophy. And there was a female professor teaching it, and she was feminist. And of course, she was bringing in her own personal biases. And so she just destroyed Descartes and Socrates and Aristotle and some more that I can't pronounce their names. And she said, "Do you understand that there were no women in this group?" She said, "Why do you think that is? They all had mothers. . . . You know why? Because the women were considered nothing. And it was all about the earth and the church and the men. And why do you think in the Bible in Timothy it says that women should not preach?" She was like, "Because they believe that we are too emotional, and we're not rational and we're not logical." . . . So she was teaching us from that perspective how women were never considered important enough, but what's more important than bringing you into the world? And she was like, "How do you think it got so twisted that men who had to be raised up from a baby couldn't respect women once they became men? Why do you think that is?" And we were trying to figure it out. And she said, "Because men are stupid [laughing]! 'Cause how else could you turn your back on what brought you here?" It made a lot of sense. That was a really good course that I took with her.

. . . Islam, I've been studying five years now. I get the books from the chaplain. She'll go to the Cleveland Public Library and get it. Like, the philosophy of the hijab, which is what this [head wrap] is called, it's in the Qur'an as a commandment. It says that the Muslim woman should be covered so that she'll be known and respected. . . . Now it's a sharia; a sharia is the law that Muslim women should adhere to the commandments, but they don't always do it. It's still a personal choice. Like, you have some Muslim women will wear it only when they make their prayers. . . . I always have to wear white in here. That's the rule. But I can't wait to wear bright, vibrant colors. . . . It's going to be fashionable. And I'm not gonna have that shrouded look like that barbarous stuff they were doing in Afghan[istan].

With this [head] covering comes a big responsibility. People see me coming, so I can't be on the yard cursing. I can't get in homosexual relationships. I can't disrespect staff. . . . This is a discipline that makes me know I'm serving God. . . . If I have a concern about something in Islam, [the imam][16] will get a book and bring it in, and I'll read it. And one of my concerns right now is that there are not many Muslim women teaching. Because the term for teacher is imam, and traditionally that's men. It's a man that comes in here. If a woman comes in, she's just coming in as a advisor. Because in Islam, the man prays in the front and the woman prays behind. . . . And I question stuff. Well, why is this? But I understand why because we bend over and you know, your shape is revealed. And men . . . are not as logical as we think, and they'll be distracted quick. . . . God knows it 'cause he created us, so to avoid that temptation, don't have the women bending over.

Then, I'm supposed to pray five times a day at certain times of the day. I questioned that. But now I understand it. That's done to regulate your day, to keep your mind on the right things. Because if I can stop in the middle of the day around 3:00, no matter how much money I'm making at a business, and I say no, I got to go and pray, that's going to keep me balanced. . . . [In the spiritual library,] there's an entire volume of Hadifs. The Hadifs are sayings of Prophet Mohammed written down. And some of them, I question them. Some of them, I *really* question them. Like the makeup for the Muslim women. But you have to put it in the context of where they were. Like, they were really only allowed to use like henna and some sort of pomegranate. So that tells me I can still wear makeup. You just can't have it made from pork base. So it's not as constraining as people think. It's all in how you perceive it, you know. And during the course of these years of me studying it, I think it's more of a liberation to me. And I just can't wait to be free with it. . . . If you adhere to all the tenets of the religion, it pretty much guides your life. And I think I needed this as opposed to Christianity. . . . It's just an orderly way to live your life. . . . Everything's supposed to be in balance. . . . They're systems with an outcome that I can kind of predict.

I wanted to read the Qur'an in Arabic . . . so now I know how to read Arabic. I can pronounce it and I can read it, and I know what I'm reading. I'm not fluent in it, but I'm well enough to read my Qur'an. . . . I read the Qur'an every day. You're supposed to read it every morning. . . . Ramadan is coming up this month. That's when we fast for thirty days, and you have to read a section called the juz. There are thirty juz in the Qur'an and you're supposed to read one every single day. And some of them are like fifteen, twenty pages. So you get up early in the morning and you read. It's sort of like a meditation. You meditate on it the same way you would if you had a devotional Daily Bread or something like that. And it pretty much covers everything. They have a section on nothing except women's issues.

. . . For instance, if a man has a daughter and son, and he dies, the son gets two-thirds and the daughter gets one-third. And the reason being the son is going to marry someone, and he's going to need more. The daughter's going to get married, and the husband is to provide for her. Of course, in some Islamic countries, they've abused that. . . . But if they follow it the right way God intended, then it's very equitable for the woman. And it even goes into how long you should nurse. You should nurse a baby for two years, and it's really explicit. And just like Deuteronomy talks about the woman's menstrual and all that, well, it's very detailed in the Qur'an as well. . . . Basically, it's a time to leave the woman alone. And we know PMS,[17] so I mean, God knew. Leave her alone. You won't get your feelings hurt [laughing]. . . . So it pretty much tells men how to treat you all the way around, you know.

And there's even a section in there on chastising, which I questioned that. It says that if a husband has a disobedient wife, that he should first admonish her and then refuse to sleep with her, and then third, strike her lightly. So I asked the imam about this, and I said, "Well, this here is real close to domestic violence. If somebody gets this, they might read it wrong." He said, "Well, if you get to this third stage, you should really consider not being there." And so I said, "What constitutes disobedience?" And he said, "Well, that was made in the Qur'an because of the fact that men and women argue. They don't always agree, but if you're in a relationship where every time your husband tells you something, you want to question it or argue about it, then there's a problem there. And so, if you don't respect him, and he admonish you or sort of chastise you verbally and you continue to do it, then it's a problem. But if it gets to the point to where you think he's going to hit you, then that problem has escalated too far." So that's really how it's meant. It's not meant to be, "Look, didn't I tell you to stop?" Pow!

. . . A lot of my reading is for my job as a law clerk. That was one of my assigned jobs. I knew nothing about it. And when I started reading the [law] books, I was angered at first because I could have gotten out of prison that last time a lot sooner had I known the law. And then I was impressed with the male inmates who do become jailhouse lawyers. . . . And then I started winning cases, so then I felt powerful a little bit. And then you get a reputation. So the women now when they see me, "That's the lady that helps you with law," you know, so it feeds my ego. Its feeds that instant gratification thing that I still have. And it also helps me do right by other souls. And then I'm able to empower them when they sit in my chair. . . . I do my best, so I just read every single law book that comes through there. . . . I read something legal every day.

. . . The way I like to read law cases, I'll get a law book, and I'll just read down the table of contents, and whenever I see cases that say *State v.,* I already know those are inmate cases. So I read them just to see what type of cases there are. And I find it very interesting what male inmates particularly get back into the courts with. And sometimes they're successful because I guess they go to prison with a different mindset than a woman. It's always a battle with them, where we [women] become complacent and we form these little communities, you know. Men, they're constantly in a fight. . . . The more astute ones battle in the courtroom rather than out in the yard.

. . . I don't even have access to an Internet. I do all my research just by reading. And every single book in that library that pertains to law, I've gotten a sense of what it means. . . . It's my job to do all the inventory, and every week we get something on the Supreme Court, federal, and state. . . . What interests me is anything pertaining to jail credit. Reduction in sentences, 'cause that's what the women need. . . . I do a lot of domestic stuff as far as getting your kids back. Divorces, custody, child support issues. . . . Mainly what I do is criminal stuff, trying to get out of prison, trying to win an appeal, trying to get jail credit or judicial hearings.

. . . What I think about the law, I understand now why lawyers start out doing it. I think they really sincerely believe in the system. Because if it's right, it works. That's what I have learned. And it's constructed beautifully, because there's a pro and a con to every single law. And you're protected by the Constitution and your right to due process. Those are beautiful rights. . . . But now that I know the law, I know that it's corrupt. It's racist. There's a whole lot of stuff that goes on with it. . . . I know that they play with it, and they use so many words 'til you really do get dizzy. . . . I know that the attorneys I had didn't work as hard for me. They couldn't have, because it's too accessible to me. If you were to put forth some effort, you could have found it, too. . . . I know that there's issues of racism, and when a judge knows the penalty and he leans more this way because of his personal biases, because I've read cases where I was biased. When I read those cases of those guys raping kids and they have the nerve to be in court again, I'm biased. So I know a judge sitting on a bench hearing this stuff and seeing the graphics, he's got to be biased.

But if they were to take it on face value, law is beautiful, and that's what I've learned. Had I had the knowledge of law that I have now, I would not have become a criminal. I probably would have become a lawyer because it still satisfies that drive, and that instant gratification, and that sense of controlling something. And also, predicting the outcome like I do [with] my clients. . . . I used to think like, "Oh god, they go to school so long. They have to pass the bar." I believe I could pass the bar now. I really believe that because I apply myself. . . . I know now that law for real is how effectively you argue. That's it.

. . . One thing they do a lot, they say "pursuant to, pursuant to, pursuant to." You're the judge and I say "pursuant to Sections 777." I'm letting you know that I have gone through this book. And those cases they take more serious. If I don't put that in there and I say "pro se," they're just, "She's just an inmate.

She don't know what she's doing." So I make sure I say what they say. I use their language. I look at cases in the law books and I use what I see real attorneys use. I just straight out plagiarize their language. . . . If you don't use their language, they know you're not from their club. So I use their language "pursuant to" and some of the Latin. We have a *Black's Law Dictionary.* I look up the Latin, and I put it in there. Their little codes. I've learned how to put them in there with the computer, the little legal squiggly. I put that in there, and the term "defendant humbly prays." I use that because that shows humility rather than "defendant requests," "defendant demands." That doesn't get it. But if you say "humbly prays," or if I say "wherefore defendant respectfully requests," I've learned how to embellish it to where when this judge reads it, he'll feel good inside, you know [laughing].

. . . I have written things, and some things have been published. I've written what it was like to be a Muslim on 9/11 in a maximum state prison. That got published in a Muslim magazine. That got me a scholarship for a year through a Islamic university. But you had to maintain a C average, and I got a D on one paper 'cause I didn't have the resources to do a thorough job. So I lost that scholarship after two semesters. And I've written things in magazines like *VIBE*. . . . Will Smith, the actor, was criticizing his father, who had been a maintenance man when he was growing up, and he was saying how he used to go with his father to fix people's refrigerators, and there would be dead rats on the floor. So I got angry, and I wrote back. And I said, "You've blown up so much that now your father's beneath you, dah, dah, dah." Whatever I said, they liked it. They put that in there. And I've written to *Ebony,* mostly letters to the editor. And when the fanatical Muslims blew up a train, I wrote a piece to the [newspaper] and I called it "Islam: The Good, the Bad, and the Ugly." . . . I was saying the good of it. The bad of it is the media depicting all Muslims as those idiots were.

I wrote one piece that was published in a prison magazine, and it was a tribute to a friend of mine who is deceased now. She was an inmate, and she died of AIDS. But before she passed away, she educated all of us to her disease. And she started the first AIDS awareness program in [the prison], and she was very honest. This was at a time when we didn't know a lot about it, and a lot of people ostracized her, but I thought she was so courageous. . . . We watched her just waste away because her sentence was longer than her condition. . . . She was always telling me, "My cell count, if I can just get my cell count up. I gotta get my T cells up." . . . And she was like really rushing to get her program together 'cause she wanted something to last, and she was like, "[Solo], promise me that you'll write to the Red Cross, and promise me that you'll write to the Disease Center in Atlanta, and promise me," and all these promises. . . . There's a team of girls now who do come around and educate you about AIDS. And they do write to the Disease Center, and they do write to the American Red Cross, all the things I promised but didn't do. So I felt kind of guilty. So I wrote an article, and it's called "Cell Count." It starts out describing her and her vibrant personality and everything, and how her life ended up just being a count. 'Cause in prison we get counted, and it's in our cells. So I thought it was really ironic that we stand up for count, cell count, and then her life ended up just being nothing except a cell count. . . . I sent it to *Angola Speaks*. The men produce it in the prison in Louisiana. And one of the editors, he wrote me back, and he's been in solitary confinement for thirty years. . . . So I wrote him back, and we corresponded for about a year. And he made sure that it got published in its entirety.

. . . I'm thankful for [a reading group led by the unit manager] 'cause that keeps me healthy intellectually because that's all we deal with is the intellect.[18] It's not a group where you go and cry or get built up. It's just a group where you go, and you logically talk about something. He sets it out, and then we research, and we come back. And he allows us an opportunity to write short stories. He'll give us the vocabulary words that we have to learn, like one of the words we had was "nocturnal," which I did know what that meant. "Incident," I didn't know what that meant. Had to look it up. "Macrocosm," I didn't know what that meant. I had to look it up. And then you had to put it in a short story. . . . When I'm going to his room, I know that I'm going to have to be sharp, and I know that he expects me to bring my best. He won't accept papers with misspelled words or scratchy-outs. You know, if you're going to present it, present it right. And it should have a logical flow. . . . If he gives you an A, that means he was really impressed with it. And then you want to see an A on your paper. . . . Then he gives us these titles of books to read, and it's an assignment so you have to read it and then you have to give a summary on it. And then you have group discussions, and you have to articulate, and you have to explain yourself. So you stay sharp, you know. You don't get dull, for lack of a better word.

. . . In a lot of groups, you start digging in, and when you dig in, stuff comes out and you cry. So it's good to have a group where I know I'm not going to be dug into. He's not even trying to get there. He's only here [pointing to her head]. We don't talk about my childhood or my past or my crime or addictions or men or relationships or my self-esteem. None of that comes up. So I don't have to deal with it. All he's dealing with is my intellect. . . . Everybody in the room is here [pointing to her head] . . . and I'm not passing tissues, you know. And in some groups that happens. . . . Even in the law library I have started crying with people. Just sheer knowledge of what they're telling me sometimes just tears me up. And I end up crying and they're crying, too. Even when I go to my Islamic services, I cry at some of the things the imam will say about the prophet or the mercy of God and how he loves me so much. . . . In this group, the posture is totally different. Everybody's sitting there with a folder. They're sitting up erect. And he's at his desk. And we're like surrounding him, and he plays real soft jazz in the background. And he just throws stuff out there. He'll say, "What do you think about that?" And he'll wait a moment and he'll say, "You do have an opinion?" And we say, "Of course." He says, "Well then, what do you think about it?" . . . And before it's over everybody has said something, and you feel like, wow!

. . . I believe tears have their place. It's just I don't want to cry all the time 'cause it bogs me down. I can't see the end when I'm stuck in that emotion. And I couldn't proceed. It's like inertia. You cannot move, and I don't like that. But it's okay sometimes because it's a slowing down. Sometimes I hear spiritual music, and I'll slow down and I'll cry. I keep my family pictures [hidden] on purpose so that when I pull them out, I can be like, whoa. You know, I don't want to see them all the time . . . so I can bring them out and feel the whole emotion rather than pass them everyday and they become blurs. So yeah, those groups are good, you know, because a lot of pain gets out. But you have to be careful when you're exposing pain because we become vindictive here. And I'm okay with you today, but do something to me next week, and I'm gonna mention what happened to you in group, and I'm gonna hurt you with it.

. . . I want to be impacted when I read. Like for instance, the one book that he had us read [in the group], *Wake of The Wind*,[19] that book impacted me, and I was also able to carry something with me because . . . it wasn't just a slave story. It was a love story, and then it was a story of survival. . . . And the woman in the book, her name was Lifey, and she was biracial and she knew it because of her lighter complexion. The real wife didn't want her in the house because she knew that [her husband] was Lifey's father. . . . That story impacted me, and I was able to feel the hurt of the slave, but then I was also able to rejoice with Lifey when at the end [she and another former slave] had settled in Georgia. She had saved up enough money, and here's this man she loved. He couldn't read, he couldn't write, he couldn't do nothing, but he was a hard worker, and he was able to build them a home. . . . And in the end, you know, it was happy ever after type of thing. So I rejoiced with her, and then I was able to move forward knowing, wow, I can do it. Lifey did it.

I mean, I loved it so much I made a crossword puzzle about it. That's how much that impacted me.

... [For one assignment,] the group leader said, "Okay, I want you to write a poem about freedom," and everybody else was writing all this historical stuff and all that. I just sat down, and I just started thinking about myself. And I wrote this poem called "Freedom," and after I reread it to myself, then I went to the class and I had to read it out loud. You have to stand up and you have to present yourself. And he listened and everybody else listened. Then he asked them what they thought about it. So after I heard all their opinions of it, I really liked it a lot more. And now it's like my mantra. I love that poem. ... And when I had to read it outside at the poetry fest, I read it, and I just was feeling it, and I had put on a black—I was defiant that day; I wouldn't wear white—I had a black headpiece on, and I was standing out there in that hot sun, and I read it like this:

> The essence of the word freedom is a state free of restraints, liberated, independence, exempt from unpleasant or onerous conditions, free will, unrestricted access and the ability to pursue unalienable rights.
>
> I, [Solo], exemplify freedom in its totality of this description. From the covering of my splendidly natural hair, to my brown eyes which no longer endure the pain of blue and blackened eyes swollen from abuse, to my mouth unclosed and expressive, to my ears now open to receive instruction, advice, and acknowledgment, to my neck, elegant, loosed from shackles of ignorance, to my shoulders erect and bold, not bent from shame, to my heart filled with optimism and expectancy, to my stomach less flat yet more satisfying, to my broader hips, which still retain the rhythm of the drum beats, clear down to the very soles of my Black feet, calloused from all the years of walking towards freedom.
> I am Free!
>
> For me, freedom has been an *evolution,* not a *revolution.* See, my freedom was gained through years of self inflicted struggle, through increments of embraced ignorance, which was demonstrated in collective acts of pure foolishness. Freedom for me was elusive. I could not purchase it; consequently, I saw no way to ever own it. I could not believe in this reality because I had no faith. Freedom for me was always close like my baby sister and like my child. I had birthed it but I would not name it, consequently, I could not claim it. Remember, freedom for me was an evolution and not a revolution. For me, freedom crept in slowly on cat's paws, quietly and unassuming.

It happened like this. One day I opened my mouth and said exactly what I meant to say and I liked it. Then, I stood up refusing to dine on entrees of morbid lies and delicacies of hypocrisy and petite deception, and I liked it. I walked away from plentiful dependence to limited independence, and I liked it too! Freedom for me was an evolution and not a revolution.

There were no star-spangled banners, no rockets' red glare. Instead, it was dark and I was naked, just standing there. Standing for my faith, standing for my unalienable right to exist, standing for my children's children to have a voice and standing for my choices, which today define who I am.

Freedom for me was an evolution and not a revolution. Yes, I have run the longest race, but I have not reached the finish line. Indeed, I have developed, but only God can create. Surprisingly, I have harbored, but few have I actually helped to freedom and for this, I apologize.

Each day, I evolve the woman you perceive me to be, yet tomorrow, I will rise a new creature conceived in love and renewed hope. Freedom for me was an evolution and not a revolution. America, America, God shed his grace on thee, and crowned thy good with brotherhood from sea to shining sea! Not so, sista! Freedom for me meant shaking off the dust from the Mississippi slave cabins hot and stifling like the heavy air hanging over unpicked cotton fields to a cold and barren empty grave with the letter X as its marker.

Freedom for me crept in around my edges and around my corners, in places so unprotected that I became helpless to stop its advancement, hallelujah! Freedom landed on my shore, set up camp, declared victory, and pledged allegiance to my soul!

For me, freedom came and slept with me, it held me close during the midnight of my existence, and baptized me with my own tears until I was thoroughly, thoroughly cleansed of inferiority, low esteem, and self loathing.

Then I awoke in the beautiful morning of my middle-age, early before the sun came up, then I *stood* up a woman who knew her name, knew her purpose, knew her past was that and nothing more than that, knew her life was meaningful, worthy of saving from both prison and abuse, and knew that her spirit was a merciful and most precious gift from God Almighty.

Freedom for me was an evolution, not a revolution.

Then I ended it like that. I just love it. I was proud of that. And I wouldn't have gotten that had it not been for that class. . . . I've never written anything that has impacted me back, you know what I'm saying? And I like it. Because when I read it, see, I'm all of what I'm saying. I evolved into who I am. I didn't just like break out and be, like some sort of revolution. It was slow, and everything that's been done to me, I did it. I mean, nobody made me do anything. . . . I know now that I was just foolish. There was absolutely no reason for me to come back and forth to prison, but I chose the lifestyle that could only result in prison. . . . I chose to limit my potential. So it wasn't like my environment. It wasn't because of my poverty. It wasn't any of that, or lack of education. It was a conscious choice to live on the edge and do illegal activities. So there's no man to blame or drugs or any of that. None of that. It was just a conscious decision.

And I didn't know that freedom was this easy because had I known it, I would have had it a long time ago. I birthed it, but I couldn't claim it. I couldn't name it 'cause I didn't know what it was. I thought being with a man maybe was freedom, or having a lot of money was freedom. But really it's none of that. It's just knowing who I am, the woman that I am, and knowing my history. Not per se black history; just knowing my part of it. Where did I come from? And who am I? And just taking a real good look at me. And like, when I say it was no star-spangled banner, it was no big celebration. Didn't nobody say, "Oh [Solo], you've arrived." That's not how it was. I was just by myself in this prison cell. Naked, not literally, but void of all the material wrapping and trappings, you know.

. . . I have already missed my children's little voices. They're adult voices now, but they have kids. So I gotta make a stand now for them. Stand for something, and my choice to stay free. And you know, I'm an American, and I love that. I wouldn't trade it, but I know what I am in America, too. And I know on any given day depending on where I am, I won't be accepted. . . . I don't have the same freedom in America. 'Cause there's not no brotherhood from sea to shining sea, now. That's not it. 'Cause see, that Mississippi slave cabin still goes with me, and somebody without a name, like X, still goes with me. . . . But I can honestly say that my mother, I think she'd be proud of me because I didn't turn out a racist. I didn't turn out a bigot. . . . I understand that it's not just a person waking up hating me. That it's a lot of stuff going into that. . . . And I understand the fear that feeds that hate because I saw a lot of that stuff.

. . . When I say, "I evolve the woman you perceive me to be," they see me one way here, but really I'm different every day. I mean, they're very quick to tell me who I am here. . . . 'Cause they watch me, you know, and they tell me who I am or who they perceive me to be, at least. But what they don't know is that every day I wake up, I'm different. Some of what I was yesterday comes with me . . . but each day brings a new challenge.

. . . And I keep repeating the refrain "Freedom for me was an evolution and not a revolution" moreso for me to hear it. That where I've come so far, just remember girl, you didn't always have this. You have evolved and evolution is continuous. Revolutions come and go. . . . It wasn't like a violent change for me that would require me to always be on the ready. It's gradual. . . . Things change with me, and I don't see them. . . . So it's like an evolution. Things happen in your sleep, you know. . . . I repeat it for me, to know that I'm steadily evolving, and then I end it with "freedom crept in around my edges" 'cause I didn't see it coming [laughing]. I didn't see that, you know. It must have landed on my shore and just set up camp 'cause I didn't even know it. It must have got down and said, "Hey, I'm here to stay." I did not know it, and it must have slept with me and just held me close or something because I just didn't know it, and I know I cried a lot, but I didn't know that crying was cleansing me. . . . And then I woke up in my middle age. I'm not sad about that because I got up early enough before the sun came up, and I saw me first before the world saw me, and by the time you met me about eight or nine [o'clock], I was a middle-aged woman. And I'm okay with it. And now I know my purpose.

True Stories about Prison

"I HAVEN'T READ a book yet that wrote a true story about prison," says Denise in her reading narrative. Although no single story can capture the diversity of women prisoners' experiences, the women featured in *The Story Within Us* create a tapestry of important insights about women who are currently incarcerated in the United States. Read together, their individual narratives tell a different kind of story about women in prison.

In these true stories, incarcerated women urgently seek to make meaning from their experiences and to situate them within broader contexts. As they reflect on their simultaneous roles as women, daughters, mothers, victims, perpetrators, prisoners, readers, mentors, and friends, the interviewees illuminate their full human complexity, thereby challenging the reductive stories that our culture tends to tell about women who have experienced or inflicted harm. Women's narratives also draw attention to the ways in which our profound social problems—including gendered violence, addiction, mental illness, racism, and poverty—manifest themselves at the level of individual bodies, psyches, and relationships. In these true stories, "everybody [is] trying to get the next good book." Women draw on available reading materials as sources of inspiration and guidance for rescripting their lives: for reinterpreting their painful pasts in ways that may allow for growth and healing, and for charting new ways of being in the world. In these true stories, prisoners also diligently strive to maintain vibrant intellectual lives in resource-poor environments. With remarkable resourcefulness and openness to difference, they use the limited books at hand to deepen their understanding of others' experiences, cultures, and ideas. And in these true stories, incarcerated women eloquently critique the justice system, countering dominant narratives that allow us to forsake incarcerated members of our community and disavow the role that each of us plays in perpetuating the world's largest penal system.

The women featured in *The Story Within Us* thus tell a collective story that merits keen attention and compassionate response. I invite you, in these final pages, to reflect on the insights that emerge from the women's stories.

"Well, who takes care of you?"

"Well, who takes care of you?" is a question that Bobbie introduces when she is describing how she has been taking care of others since she was a very small child. Bobbie recounts that she struggled to answer the question when someone posed it to her, responding, "I don't know. I think I do. I'm not sure." The narratives featured in *The Story Within Us* have helped me to understand how this seemingly simple question can assume great complexity for many women in prison. As women reflect on their experiences as children and adults—trying to come to terms with relationships that are often layered and highly complex—they draw attention to myriad factors that have shaped their ability to care for their own and others' needs. Lending depth and texture to abstract concepts such as abuse, cycles of violence, victim, and perpetrator, the interviewees illuminate how experiences of sustaining and inflicting harm almost always go hand-in-hand. Furthermore, they model the difficult work—including forgiving oneself and others—involved in salvaging relationships marred by inadequacies in giving and receiving care. By thus highlighting women prisoners' full complexity as human beings, the featured narratives counter dehumanizing stories that allow us, as a society, to relinquish care for those who fill our nation's prisons.

On one level, "Well, who takes care of you?" speaks to the fact that many incarcerated women "skipped over childhood" because they had to play the role of parent when they were children. As several women's narratives reveal, intergenerational cycles of abuse, violence, addiction, and mental illness profoundly shaped their parents' ability to care for their own and their children's needs. The complexity of such parent/child relationships seems evident, for instance, in Olivia's layered description of her father as someone who at once shared and enabled her addictions, opened his door for her every time she was seeking refuge from abuse, and encouraged her by his example as an avid reader and public library patron. Such complexity likewise seems evident when Audrey says of her mother, "I think I respect her a little bit more than I love her, because . . . she raised all six of us by herself. And I seen her go through hell with my stepdaddy beating on her . . . and they went all over her when she was little." Like Audrey, whose painful feelings of abandonment and betrayal are tempered by respect, gratitude, and compassion for the terrorizing violence that her mother endured, many of the interviewees are struggling to reconcile competing emotions of anger, hurt, and compassion as they work to repair relationships with inadequate caregivers who received insufficient care themselves.

On another level, "Well, who takes care of you?" evokes the complicated relationships that many incarcerated women have with their own children. Women struggle with overwhelming feelings of guilt, shame, anxiety, and regret for their failures to meet their children's needs both prior to and during incarceration. As Bobbie laments in acknowledging that her daughter is now playing the role of parent just as Bobbie did as a child: "[T]he child shouldn't have to take care of her parents." Audrey captures the complex range of emotions that many incarcerated mothers feel when she emphasizes her debilitating regret that she "messed up [her children's] life," her joyful wonder at her children's loyalty and near-weekly visits, and her painful recognition that she cannot "freeze" time and must accept how her children have changed during her incarceration; her current challenge, Audrey explains, is "letting my children grow up in my mind." The question, "Well, who takes care of you?" assumes additional complexity in light of the fact that 1.7 million children have parents who are incarcerated (Brown 11). According to the 1997 Adoption and Safe Families Act, states must file a petition to terminate parental rights when a child has been in foster care for fifteen of the most recent twenty-two months. Women with longer prison sentences thus "face the continual threat of termination of their parental rights unless the children are placed with a spouse or relative" (Brown 11).[1] When children are permanently removed from their parents, they often drift through foster homes until adulthood (Brown 12), experiencing a lack of nurturing that can contribute to cycles of inadequate caregiving.

Women's fierce determination to interrupt such cycles—and to teach their children alternative ways to script their life stories—emerges as a powerful theme across their narratives. "My baby will not go through what I went through," Sissy insists. "I took all the abuse that we're gonna take," Denise tells her daughters and nieces. "The cycle stops with me," Audrey declares to her son-in-law. And determined to interrupt her family's legacy of untreated mental illness, Valhalla vows, "I will educate my children. I will watch my children. If I'm not sure what's going on, I will get them help."

"Well, who takes care of you?" also speaks to many women prisoners' efforts to address their ongoing needs for nurturing, because feeling like a parent at age five can leave one feeling like a needy child at age forty-five. Learning to care for themselves takes many forms in women's narratives. It includes learning to establish boundaries, to balance their own and others' needs, to face new challenges and develop newly discovered talents, and to accept help from others. Although the interviewees occasionally mention penal employees who have served as important "nurturers," they far more often discuss other prisoners as their mentors and helping hands. Supporting one another is not easy in prison; penal environments breed tension and a lack of trust, and women sometimes betray each other's confidences. Some women nonetheless manage to develop a sense of solidarity in recognizing their shared experiences. As Bobbie realized in hearing another prisoner speak about her experiences with molestation, addiction, and domestic violence, "It's a whole city of women just alike!" Within this city of women, prisoners serve as "mother-sisters" and "big sisters" for each other, offering words of wisdom, pushing one another to "stand up and be a woman," serving as models to emulate, and tenderly teaching each other "about life." And like Solo says of her Act Up program—that mentoring other women helps her to realize that she merits respect even in her "tarnished" state—supporting each other enables some women to come full circle in learning to care for themselves.

"You need a book to come at you like your best friend"

Within the "city of women," reading also serves as a crucial means for prisoners to give and receive care. Countering the erasure and isolation that imprisonment fosters, women sometimes read to one another as a form of nurturance, and they forge and maintain connections with people on both sides of the prison fence by sharing and discussing books. At the same time, women prisoners often gain guidance and support from the act of reading itself. Using books as "equipment for living" (Burke 10)—as sources of practical knowledge for addressing the challenges they face—women turn to the characters and people featured in books as mentors, guides, quasi-parental figures, and friends. Through complex processes of identifying with such personae, prisoners make meaning from their experiences, learn to recognize and reckon with suppressed emotions, gain wisdom and inspiration, and discover how to become authors of their own lives. Like Solo, who "transition[s] from who I am to being what I want to be" by performing "a new script," these women draw on available reading materials as resources for reframing their pasts and creating alternative storylines for their futures.

Although violence and mental illness tend to be passed down through generations, the work of healing ultimately defies the laws of inheritance; it must be performed on an individual basis. Reading others' stories offers women companionship and assistance for performing this lonely, difficult labor. As Valhalla explains in discussing her strong sense of connection with the protagonist of Wally Lamb's *She's Come Undone,* "Some of the books I've read are like my friends. There's characters I've met who I keep with me inside of me." Denise's discussion of self-help books about domestic violence offers another striking illustration of women's reliance on books as helpful companions. "When you've been in [an abusive relationship] for ten or fifteen years," Denise argues, "you need a book to come at you like your best friend. You need a book that come at you strong like you care, a book really to snatch you out of it." The slippage between "a book" and "you care"—rather than "a book that comes at you strong like *it* cares"—suggests the extent to which Denise personifies books as mentors and sources of support.

Reading plays an especially important role in many incarcerated women's efforts to understand, and to counter, the cycles of violence and silence that have shaped their lives. With uncanny repetition, the interviewees underscore myriad forces that contribute to ongoing silences about abuse, including self-silencing and the prevailing view that what happens in the family is "nobody's business outside of the house." Prisoners also emphasize how the penal system serves as a silencing force by failing to provide opportunities for women to discuss their histories. "The first thing they ask you," Olivia notes, "is, 'Do you want to take some meds?'" The interviewees counter these silencing forces by reading a range of books that address issues of incest and abuse, from V. C. Andrews's lurid teen fiction to Joyce Meyer's Christian self-help books. For many women, reading such books entails difficult cognitive and emotional labor. Like Olivia, who used to feel totally overwhelmed from reading self-help books, women must learn to "pace" themselves in reading emotionally challenging material.

As the foregoing examples illustrate, imprisoned women draw on a surprising variety of fictional and nonfictional genres in their efforts to come to terms with their pasts and rescript their futures. However, penal officials fail to recognize this fact in determining library and censorship policies. "The people who decide what we can and cannot get tends to be a white man," Valhalla astutely observes in critiquing her prison's ban on urban fiction.[2] "I'm sure it's not a bunch of urban project women with a bunch of kids. You know, I'm sure it's highly educated men that went to a good college and had a good life, and they don't understand. That book's ridiculous to them, and it's disgusting." Although some prisoners support censorship of urban fiction on the grounds that it glamorizes crime and "does black life injustice," women such as Bobbie relish and learn from urban books' focus on "reality," including problems such as poverty and violence against women. Some incarcerated women also make resourceful and important uses of true crime books, another genre that is often banned in prisons. Melissa, for instance, suggests that her intense sense of identification with women featured in true crime books enables her to increase her emotional literacy: her ability to recognize and process difficult feelings, such as anger and pain, rather than attempting to manage them by cutting herself or getting high.

Like so many women in prison, the interviewees also find inspiring models of change in a wide range of genres. While Melissa looks to the women featured in true crime books, Jacqueline feels inspired to "get it together" and "take advantage of every minute" by reading biographies and autobiographies featuring Booker T. Washington, Malcolm X, Natalie Cole, and Whitney Houston, as well as Terry McMillan's fictional portraits of black women. Deven cultivates her burgeoning belief that "people do change" by reading *Chicken Soup for the Prisoner's Soul,* and she turns to "spiritual books" for practical suggestions about altering her own habits and behaviors.

Women prisoners' ability to find useful knowledge in unlikely reading materials further testifies to their resourcefulness and creativity. As we have seen, both Olivia and Mildred feel unable "to understand the law books," so they seek practical legal knowledge from John Grisham's legal thrillers. Mildred explains that learning "how to talk to the judge and the prosecutor" is crucial because she does not "want to see [her] child in prison." Toni Morrison's fiction enables Denise to reflect on a host of issues related to growing up in a rural, southern town: poverty, exclusionary class pretensions, the power of communal belonging, and the intense shame and pain of communal judgment. And in a particularly moving example, Sissy suggests that Sidney Sheldon's novels have served as her surrogate parents and gentle lovers, teaching her about physical tenderness and intimacy, and teaching her how to love herself.

Women's engagements with these varied materials also highlight their status as active, critical readers who sift and sort through available materials, sometimes pushing back against dominant narratives and complicating or supplementing them to better suit their needs. For instance, insisting that the author was not "writing that book right," Audrey fills in what she believes is missing from the true crime account of Aileen Wuornos's experiences with abuse and violence. Deven similarly draws on her own experiences in questioning Christian self-help books' claim that men should be "head of the house" and "women should be submissive." "I like the fact that [self-help] books make you think," Deven explains, "because this is a very dormant place, and you can just lay here, you know, with the life sucked out of you, or you can seek life. And today I'm seeking life and what it has to offer and how I can make the best of it."

"If you can't relate to it, then read about it"

Deven's efforts to counter the numbing, dormant atmosphere of the prison resonate with many prisoners' valiant efforts to maintain a life of the mind in settings that radically circumscribe that possibility. As numerous examples from women's narratives illustrate—the scholarship that Solo lost because she "didn't have the resources" to write satisfactory papers, the ban on books about Wicca, the space limitations that require Sissy to write about her experiences in the most concise manner possible—penal officials routinely limit prisoners' opportunities for intellectual engagement. A devastating instance of this fact occurred during my research. Upon Solo's recommendation, I requested permission to interview the unit manager who started the reading group that Solo credits with keeping her "healthy intellectually." The penal administration was not aware of the group until I brought it their attention, and much to my chagrin, they promptly shut it down because it was not operating under official approval. Given such limitations, the fact that some prisoners maintain vibrant intellectual lives testifies to their ingenuity and determination to make a way out of no way.

Indeed, although they may not fit the presumed profile of an intellectual, the women featured in this collection perform crucial intellectual work through their engagements with available reading materials. Their intellectual curiosity takes many forms, including interests in African American history, famous political figures, the Holocaust, women's history, and world religions. In an environment that is sorely lacking in sensory delight, Sissy takes particular pleasure in reading art books that allow her to trace "how art has changed" over the centuries. Given her desire to "experience new and different things," Deven appreciates Toni Morrison's *The Bluest Eye* for introducing her to "another era" and "another class of people" about whom she had little knowledge. Solo is both actively investigating the precepts of Islam and discovering the beauty and limitations of the law. "Had I had the knowledge of law that I have now," she astutely observes, "I would not have become a criminal. I probably would have become a lawyer because it still satisfies that drive, and that instant gratification, and that sense of controlling something." Denise brings her active imagination to bear on everything that she reads, creating her own story for things—such as the NASDAQ—that she does not understand. She finds it especially satisfying, Denise explains, to read a book "that outsmarts me," that yields new insights upon rereading, and that "change[s] something about the way I view tomorrow."

Many incarcerated women also strive, through reading, to keep up with rapid social change in the outside world and to maintain a sense of human interconnectedness. Such efforts are crucial for women who may spend the rest of their lives in prison. "I've grown up basically in prison," explains Sissy. "And it has impacted my life a lot because there's things that I don't know about society . . . 'cause I haven't lived out there in twenty-seven years." Keeping up with "the politics, radios, papers, all that's in the news" is essential, Sissy argues, because "even though I'm in prison, the different things that's happening out there still affects me."

Although identifying with others is a key feature of many prisoners' reading practices, reading also enables women to engage with difference and to develop understanding and empathy for those whose perspectives differ from their own. Denise highlights this important intellectual work in describing her desire to reread Dorothy Allison's *Bastard out of Carolina* from the perspectives of the mother and stepfather rather than of the abused daughter. "I know a lot of people in here that are child abusers, and I got this wall against child abusers," Denise explains. "I want to read this book [again] to look at the person that's doing the abuse so I can better understand where they're at in their head. And that way . . . I won't be so judgmental towards the next woman who lets a man beat her kids or who let her boyfriend molest her children." Sissy describes her motivations for reading in similar terms: "It teaches me about people, their culture, their way of thinking, their way of doing things. And that keeps you from being prejudiced." Foregrounding the role that reading plays in her openness to difference, Sissy continues, "Whether you're in jail . . . or whether you're out in the world's society, we still have a responsibility to treat each other as human beings. And to learn and understand you have to put yourself out there. And some people are afraid. . . . And because they're afraid, they need to read. To me, if you can't relate to it, then read about it. And if you still can't relate to it, at least . . . you can't say I never tried to understand." Offering powerful insights about tolerance and interconnectedness, Sissy suggests that "the problems we have now" stem from our refusal to "try to understand" others.

"Don't count me out"

Our "responsibility to treat each other as human beings" assumes added significance in light of current penal policy and prevailing attitudes about incarcerated people. Deven draws attention to the social erasure and dehumanization of prisoners when she says, "Have you ever watched *Star Trek,* where they have like societies within a society? There's a big community out around us, and it's like we don't even exist. . . . I really think other people need to realize that just because we are in prison, we are still human beings. We are not second-class citizens." Yet in myriad ways—such as restricting prisoners' access to reading materials, increasing the difficulty of visiting or calling prisoners, and placing prisoners in "maximum isolation units" for indefinite periods that "can last for decades" (Dayan)[3]—current penal policy is predicated on rupturing social ties between incarcerated and nonincarcerated people. In Mildred's words, "People on the outside don't think of us as society at all. They think of us as these low-down humans." And as Solo underscores in describing solitary confinement—"You're in a grave and you're trying to live" but "nobody hears you when you call out, 'Hey, I'm alive!'"—U.S. penal practice tends to operate on an "out of sight, out of mind" basis. Rather than addressing the profound social problems that pave the path to prison, we "disappear" the human evidence of our social failures behind prison walls.

The women featured in this collection forestall such erasure, however, insisting—in Sissy's words—that "life goes on" even if "you're locked up," and claiming their places as integral members of our community. "Don't count me out," says Jacqueline in asserting her determination to chart a new path: "[N]o matter how bad it looks, don't count me out because as long as I'm breathing, I'm not gonna stop fighting." Like Jacqueline, and like many incarcerated women, the interviewees are engaged in ongoing efforts to "make a life" as healthy citizens, whether or not they will be released from prison. "Don't count me out" is a sentiment that all of the women share.

Women's narratives nonetheless highlight the diversity and uniqueness of their aspirations and their differing senses of their own development. Pursuing further education is a priority for Mildred and Olivia. "Sharpening [her] mind" feels important to Olivia because she "lost a lot of that sharpness" from using drugs. Melissa, Valhalla, and Deven emphasize their ongoing processes of self-discovery. Melissa remains "full of anger" yet feels hopeful that efforts to "rebuild" her will succeed. Valhalla explains, "I'm trying to look deeply into my soul 'cause I don't know who I am," while Deven is learning to be more "open-minded" and getting in touch with her "inner self." Jacqueline and Denise express a similar sense of urgency in conveying their desire to change, their uncertainty about how to do so, and their fear that "it's too late." Declaring, "I can't waste any more time," Jacqueline emphasizes her determination to forgive herself, "let the past go," and "move forward." Denise views her post-shoplifting future as "a blank white wall" that she can paint however she chooses. "I don't know how far I can go now," she acknowledges. "But I gotta see. I gotta try."

The sense of excitement and urgency in these women's narratives contrasts with the sense of calm—even peace—that other interviewees' narratives convey. Explaining that she has "been self-helped enough," Bobbie's current aspiration is simply to enjoy "being alive, 'cause I consider myself really blessed." Audrey wants to let her children "grow up in [her] mind" and enable her mother to "sit down and not do nothing." Sissy's many years of rigorous self-reflection seem evident when she says, "I know me today. And I know which way I'm going, and I know how to get there." In the spirit of living life "to the best of our ability," Sissy's daily goal is to "know that I made a positive impact in some way for somebody." Although Solo is still struggling to let "the little kid" inside of her heal, freedom has "crept in around [her] edges," and she continues to evolve as a woman who knows "her name" and "her purpose," knows her past is "nothing more than that," and knows that her life is "meaningful, worthy of saving from both prison and abuse."

The fact that these women are making meaning from their experiences and forging new paths is a testament to their creativity, resilience, and determination; it is *not* a testament to the rehabilitative power of the prison. As the interviewees suggest, and as scholars involved in the Critical Resistance movement and the International Conference on Penal Abolition corroborate, imprisoning people often makes them more likely to commit additional crimes. Although counseling or an educational program may cause "positive life change" for some prisoners, incarceration entails alienation from society, dehumanizing and infantilizing conditions, abuse and humiliation by other prisoners and staff, and significant barriers to work, housing, and citizenship upon release (Morris 52).

Furthermore, if rehabilitation entails offering a prisoner "tools and positive resources so she or he can and will choose honest paths" (Morris 26), U.S. penal systems provide grossly inadequate rehabilitative services. As Valhalla puts it, "Most women here, something's wrong with them: depression, anxiety, violent tendencies, anger, abuse. But they don't get help." In Jacqueline's terms, "You're breaking us down while we're in these places.

That's not rehabilitation. . . . I tell myself on a daily basis, 'You're salvageable. You're worth being saved.' . . . I have to do that myself 'cause nobody in here is telling me that." Bobbie and Melissa emphasize the futility of incarcerating people for drug use rather than offering them treatment. Referring to a woman who is serving her fourth sentence for drug possession, Melissa asks, "What's gonna help her this time that didn't help her the first time, but now you've given her eight years? . . . She's gonna turn out to be this angry person . . . and ain't no telling what the hell she's gonna do when she get out! So I mean, where is there any justice at in the system?" Repeating the refrain, "Where are you getting rehabilitated?" Melissa then argues that women who enter prison as teenagers merely learn to be "better criminal[s]" because prisons offer them no meaningful programs, and "half of the time you have to fight to get into school." And as Solo argues, eliminating federal Pell grants for prisoners greatly increases the likelihood that they will get involved with drugs again because "you won't let [them] go to school." In fact, the Higher Education Act of 2006 states that anyone convicted of a drug offense while receiving federal financial aid is ineligible to receive further aid for prescribed time periods, and subsequent offenses can lead to a lifetime ban on financial aid (Levi and Waldman 252; Brown 15–16). Moreover, the Personal Responsibility and Work Opportunity Reconciliation Act renders drug offenders permanently ineligible for federal food stamps or Temporary Assistance for Needy Families,[4] and public housing agencies can legally evict or refuse to house people with drug offenses (Levi and Waldman 253). "In ten years, they're going to regret these decisions," Solo contends. "You just want to beat me, beat me, beat me, punish me, punish me, punish me. And then expect me to come out of prison reformed. At some point I'm just going to become what you expect me to. I'm gonna become that monster."

Perhaps the most damaging aspect of the penal system is that it "underwrites the social problems that it purports to solve" by siphoning off resources that should be used to address the profound social problems that create a pipeline to prisons (Davis and Dent 1238). Indeed, imprisonment has become our primary means of managing social problems in the United States. Deven draws attention to this fact when she observes, "We're paying $30,000 a year to house an inmate and only $10,000 for a child in our public school system." If we offered better educational opportunities, Deven suggests, fewer people would end up in prison because they would be "able to support their family." Instead, we pay $30,000 a year "to have some overpriced babysitter" treat prisoners like "a piece of garbage, but yet we're not gonna give our kids a chance."

Given these fundamental flaws in our penal system and the deep-rooted social problems that fuel crime, it may seem counterproductive to emphasize women prisoners' efforts to transform themselves through reading and self-education. Focusing on women's individual processes of healing risks occluding our pressing need to heal the social body: to address the social and structural problems that become manifest at the level of individual lives. However, because autobiographical narratives are also "stories about our shared social world" (Peck 153), prisoners' efforts to restory their lives illuminate our collective need to "renarrativize society" (Gordon 61), to imagine and create a world in which social justice, rather than imprisonment, will serve as the foundation of our social health. In offering *The Story Within Us*, I hope to perform what Angela Davis calls a "balancing act" of "passionately attending to the needs of prisoners" while at the same time "question[ing] the place of the prison in our future" (103).

The women featured in the collection generate important insights for furthering this two-pronged goal. Bobbie highlights the importance of initiatives that help to break down barriers between inside and outside,[5] such as prisoners' and college students' collaborative efforts to increase awareness that felons are not "leper people" but rather "normal people" who "made a mistake" and "got caught." Drawing attention to the economic underpinnings of many women's involvement in crime, Mildred advocates making health care and education more accessible and affordable. Solo recommends providing reading materials that will help ex-prisoners to find willing employers, overcome social stigma through effective communication, and meet the practical challenges that freedom presents. More broadly, Solo argues that all human beings need "to be nurtured . . . psychologically, emotionally, physically, spiritually" from a very young age because it is difficult to nurture those who have suffered "so much damage" and "become extremely hardened." Melissa plans to open a facility called "The Last Chance," which would offer "anybody twenty-five and under" a final opportunity to avoid prison. Her hopeful vision of a facility that includes living quarters, "all the schools they're gonna need," and "a very big variety of jobs" resonates with the assertion—and sometimes plea—that emerges across prisoners' narratives: "Don't count me out."

While I believe that our penal system ultimately damages prisoners and the wider society, I believe that "passionately attending to the needs of prisoners" also entails providing them with far greater access to a broad range of reading materials and educational opportunities. Kevin Warner, head of the

Prison Education Service in Ireland, argues that imprisoned people should "have the right to explore their needs and interests, set their own goals and decide how they wish to learn," and have opportunities "to reflect on their situation, explore new possibilities and initiate change" (176). According to Warner, "deficit models" of penal education, which focus on correcting "what is deemed to be wrong" with prisoners, depict lawbreakers "one-dimensionally, only as offenders," thereby occluding "[o]ther aspects of their lives and personalities, their complexities, their problems and their qualities (aspects of the whole person, in other words)" (180). Expanding incarcerated people's opportunities for reading and education will not diminish the economic and political centrality of prisons, decriminalize drug use, or eliminate violence against women. Furthermore, reading does not play a uniformly educative or beneficial role for all incarcerated readers. Nonetheless, at a time when prisoners are rarely regarded as complex human beings capable of deep thought, growth, and change, I believe that it is crucial to recognize how some women in prison use reading as a means to minimize "the detrimental effects of imprisonment" (Warner 175), redress their educational disadvantages, engage in self-reflection and self-creation, and maintain a sense of connection with their fellow citizens on both sides of the prison fence.[6]

Indeed, women prisoners' stories do not end with incarceration. Despite their erasure in popular and scholarly accounts, and despite the dehumanizing policies that restrict their intellectual lives, imprisoned women find myriad ways to claim their humanity and practice freedom in the midst of "a death-generating institution" (Rodríguez 211). As you close the pages of this collection, I invite you to reflect on the ways in which women's true stories may have changed you or inspired you to participate in rescripting our collective story. For each of us plays a role in perpetuating the penal system, and each of us can play a role in changing the structures, policies, and institutions that keep so many members of our community in prison. As Sissy reminds us, "Whether you're in jail . . . or whether you're out in the world's society, we still have a responsibility to treat each other as human beings," and "as human beings, we're affected by everything each other does."

APPENDIX

Study-Related Materials

Pseudonym	Racial Self-Identification	Age	Education Level
Mildred	African American	42	12th grade, some college
Sissy	African American	46	12th grade
Olivia	Caucasian	27	11th grade
Denise	black	46	12th grade
Bobbie	black	42	12th grade, medical assistants' school
Melissa	American Indian	27	10th grade
Valhalla	Caucasian	29	12th grade
Jacqueline	black	41	12th grade
Audrey	black	43	junior high school
Deven	white	36	12th grade
Solo	African American	56	associate's degree

RESEARCH SETTINGS

The North Carolina Correctional Institution for Women (NCCIW) is located in a rural setting in Raleigh, North Carolina. The facility houses women prisoners of all custody levels and control statuses, from minimum security to death row. When I was conducting my research, NCCIW housed approximately 1,200 women, and as of 2007, it housed 1,300 women.

The Northeast Pre-Release Center (NEPRC) is a minimum- to medium-security prison located in an urban setting in Cleveland, Ohio. The facility houses women who have been refused parole but have fewer than five years left to serve. The majority of women have been convicted of crimes such as drug selling, drug use, and theft, and 85 percent are from Cleveland. As of January 2008, NEPRC housed 579 women, of whom roughly one-half are white and one-half are black. The prison is consistently filled beyond capacity, reflecting the fact that Ohio has one of the fastest growing incarceration rates in the United States (Sabol, Couture, and Harrison 14).

STUDY ADVERTISEMENT

Doing Time, Reading Crime
Cultures of Reading in Women's Prisons

- Do you like to read?
- Would you like to be part of a book discussion group?
- Would you like to talk about women, crime, punishment, or healing?

If you answered "yes" to *any* of these questions, you may want to participate in this study.

I'm a professor at the University of Michigan, and I'm conducting research about:

- books that are popular in prison
- the role that reading plays in women prisoners' lives
- prisoners' ideas about crime, punishment, and healing

Volunteering for this study will involve:

- participating in three tape-recorded, individual interviews
    - one interview will focus on your life experiences
    - two interviews will focus on your reading practices
- reading between four and six books that we'll select for the group discussions
- participating in four to six group discussions about those books
- discussing issues relating to women, crime, punishment, and healing

If you choose to participate in this study, your privacy will be protected.

To hear more, please attend the meeting on:
Day, Date
Time
Location

GUIDING QUESTIONS FOR INDIVIDUAL INTERVIEW #1 (LIFE HISTORY/NARRATIVE)

1. Could you please tell me your age? Race? Marital status? Education level?
2. Can you tell me a little bit about where you were born and the people who raised you?
3. What was family life like for you?
4. What was school like for you?
5. What are some of the joys that you've had in your life?
6. What relationships have been important in your life?
7. Have you helped to raise any children and/or had children of your own?
8. Has violence been a part of your life in any way?
9. Have drugs or alcohol been a part of your life?
10. What was happening in your life around the time that you came to prison?
11. What has it been like for you to be in prison?
12. From your experiences, why do you think that women end up in prison?
13. Do you have any ideas about what society should do to keep more women from coming to prison?
14. What's next for you?
15. Are there other parts of your life story that you would like to share?

GUIDING QUESTIONS FOR INDIVIDUAL INTERVIEW #2 (GENERAL READING PRACTICES)

1. How would you describe yourself as a reader?
2. What sorts of books do you like to read?
3. How do you decide which books to read?
4. Where do you get the books that you read?
5. How often, and when, do you read?
6. What is your favorite setting for reading?
7. What role, if any, did reading play in your life before you came to prison?
8. What role does reading play in your life now that you're in prison?
9. What role, if any, does the prison library play in your life?

10. Why do you read? What do you get out of reading?
11. What's your favorite thing about reading?
12. Do you ever like to read books that make you think about your own life?
13. Do you ever like to read books as a form of escape from the "real world"?
14. Do you ever talk with friends or family about what you're reading or have read?
15. Have you read anything lately that you've really liked or disliked?
16. Does it matter to you whether or not you feel like you've learned something from reading a book?
17. What kinds of things, if any, do you like to learn from reading books?
18. Do you have a favorite type of book? If so, what do you like about that kind of book?
19. Do you have a favorite book and/or author? If so, what do you like about that book or author?
20. If you could have greater access to any type of book or to particular books, what would you most like to read?
21. Has any book ever made a big impression on you, changed your life in some way, or changed the way you think about yourself or the world?
22. Do you ever read legal materials now that you're in prison?
23. What else would you like to tell me about the role that books and reading play in your life?

INDIVIDUAL INTERVIEW #3 (SPECIFIC READING PRACTICES)

The trajectory of this interview was determined by the particular reading practices of each participant. I asked each participant to come ready to discuss one or two books that she has read, and I allowed her to guide the conversation. My aim in leaving this interview open-ended was to allow participants, as much as possible, to frame their experiences of reading in their own terms.

ORGANIZATIONS THAT GATHER BOOKS FOR PRISONERS: A REPRESENTATIVE SAMPLE

The Appalachian Prison Book Project
P.O. Box 601
Morgantown, WV 26506
aprisonbookproject.wordpress.com

Asheville Prison Books Program
67 N. Lexington Ave.
Asheville, NC 28801
www.main.nc.us/prisonbooks/who.html

Book 'Em
The Thomas Merton Center
5129 Penn Ave.
Pittsburgh, PA 15224
www.thomasmertoncenter.org/projects/prisoner-rights/
bookem/index.html

Books Through Bars
4722 Baltimore Ave.
Philadelphia, PA 19143
(215) 727–8170
www.booksthroughbars.org

Books Through Bars—Ithaca
c/o Autumn Leaves Bookstore
115 The Commons, 2nd Floor
Ithaca, NY 14850
(607) 645–0250

Books Through Bars—NYC
c/o Bluestockings Bookstore
172 Allen St.
New York, NY 10002
(212) 254–3697, ext. 322
www.abcnorio.org/affiliated/btb.html

Books to Prisoners
c/o Left Bank Books
92 Pike St., Box A
Seattle, WA 98101
www.bookstoprisoners.net

Chicago Books to Women in Prison
c/o Beyondmedia Education
4001 N. Ravenswood Ave. #204C
Chicago, IL 60613
www.chicagobwp.org

Cleveland Books to Prisoners
4241 Lorain Ave.
Cleveland, OH 44012
clevelandbooks2prisoners@hotmail.com

The DC Books to Prisons Project
Quixote Center
P.O. Box 5206
Hyattsville, MD 20782
www.quixote.org/ej/bookstoprisons/

Gainesville Books for Prisoners
P.O. Box 12164
Gainesville, FL 32604
www.civicmediacenter.org/links/2003/11/01/13.29.05.htm

Inside Books Project
c/o 12th St. Books
827 West 12th Street
Austin, TX 78701
www.insidebooksproject.com

Internationalist Prison Books Collective
405 West Franklin St.
Chapel Hill, NC 27514
www.prisonbooks.info

Midwest Books to Prisoners
c/o Quimby's Bookstore
1321 North Milwaukee Ave. pmb #460
Chicago, IL 60622
mwbtp@riseup.net

The Midwest Pages to Prisoners Project
c/o Boxcar Books and Community Center, Inc.
118 S. Rogers, Suite #2
Bloomington, IN 47404
www.pagestoprisoners.org/

Oregon Books to Prisoners
1112 NE Morton St.
Portland, OR 97211
www.bookstooregonprisoners.org

Prison Book Program
c/o Lucy Parsons Bookstore
1306 Hancock Street, Suite 100
Quincy, MA 02169
(617) 423-3298
info@prisonbookprogram.org

Prison Book Project
c/o Food for Thought Books
P.O. Box 396
Amherst, MA 01004
prisonbookproject@riseup.net

The Prison Library Project
915 W. Foothill Blvd., pmb #128
Claremont, CA 91711
www.inmate.com/prislibr.htm

Women's Prison Book Project
c/o Boneshaker Books
2002 23rd Ave. South
Minneapolis, MN 55404
www.wpbp.org

Notes

Introduction

1. Although prisoners received less than 1 percent of yearly Pell Grant funds, these merit-based grants greatly increased the availability of higher education in prisons.

2. I conducted one round of research in North Carolina, from April through July 2001; two rounds of research in Ohio, from September 2006 through July 2007; and one round of research in Pennsylvania, from July through December 2007. I solicited participants for my study by posting an advertisement in each prison's dormitories, common areas, educational area, and library (see appendix). At each facility, I held a meeting for all interested participants in which I explained the aims and methods of my study, and women who decided to participate signed a consent form at the conclusion of the meeting.

3. I include women's racial self-identifications to signal the importance of race, but I want to caution readers not to assume that a woman's racial self-identification provides an easy key to understanding the totality of her experiences.

4. Although I did not actively solicit such information, several women openly discussed their offenses.

5. Current statistical information about the average education level of incarcerated women is scarce. The 2006 Educational Testing Service Policy Report, *Locked Up and Locked Out: An Educational Perspective on the U.S. Prison Population,* focuses exclusively on men. A 2007 publication, *Literacy Behind Bars: Results from the 2003 National Assessment of Adult Literacy Prison Survey,* indicates that incarcerated women have lower prose, document, and quantitative literacy levels than women living in households (Greenberg, Dunleavy, and Kutner, *Literacy Behind Bars,* 38).

6. See Paula Johnson, *Inner Lives: Voices of African American Women in Prison,* 45–48. Between 1997 and 2006, women's arrests for drug abuse violations rose by 29.9 percent, while men's arrests for the same type of crimes rose by 15.7 percent (Institute on Women and Criminal Justice, http://www.wpaonline.org/institute/index.htm).

7. See, for instance, the work of Geneva Brown, Paula C. Johnson, Beth Richie, Kimberlé Williams Crenshaw, Angela Davis, Joy James, Avery Gordon, Cassandra Shaylor, Ellen Berry, Karlene Faith, Joanne Belknap, Juanita Diaz-Cotto, Luana Ross, Adrien Wing, Nancy Kurshan, Linda Whitehorn, and Marilyn Buck. Organizations such as Justice Now, the National Network for Women in Prison, and Incite! Women of Color against Violence have also generated awareness of issues affecting imprisoned women of color.

8. Since 2000, the percentage of white women among sentenced female prisoners has increased from 40 percent to 48 percent, while the percentage of black women has declined from 38 percent to 28 percent. Vis-à-vis white women, the rate of incarceration for both black and Latina women has also declined. In 2000, black women were 5.3 times more likely to be incarcerated than white women, and Latinas were 2.4 times more likely. These groups are now, respectively, 3.1 and 1.7 times more likely to be incarcerated than white women (Sabol, Couture, and Harrison, "Prisoners in 2006," 8).

9. See Jacobi, "Slipping Pages" and "Writing Workshops." Through her "Woman is the Word" program, Michele Tarter and a few undergraduates from the College of New Jersey offer a memoir-writing workshop in a women's prison. At the conclusion of the workshop, the undergraduates create a typed and bound copy of each incarcerated woman's memoir and present the books to the women as graduation presents.

10. Brandt, *Literacy*, 11; Dingwall, qtd. in Fontana and Frey, "The Interview," 664.

11. For further discussion of this topic, see Benwell and Allington, "Reading the Reading Experience."

12. Of women involved in my overall study, 89.4 percent reported sustaining physical or emotional abuse, sexual abuse, or rape, and many witnessed significant violence in their childhood homes.

13. The International Conference on Penal Abolition, founded in 1983 by the Quaker Committee on Jails and Justice, seeks to promote alternatives to incarceration. Critical Resistance was formed in 1997 by U.S. scholars and activists interested in challenging the growth and centrality of the prison-industrial complex. The Institute on Women and Criminal Justice, founded by the Women's Prison Association in 2004, is a U.S. think tank that focuses on reducing our reliance on prisons and investing more in our communities.

14. Prisoners whose highest level of educational achievement is a GED scored ten points higher on the prose literacy scale than nonincarcerated people with an equivalent education (73). The prose literacy scale measures one's ability to search, comprehend, and use information from materials such as editorials, news stories, brochures, and instructional materials. Almost one-third of incarcerated people, versus only one-fifth of nonincarcerated people in this pool, indicate that they watch television one hour or less a day (83).

15. Kerman often adopts an "anthropological distance" (Grose) that lends her account the feel of a short-term excursion into a foreign land. She emphasizes

her exceptional status—in her husband's words—as "a pretty, blond Smith grad who looks as if she descended from Mayflower stock: the last girl you'd expect to end up behind bars" (L. Smith), and most media coverage of the book adopts a corresponding tone of "What was a nice girl like you doing in a place like that?" In the meantime, the experiences of most women prisoners—who are disproportionately women of color, who come from less-privileged class and educational backgrounds, and who often serve sentences far longer than thirteen months— rarely count as news. In the words of Brenda V. Smith, director of the Program on Gender, Crime, Sex and Community at American University, "Ms. Kerman's imprisonment gets a book deal, while the majority of women are 'booked' and forgotten" (B. Smith).

16. Some members of groups that promote reading in prison—including the Changing Lives Through Literature program, The Reader Organization, and various Writer-In-Residence programs—argue that only literary texts, not "light stuff," can foster prisoners' growth and change.

17. Protecting this woman's anonymity seems important in this context.

18. Reflecting on strictures against bodily contact in penal contexts, prisoner Dan Pens writes, "Touch is life. It is vitality. It is the music of the skin. . . . To be deprived of touch can wreak devastation on the psyche. To touch is to be human" (151).

Chapter 1. Mildred

1. Mildred's prison is the most permissive in terms of library visits; the other prisons featured in this book limit women's library visits and require them to schedule visits one week in advance.

2. Some women are enrolled in therapeutic groups that involve educational or motivational activities.

3. John Grisham, *The Pelican Brief* (1992); *The Summons* (2002); *Bleachers* (2003); *The Runaway Jury* (1996); *The King of Torts* (2003).

4. Women use the phrase "Daily Breads" to reference a variety of devotional materials distributed by Christian publishers.

5. Driving Under the Influence of alcohol.

6. Terry McMillan, *Waiting to Exhale* (1992); *How Stella Got Her Groove Back* (1996).

7. John Grisham, *A Painted House* (2001); *The Street Lawyer* (1998).

Chapter 2. Sissy

1. A "kite" is a written request that prisoners send to prison administrators.

2. Percy R. Welsing, *Prayer and Fasting* (2005).

3. Sidney Sheldon, *If Tomorrow Comes* (1985).

4. Sidney Sheldon, *Master of the Game* (1982).

5. Sissy seems to be referencing Harold Robbins's *79 Park Ave. S.* (1955).

6. Prison libraries or educational programs sometimes sponsor activities related to Black History Month or Women's History Month.

Chapter 3. Olivia

1. In the prison where Olivia is incarcerated, women are eligible for GED classes only when their remaining sentence is three years or less.

2. Herman Melville, *Moby Dick* (1851).

3. Pearl S. Buck, *Pavilion of Women* (1946).

4. Nathaniel Hawthorne, *The Scarlet Letter* (1850).

5. Karen Kingsbury, *Oceans Apart* (2004).

6. Karen Kingsbury, *A Time to Dance* (2001); *A Time to Embrace: A Story of Living Life to the Fullest* (2002).

7. Jude Deveraux, *An Angel for Emily* (1998).

8. Ellen Bass and Louise Thornton, eds., *I Never Told Anyone: Writings by Women Survivors of Child Sexual Abuse* (1983).

9. Olivia seems to be referencing Anne Graham Lotz's *Heaven: My Father's House* (2001).

10. Max Lucado, *Come Thirsty: No Heart Too Dry for His Touch* (2004).

11. Joyce Meyer, *Beauty for Ashes: Receiving Emotional Healing* (2003).

12. Joyce Meyer, *Battlefield of the Mind: Winning the Battle in Your Mind* (1995).

13. Anne Graham Lotz, *My Heart's Cry* (2002).

14. Tim S. Perry, *Blessed Is She: Living Lent with Mary* (2006).

Chapter 4. Denise

1. "Boosting" means shoplifting.

2. Denise defines a "rogue" as a thief.

3. Ludwig Bemelmans is author of the Madeline series.

4. Alice Sebold, *The Lovely Bones* (2002).

5. Eric Jerome Dickey, *Milk in My Coffee* (2000).

6. Carl Weber, *The Preacher's Son* (2003).

7. Stephen King, *Pet Sematary* (1983).

8. Rosanne Bittner, *Tame the Wild Wind* (1996).

9. Anne Frank, *Anne Frank: The Diary of a Young Girl* (1952).

10. Toni Morrison, *Song of Solomon* (1977).

11. Maya Angelou, *I Know Why The Caged Bird Sings* (1969).

12. Toni Morrison, *The Bluest Eye* (1970).

13. Toni Morrison, *Sula* (1973); *Tar Baby* (1981); *Beloved* (1987).

14. Tom Lagana, Jack Canfield, and Mark Victor Hansen, eds., *Chicken Soup For*

The Prisoner's Soul: 101 Stories to Open the Heart and Rekindle the Spirit of Hope, Healing and Forgiveness (2000).

15. Tyler Perry, *Madea Goes to Jail* (2006); Tyler Perry, *Madea's Family Reunion* (2002).

16. Tyler Perry, *Don't Make a Black Woman Take Off Her Earrings: Madea's Uninhibited Commentaries on Love and Life* (2006).

17. Dorothy Allison, *Bastard Out of Carolina* (1992).

18. Dave J. Pelzer, *A Child Called "It": One Child's Courage to Survive* (1995).

Chapter 5. Bobbie

1. "Mother-sister" is a term of endearment for a mentor.

2. Toastmasters is a club that focuses on the art of public speaking.

3. Author and publication date unknown.

4. Author and publication date unknown.

5. Mary Wilson, *Dreamgirl: My Life as a Supreme* (1986).

6. Shannon Holmes, *Bad Girlz: A Novel* (2003).

7. Triple Crown Publications is a major publisher of urban fiction. Black Expressions is an online book club that sells books by and for African Americans.

8. James Ellroy, *Black Dahlia* (1987).

9. In *Pretty Woman*, a 1990 film starring Richard Gere and Julia Roberts, a wealthy businessman hires a lower-class sex worker to play the role of girlfriend. He provides her with a lavish new wardrobe and hotel suite, and the two eventually fall in love.

10. Wahida Clark, *Payback Is A Mutha* (2006).

11. T. N. Baker, *Sheisty* and *Sheisty II* (2004).

12. The Huxtable family is the upper-middle-class black family featured on *The Cosby Show*, a television program that ran from 1984 to 1992.

13. Noire, *G-Spot: An Urban Erotic Tale* (2005).

14. Y. Blak Moore, *Slipping* (2005).

15. Mario Puzo, *The Family* (2001); *The Godfather* (1969).

16. Mary Monroe, *God Don't Like Ugly* (2000).

17. Mary Monroe, *God Still Don't Like Ugly* (2003).

18. Dan Brown, *The Da Vinci Code* (2003).

19. E. Lynn Harris, *Invisible Life: A Novel* (1991).

Chapter 6. Melissa

1. True crime books offer allegedly factual accounts of actual criminals. The subjects featured in the books are almost always white and middle-class, and they are typically serial killers or women who kill their husbands or children for selfish ends.

2. Stephen Williams, *Invisible Darkness: The Strange Case of Paul Bernardo and Karla Homolka* (1996).

3. Dolores Kennedy, *On A Killing Day: The Bizarre Story of Convicted Murderer Aileen "Lee" Wuornos* (1992).

4. Rena Vicini, *Fatal Seduction* (1994).

5. Stephen Singular, *Charmed to Death* (1995).

6. Aphrodite Jones, *Cruel Sacrifice* (1994).

7. Patrick Carnes, *Don't Call It Love: Recovery From Sexual Addiction* (1991).

Chapter 7. Valhalla

1. Ann M. Martin is author of the books in the *Babysitters Club* series.

2. Francine Pascal is author of most of the books in the *Sweet Valley High* series.

3. Wilson Rawls, *Where The Red Fern Grows* (1996).

4. S. E. Hinton, *The Outsiders* (1982).

5. C. S. Lewis, *The Chronicles Of Narnia* (1950–1956).

6. Lewis Carroll, *Alice's Adventures in Wonderland* (1865).

7. V. C. Andrews, *Flowers in the Attic* (1979).

8. Jeannette Walls, *The Glass Castle: A Memoir* (2006).

9. Ann-Marie MacDonald, *Fall on Your Knees* (2002).

10. Jane Hamilton, *The Book of Ruth* (1988).

11. Wally Lamb, *She's Come Undone* (1992).

12. John Steinbeck, *Grapes of Wrath* (1939).

13. Author and date of publication unknown.

14. J. K. Rowling is author of the *Harry Potter* series.

15. Tom Robbins, *Skinny Legs and All* (1990); *Still Life with a Woodpecker* (1980); *Jitterbug Perfume* (1984).

16. Gregory Maguire, *Wicked: The Life and Times of the Wicked Witch of the West* (1995).

17. Olivia Montgomery and F. D. Gatlin, *Diaries of a Chocolate Cruise* (2005); Ashley JaQuavis, *Diary of a Street Diva* (2005); Noire, *G-Spot* (2005).

18. C. S. Lewis, *The Lion, the Witch, and the Wardrobe* (1950). The novel is the first of seven books in *The Chronicles of Narnia* series.

Chapter 8. Jacqueline

1. Booker T. Washington, *Up from Slavery: An Autobiography* (1901).

2. Malcolm X and Alex Haley, *The Autobiography of Malcolm X: As Told to Alex Haley* (1965).

3. Natalie Cole and Digby Diehl, *Angel On My Shoulder: An Autobiography* (2000).

4. Terry McMillan, *Mama* (1987); *Waiting to Exhale* (1992); *How Stella Got Her Groove Back* (1996).

5. Terry McMillan, *A Day Late and a Dollar Short* (2001).

6. Kevin Ammons, *Good Girl, Bad Girl: An Insider's Biography of Whitney Houston* (1996).

7. Octavia E. Butler, *Kindred* (1979).

Chapter 9. Audrey

1. Ann Rule, *Small Sacrifices: A True Story of Passion and Murder* (1987).

2. Ann Rule, *The Stranger Beside Me* (1980).

3. Ann Rule, *Dead by Sunset* (1995).

4. Barbara Davis, *Precious Angels* (1999).

5. Michael Reynolds, *Dead Ends: The Pursuit, Conviction and Execution of Female Serial Killer Aileen Wuornos, the Damsel of Death* (2003).

Chapter 10. Deven

1. V. C. Andrews, *Flowers in the Attic* (1979); *Petals on the Wind* (1980); *If There Be Thorns* (1981).

2. William Sears and Martha Sears, *The Birth Book: Everything You Need to Know to Have a Safe and Satisfying Birth* (1994).

3. Corrections officers.

4. Max Lucado, *When God Whispers Your Name* (1994).

5. Rick Warren, *The Purpose Driven Life: What On Earth Am I Here For?* (2003).

6. Kay Arthur, *Our Covenant God: Living in the Security of His Unfailing Love* (1999).

7. Gloria Copeland, *God's Will for You* (1995).

8. Joyce Rupp, *Dear Heart, Come Home: The Path of Midlife Spirituality* (1996).

9. Joyce Meyer, *Me And My Big Mouth: Your Answer Is Right Under Your Nose* (1997).

10. Author and publication date unknown.

11. Stormie Omartian, *The Power of a Praying Woman* (2002).

12. Tom Lagana, Jack Canfield, and Mark Victor Hansen, eds., *Chicken Soup For The Prisoner's Soul: 101 Stories to Open the Heart and Rekindle the Spirit of Hope, Healing and Forgiveness* (2000).

13. Nancy Nason-Clark and Catherine Clark Kroeger, *Refuge from Abuse: Healing and Hope for Abused Christian Women* (2004).

14. Joan Baez, *And a Voice to Sing With: A Memoir* (1987).

15. Women are sent to "the hole"—a segregation cell—as a disciplinary measure.

Chapter 11. Solo

1. Solo and Denise, African American women who differ in age by ten years, offer remarkably similar accounts of using the Sears and Roebuck catalogue as a tool for imaginative self-invention.

2. Mark Twain, *The Prince and the Pauper* (1881).

3. Marcus Garvey was a Jamaican intellectual, publisher, journalist, and entrepreneur who was a staunch proponent of black nationalism and Pan-Africanism (http://en.wikipedia.org/wiki/Marcus_Garvey).

4. Huey Newton, Eldridge Cleaver, Angela Davis, and George Jackson were all involved in the Black Power movement.

5. George Jackson, *Soledad Brother: The Prison Letters of George Jackson* (1970).

6. Kyle Onstott, *Mandingo* (1957); *Master of Falconhurst* (1964).

7. Department of Rehabilitation and Corrections.

8. Corrections officer.

9. A "judicial" is a petition for early release.

10. Solo's comment echoes Jacqueline's earlier reference to the foster care system as a "new form of slavery" for African American children.

11. Alice Walker, *The Color Purple* (1982).

12. Robert Greene, *The 48 Laws of Power* (1998).

13. Niccolo Machiavelli, *The Prince* (1532).

14. Dante Alighieri, *Inferno* (c. 1317).

15. Sarah L. Delany, A. Elizabeth Delany, and Amy Hill Hearth, *Having Our Say: The Delany Sisters' First 100 Years* (1993).

16. An imam is a Muslim religious teacher or leader.

17. Pre-menstrual syndrome.

18. Upon the recommendation of a few women participating in this group, I requested permission from penal officials to interview the group's organizer. Unbeknownst to me, the administration was not aware of the group until I brought it their attention, and they promptly shut it down because it was not operating under official approval.

19. J. California Cooper, *The Wake of The Wind: A Novel* (1998).

Afterword

1. Women serve an average of forty-four months for drug offenses and fifty-four months for property offenses (Brown 11).

2. Prison librarians in both Ohio and Pennsylvania exclude urban fiction because of its emphases on drug dealing, hustling, prostitution, and violence. Prisoners who can afford to do so sometimes ask family members and friends to order urban books for them. When a book arrives in the mailroom, a prison official decides whether it is acceptable, and if it is not, the prisoner must destroy it or return it to the sender.

3. For further information about such practices in California prisons, see Dayan, "Barbarous Confinement."

4. States may opt out of or modify this ban by adopting specific legislation. As of 2009, nine states had permanently denied benefits to anyone convicted of a drug offense, another nine states had eliminated the ban, and thirty-three states had

modified the ban, allowing people with drug convictions to obtain benefits if they met particular requirements (Levi and Waldman 254).

5. One such initiative is the Inside-Out Prison Exchange Program, which sponsors semester-long college courses that involve incarcerated and nonincarcerated students. Typically, fifteen to eighteen nonincarcerated students and an equal number of incarcerated students attend a weekly class in the prison. All participants read a variety of texts, write several papers, discuss issues in small and large groups, and work together on a class project. Inside-Out hopes to establish programs in all fifty states by 2012. Michele Tarter's New Jersey–based program, "Woman is the Word," is another initiative that brings together incarcerated and nonincarcerated students. For information about additional programs that foster conversation among incarcerated and nonincarcerated people, see Jacobi, "Slipping Pages through Razor Wire: Literacy Action Projects in Jail"; Weil Davis, "Inside-Out: The Reaches and Limits of a Prison Program"; Yaeger, Special Issue: "Incarceration and Social Justice"; Wiltse, "Hope Across the Razor Wire: Student-Inmate Reading Groups at Monroe Correctional Facility"; and Winn, *Girl Time*.

6. Several studies link prisoners' educational participation and achievement to increased levels of postrelease employment and lower recidivism (Harlow, Jenkins, and Steurer 69).

Bibliography

Alexander, Michelle. *The New Jim Crow: Mass Incarceration in the Age of Colorblind-ness*. New York: The New Press, 2010.

Benwell, Bethan, and Daniel Allington. "Reading the Reading Experience: 'Book-talk' and Discursive Psychology." 2008. Unpublished essay.

Berger, John. "Undefeated Despair." *OpenDemocracy*. January 13, 2006, http://www .opendemocracy.net/globalization-debate_97/palestine_3176.jsp. Accessed April 2008.

Brandt, Deborah. *Literacy in American Lives*. Cambridge, U.K.: Cambridge University Press, 2001.

Breyer, Stephen. Majority opinion. Beard, Secretary, Pennsylvania Department of Corrections v. Banks. No. 04-1739. Supreme Court of the United States. June 28, 2006.

Brown, Geneva. "The Intersectionality of Race, Gender, and Reentry: Challenges for African-American Women." American Constitution Society for Law and Policy. November 2010, http://www.acslaw.org/files/Brown%20issue%20brief %20-%20Intersectionality.pdf. Accessed August 2, 2011.

Burke, Kenneth. "Literature as an Equipment for Living." *Direction* 1, no. 4 (April 1938): 10–13.

Davis, Angela Y. *Are Prisons Obsolete?* New York: Seven Stories, 2003.

Davis, Angela Y., and Gina Dent. "Prison as a Border: A Conversation on Gender, Globalization, and Punishment." *Signs: Journal of Women in Culture and Society* 26, no. 4 (Summer 2001): 1235–41.

Davis, Simone Weil. "Inside-Out: The Reaches and Limits of a Prison Program." In *Razor Wire Women: Prisoners, Activists, Scholars, and Artists*, edited by Jodie Michelle Lawston and Ashley E. Lucas. Albany: State University of New York Press, 2011.

Dayan, Colin. "Barbarous Confinement." *New York Times*. July 17, 2011, http://www .nytimes.com/2011/07/18/opinion/18dayan.html. Accessed July 17, 2011.

Dickens, Charles. *David Copperfield*. New York: Tor Classics, 1998.

Faith, Karlene, and Anne Near, eds. *13 Women: Parables from Prison*. Vancouver: Douglas & McIntyre Ltd., 2006.

Fontana, Andrea, and James H. Frey. "The Interview: From Structured Questions to Negotiated Text." In *Handbook of Qualitative Research*, 2nd ed., edited by Norman K. Denzin and Yvonna S. Lincoln, 645–72. Thousand Oaks, Calif.: Sage, 2000.

Foucault, Michel. *Discipline and Punish: The Birth of the Prison*. 1975. New York: Vintage Books, 1979.

Frost, Natasha, Judith Greene, and Kevin Pranis. "Hard Hit: The Growth in the Imprisonment of Women, 1977–2004." Institute on Women & Criminal Justice. 2008, http:// www.wpaonline.org/institute/hardhit/index.htm. Accessed February 12, 2008.

Gibran, Kahlil. *The Prophet*. New York: Alfred A. Knopf, 1923.

Gordon, Avery. *Keeping Good Time: Reflections on Knowledge, Power, and People*. Boulder, Colo.: Paradigm Publishers, 2004.

Greenberg, Elizabeth, Eric Dunleavy, and Mark Kutner. *Literacy Behind Bars: Results from the 2003 National Assessment of Adult Literacy Prison Survey*. National Center for Education Statistics. May 10, 2007, http://nces.ed.gov/PUBSEARCH/pubsinfo.asp?pubid=200747330. Accessed November 2007.

Greenfeld, Lawrence A., and Tracy L. Snell. *Women Offenders: Bureau of Justice Statistics Special Report*. U.S. Department of Justice, 1999. http://www.ojp.usdoj.gov/bjs/pub/pdf/wo.pdf. Accessed June 12, 2008.

Grose, Jessica. "What's a Nice Blonde Like Me Doing in Prison? A Review of Piper Kerman's *Orange Is the New Black: My Year in a Women's Prison*." April 8, 2010, http://www.slate.com/id/2250034/558. Accessed June 14, 2010.

Harlow, Caroline Wolf, H. David Jenkins, and Stephen Steurer. "GED Holders in Prison Read Better than Those in the Household Population: Why?" *Journal of Correctional Education* 61, no. 1 (March 2010): 68–92.

Illouz, Eva. *Saving the Modern Soul: Therapy, Emotions, and the Culture of Self-Help*. Berkeley: University of California Press, 2008.

Institute on Women & Criminal Justice. "Over 2.4 Million Women Arrested in 2006; More Than 200,000 for Drug Crimes." September 27, 2007, http://www.wpaonline.org/institute/index.htm. Accessed June 14, 2010.

Jacobi, Tobi. "Slipping Pages through Razor Wire: Literacy Action Projects in Jail." *Community Literacy Journal* 2, no. 2 (2007): 67–86.

———. "Writing Workshops As Alternative Literacy Education for Incarcerated Women." *Corrections Today* 71, no. 1 (February 2009): 52–56.

Johnson, Paula C. *Inner Lives: Voices of African American Women in Prison*. New York: New York University Press, 2003.

Kerman, Piper. *Orange Is the New Black: My Year in a Women's Prison*. New York: Spiegel & Grau, 2010.

Lamb, Wally. *Couldn't Keep it to Myself: Wally Lamb and the Women of York Correctional Institution*. New York: Regan Books, 2003.

Lawston, Jodie Michelle, and Ashley E. Lucas, eds. *Razor Wire Women: Prisoners, Activists, Scholars, and Artists*. Albany: State University of New York Press, 2011.

Levi, Robin, and Ayelet Waldman, eds. *Inside this Place, Not of It: Narratives from Women's Prisons*. San Francisco: McSweeney's and Voice of Witness, 2011.

Liptak, Adam. "1 in 100 U.S. Adults behind Bars, New Study Says." *New York Times*. February 28, 2008, http://www.nytimes.com/2008/02/28/us/28cnd-prison.html ?_r=1&hp&oref=slogin. Accessed February 28, 2008.

Morris, Ruth. *Penal Abolition: The Practical Choice: A Practical Manual on Penal Abolition*. Toronto: Canadian Scholars' Press, 1995.

Morrison, Toni. Letter to Wahneema Lubiano. September 1998.

Peck, Janice. "The Mediated Talking Cure: Therapeutic Framing of Autobiography in TV Talk Shows." In *Getting a Life: Everyday Uses of Autobiography*, edited by Sidonie Smith and Julia Watson, 134–55. Minneapolis: University of Minnesota Press, 1996.

Pens, Dan. "Skin Blind." In *Prison Masculinities*, edited by Dan Sabo, Terry Krupers, and Willie London, 150–52. Philadelphia: Temple University Press, 2001.

Rodríguez, Dylan. *Forced Passages: Imprisoned Radical Intellectuals and the U.S. Prison Regime*. Minneapolis: University of Minnesota Press, 2006.

Sabol, William J., Heather Couture, and Paige M. Harrison. "Prisoners in 2006." Bureau of Justice Statistics Bulletin. http://www.ojp.usdoj.gov/bjs/abstract/p06 .htm. Accessed January 22, 2008.

Sharma, Suniti. "Contesting Institutional Discourse to Create New Possibilities for Understanding Lived Experience: Life Stories of Young Women in Detention, Rehabilitation, and Education." *Race, Ethnicity, and Education* 13, no. 3 (2010): 327–47.

Smith, Brenda V. "Prison's Untold Tales." *New York Times*. April 2, 2010, http:// www.nytimes.com/2010/04/04/fashion/04letters-1.html. Accessed June 14, 2010.

Smith, Larry. "A Life to Live, This Side of the Bars." *New York Times*. March 25, 2010, http://www.nytimes.com/2010/03/28/fashion/28Love.html. Accessed June 14, 2010.

Smith, Sidonie, and Julia Watson, eds. Introduction. *Getting a Life: Everyday Uses of Autobiography*. Minneapolis: University of Minnesota Press, 1996.

Solinger, Rickie, Paula C. Johnson, Martha Raimon, Tina Reynolds, and Ruby Tapia, eds. *Interrupted Life: Experiences of Incarcerated Women in the United States*. Berkeley: University of California Press, 2009.

Sweeney, Megan. *Reading Is My Window: Books and the Art of Reading in Women's Prisons*. Chapel Hill: University of North Carolina Press, 2010.

"Texan Klan Mailings to Prisons Approved." *Corrections Digest*, September 3, 1990, 3.

Vogel, Brenda. *Down for the Count: A Prison Library Handbook*. London: Scarecrow Press, 1995.

Warner, Kevin. "Against the Narrowing of Perspectives: How Do We See Learning, Prisons, and Prisoners?" *Journal of Correctional Education* 58, no. 2 (June 2007): 170–84.

Wilson, Anita. "Four Days and a Breakfast: Time, Space and Literacy/ies in the Prison Community." In *Spatializing Literacy Research and Practice,* edited by Kevin Leander and Margaret Sheehy, 69–90. New York: Peter Lang, 2004.

Wiltse, Ed. "Hope Across the Razor Wire: Student-Inmate Reading Groups at Monroe Correctional Facility." In *Hope Against Hope: Philosophies, Cultures and Politics of Possibility and Doubt,* edited by Janet Horrigan and Ed Wiltse, 207–21. New York: Rodopi, 2010.

Winn, Maisha. *Girl Time: Literacy, Justice, and the School-to-Prison Pipeline.* New York: Teachers College Press, 2011.

Yaeger, Patricia, ed. Special Issue: "Incarceration and Social Justice." *PMLA* 123, no. 3 (May 2008).

Index

abuse, emotional: Audrey, 165, 169, 170-71; Denise, 62-63; prevalence among women prisoners, 250n12; Sissy, 29

abuse, physical. *See* domestic violence

abuse, sexual: Bobbie, 102; Denise, 61; Jacqueline, 148; Melissa, 105, 107, 113-14, 126; Mildred, 11, 12, 13; Olivia, 46, 47, 56, 57, 58; prevalence among women prisoners, 250n12; Sissy, 27-28, 40. *See also* rape

abuse, silence about: Denise, 62-63; Melissa, 119-20, 126-27; Mildred, 11, 13; Olivia, 46, 47, 57-58; Sissy, 27, 28, 31, 32, 41, 43

addiction: Audrey, 167, 168-69; Bobbie, 93, 94, 95, 96; Denise, 60, 65, 70; Deven, 182, 183; incarceration rates for women, 249n6; Jacqueline, 151, 152-53; Melissa, 105-8, 112, 115, 116, 126-27; Olivia, 45, 47-48, 49, 50; Sissy, 29, 43; Solo, 204; Valhalla, 129, 130, 132, 133-34, 137

Adoption and Safe Families Act, 229

African American women: featured in interviews, 3, 241, 249n3; rates of incarceration for, 5, 250n8; in scholarship about crime, 4-5, 250n7

Alexander, Michelle: *The New Jim Crow*, 4, 5

Alice's Adventures in Wonderland (Carroll), 139, 254n6

Alighieri, Dante: *Inferno*, 214, 256n14

Allison, Dorothy: *Bastard out of Carolina*, 88-90, 253n17

Ammons, Kevin: *Good Girl, Bad Girl*, 158, 254n6

And a Voice to Sing With (Baez), 194-95, 255n14

Andrews, V. C.: *Flowers in the Attic* series, 139, 185, 254n7, 255n1; interviewees' enthusiasm for, 8, 41, 144, 231

Angel on My Shoulder (Cole and Diehl), 156-57, 254n3

Anne Frank: The Diary of A Young Girl, 82, 252n9

Arthur, Kay: *Our Covenant God*, 186, 255n6

Audrey: abuse, emotional, 165, 169, 170-71; activities in prison, 166; addiction, 167, 168-69; on crime and punishment practices, 173-74; criminal history, 167-68; domestic violence, 163-65, 167, 169, 170-73, 175, 177, 178-79; educational history, 161, 163, 166; family history, 161-62, 175, 228; future plans, 170, 175, 236; on learning to accept help, 174-75; motherhood, 163, 166, 168, 169-70,

171, 173, 174, 229; reading preferences, 176; on true crime books' depictions of violent women, 176-79, 232

autobiography: *And a Voice to Sing With* (Baez), 194-95, 255n14; *Angel On My Shoulder* (Cole and Diehl), 156, 254n3; *The Autobiography of Malcolm X*, 155-56, 254n2; *A Child Called "It"* (Pelzer), 90, 253n18; *Anne Frank: The Diary of A Young Girl*, 82, 252n9; *Dreamgirl* (Wilson), 98, 253n5; *The Glass Castle* (Walls), 140, 254n8; *Orange Is the New Black* (Kerman), 8; scholarship about, 5, 7, 9, 232, 238; *Soledad Brother* (Jackson), 202, 256n5; *Up from Slavery* (Washington), 155, 254n1

Babysitters Club series (Martin), 139, 254n1

Bad Girlz (Holmes), 98, 253n6

Baez, Joan: *And a Voice to Sing With*, 194-95, 255n14

Baker, T. N.: *Sheisty* and *Sheisty II*, 99, 253n11

Bastard out of Carolina (Allison), 88-90, 253n17

Battlefield of the Mind (Meyer), 56, 102, 188-89, 252n12

Beard v. Banks, 2

Beauty for Ashes (Meyer), 56, 252n11

Beloved (Morrison), 83, 86, 252n13

Berger, John, 7

Birth Book, The (Sears),185, 255n2

Black Dahlia (Ellroy), 98, 253n8

black women. *See* African American women

Bleachers (Grisham), 16, 251n3

Bluest Eye, The (Morrison), 193-94, 233, 252n12

Bobbie: abuse, sexual, 102; activities in prison, 95-96; addiction, 93, 94, 95, 96; addiction of family members, 93; on crime and punishment practices, 93, 95, 96-97, 238; criminal history, 93-94; on *The Da Vinci Code*, 103; domestic violence, 93, 96; educational history, 93; family history, 92-93, 95, 96; future plans, 97, 236; on Jackie Collins's books, 100, 101; on Mario Puzo's books, 99, 101; motherhood, 92, 94, 228, 229; reading as tool for self-education and self-reflection, 102, 230; reading preferences, 97-98, 99, 104; on self-help books, 102-3; on urban fiction, 98, 99, 100, 101

Book of Ruth, The (Hamilton), 140, 254n10

books for prisoners, organizations that gather, 269-70

Brown, Dan: *The Da Vinci Code*, 103, 253n18

Burke, Kenneth: books as "equipment for living," 230

Butler, Octavia: *Kindred*, 159, 254n7

Carnes, Patrick: *Don't Call It Love*, 126 254n7

Carroll, Lewis: *Alice's Adventures in Wonderland*, 139, 254n6

censorship in penal settings: banning of unsanctioned reading group, 256n2; banning of urban fiction, 145, 231, 256n18; *Beard v. Banks*, 2; library policies, 211-12

Changing Lives Through Literature program, 251n16

Charmed to Death (Singular), 122-23, 254n5

Chicken Soup for the Prisoner's Soul (Lagana et al.), 88, 90, 190-92, 232, 252n14, 255n12

Child Called "It" A (Pelzer), 90, 253n18

Chronicles of Narnia (Lewis), 139, 146, 254n5

Clark, Wahida: *Payback Is A Mutha*, 99, 253n10

Coldest Winter Ever, The (Souljah), 8

Cole, Natalie and Digby Diehl: *Angel on My Shoulder*, 156-57, 254n3

Collins, Jackie, 21, 100, 118, 119

Color Purple, The (Walker), 209, 256n11

Come Thirsty (Lucado), 55, 252n10

Cooper, J. California: *The Wake of the Wind*, 221, 256n19

Copeland, Gloria: *God's Will for You*, 186, 187, 190, 255n7

Couldn't Keep it to Myself (Lamb), 5

Critical Resistance, 7, 236, 250n13

Cruel Sacrifice (Jones), 123-26, 127, 254n6

Da Vinci Code, The (Brown), 103, 253n18

Davis, Angela, 202, 238, 250n7

Davis, Angela, and Gina Dent, 237

Dayan, Colin, 235, 256n3

Day Late and a Dollar Short, A (McMillan), 157-58, 232, 254n5

Dead by Sunset (Rule), 176, 255n3

Dead Ends (Reynolds), 178, 255n5

Dear Heart, Come Home (Rupp), 186, 255n8

Delany, Sarah L., A. Elizabeth Delany, and Amy Hill Hearth: *Having Our Say*, 214, 256n15

Denise: abuse, emotional, 62-63; abuse, sexual, 61; abuse, silence about, 62-63; addiction, 65, 70; addiction of family members, 60; on *Bastard out of Carolina*, 88-90; on *Beloved*, 86; on crime and punishment practices, 90; criminal history, 61, 64-65, 69; domestic violence, 61-64, 70, 87-88, 89; educational history, 60; family history, 59-60, 74, 84-85; future plans, 69, 71-73,

91, 236; motherhood, 62, 63, 64, 65, 67, 70, 71; on Native American romances, 80-81; reading history, 74-75; reading as tool for self-education and self-reflection, 75, 90-91, 231, 232, 234; reading preferences, 73-74, 75, 78, 79-80, 82, 90, 234; on self-help books, 87-88; on shoplifting, 61, 64-69, 71-73, 78, 81, 90-91; on *Song of Solomon*, 82-84, 86, 87; on Toni Morrison, 79, 84, 85; on urban fiction, 78-79

Deven: addiction, 182, 183; on *The Bluest Eye*, 193-94, 233; on *Chicken Soup for the Prisoner's Soul*, 190-92, 232; on crime and punishment practices, 183, 184, 189, 195-96, 235, 237; criminal history, 182; domestic violence, 181-82, 192-93, 194; educational history, 180; family history, 180, 192; future plans, 183-84, 196; on gender inequality, 183, 190; on Joan Baez's memoir, 194-95; on Joyce Meyer's books, 186, 188-89, 190; motherhood, 180, 181, 182, 184, 191, 196; reading as tool for self-education and self-reflection, 9, 186-90, 192-93, 194-95, 233, 236; reading preferences, 184-85, 186-88, 194-95; on self-help and spiritual books, 186-88, 232; on *When God Whispers Your Name*, 187

Diaries of a Chocolate Cruise (Montgomery and Gatlin), 145, 254n17

Diary of a Street Diva (JaQuavis), 145, 254n17

Dickey, Eric Jerome, 79, 252n5

domestic violence: Audrey, 163-65, 167, 169, 170-73, 175, 177, 178-79; Bobbie, 93, 96; Denise, 61-64, 70, 87-88, 89; Deven, 181-82, 192-93, 194; Jacqueline, 147-48; Melissa, 111, 112, 120; Olivia, 46, 49, 50, 54, 57; prevalence among women prisoners, 250n12; Sissy, 28, 29, 30; Solo, 207, 222; Valhalla, 130

Don't Call It Love (Carnes), 126 254n7

Dreamgirl (Wilson), 98, 253n5

drug selling, 18-19, 93

education, interviewees' histories of. *See under names of individual interviewees*

education in penal settings: current opportunities for, 1, 2, 3, 7, 252n1; elimination of Pell Grants for prisoners, 2, 213, 237, 249n1; Higher Education Act of 2006, 237; policy recommendations, 239, 257n6; prisoners' literacy levels, 7, 249n5, 250n14. *See also under names of individual interviewees*

Ellroy, James: *Black Dahlia*, 98, 253n8

Faber, Brenton, 7

Faith, Karlene, and Anne Near: *13 Women*, 5

Family, The (Puzo), 99, 101-2, 253n15

Fatal Seduction (Vicini), 121-22, 253n4

Flowers in the Attic series (Andrews), 139, 185, 254n7, 255n1; interviewees' enthusiasm for, 8, 41, 144, 231

48 Laws of Power, The (Greene), 213, 256n12

Frank, Anne: *Anne Frank: The Diary of A Young Girl*, 82, 252n9

ghetto fiction. *See* urban fiction

Girl Time (Winn), 256-57n5

Glass Castle, The (Walls), 140, 254n8

God Don't Like Ugly (Monroe), 102, 253n16

Godfather, The (Puzo), 101, 253n15

God Still Don't Like Ugly (Monroe), 102, 253n17

God's Will for You (Copeland), 186, 187, 190, 255n7

Good Girl, Bad Girl (Ammons), 158, 254n6

Gordon, Avery, 238

Graham, Billy, 56

Grapes of Wrath, The (Steinbeck), 141, 254n12

Greene, Robert: *The 48 Laws of Power*, 213, 256n12

Grisham, John: as source of legal knowledge, 52, 232; *Bleachers*, 16, 251n3; *The King of Torts*, 16, 17-18, 19, 21, 251n3; *A Painted House*, 21, 251n7; *The Pelican Brief*, 16, 251n3; *The Runaway Jury*, 16, 17, 251n3; *Street Lawyer*, 21, 251n7; *The Summons*, 16; 251n3

G-Spot (Noire), 100, 145, 253n13, 254n17

Hamilton, Jane: *The Book of Ruth*, 140, 254n10

Harris, E. Lynn: *Invisible Life*, 104, 253n19

Harry Potter series (Rowling), 143, 254n14

Having Our Say (Delany, Delany, Hearth), 214, 256n15

Hinton, S. E.: *The Outsiders*, 139, 254n4

Holmes, Shannon: *Bad Girlz*, 98, 253n6

"Hope Across the Razor Wire" (Wiltse), 256-57n5

How Stella Got Her Groove Back (McMillan), 21, 157, 251n6, 254n4

If Tomorrow Comes (Sheldon), 39-40, 251n3

Inferno (Dante), 214, 256n14

Inner Lives: Voices of African American Women in Prison (Johnson), 5

Inside-Out Prison Exchange Program, 256-57n5

Inside this Place, Not of It (Levi and Waldman), 5

International Conference on Penal Abolition, 236, 250n13

Interrupted Life (Solinger et al.), 5
Invisible Darkness (Williams), 118, 253n2
Invisible Life (Harris), 104, 253n19

Jackson, George: *Soledad Brother*, 202, 256n5
Jacobi, Tobi, 5, 9, 256-57n5
Jacqueline: abuse, sexual, 148; addiction, 151, 152-53; on *Angel On My Shoulder*, 156-57; on *The Autobiography of Malcolm X*, 155-56; on crime and punishment practices, 153-54, 159; domestic violence, 147-48; educational history, 148-50; family history, 147-48; future plans, 152, 235, 236; on *Good Girl, Bad Girl*, 158; on *Kindred*, 159; mental health, 149-50, 151, 152, 153, 160; motherhood, 150, 151; reading as tool for self-education and self-reflection, 155-56, 157-59, 160; reading preferences, 154-55, 160; on Terry McMillan's novels, 157-58; on *Up From Slavery*, 155
JaQuavis, Ashley: *Diary of a Street Diva*, 145, 254n17
Jitterbug Perfume (Robbins), 143, 254n15
Johnson, Paula C.: *Inner Lives: Voices of African American Women in Prison*, 5
Jones, Aphrodite: *Cruel Sacrifice*, 123-26, 127, 254n6

Kennedy, Dolores: *On A Killing Day*, 120-21
Kerman, Piper: *Orange Is the New Black: My Year in a Women's Prison*, 8, 250n15
Kindred (Butler), 159, 254n7
King, Stephen, 39, 80, 188, 252n7
King of Torts, The (Grisham), 16, 17-18, 19, 21, 251n3;

Kingsbury, Karen: *Oceans Apart*, 53, 252n5; *A Time to Dance*, 53-54, 252n6; *A Time to Embrace*, 53, 252n6
Koontz, Dean, 39

Lagana, Tom, et al.: *Chicken Soup for the Prisoner's Soul*, 88, 90, 190-92, 232, 252n14, 255n12
Lamb, Wally: *Couldn't Keep it to Myself*, 5; *She's Come Undone*, 142-43, 231, 254n11
Latina women: rates of incarceration for, 250n8
Lawston, Jodie, and Ashley Lucas: *Razor Wire Women*, 5
legislation and policies, penal: Adoption and Safe Families Act, 229; *Beard v. Banks*, 2; Higher Education Act of 2006, 237; maximum isolation units, 235, 256n3; Personal Responsibility and Work Opportunity Reconciliation Act, 237, 256n4. *See also* censorship in penal settings
Levi, Robin, and Ayelet Waldman: *Inside this Place, Not of It*, 5
Lewis, C. S.: *Chronicles of Narnia*, 139, 146, 254n5; *The Lion, the Witch, and the Wardrobe*, 146, 254n18
libraries in penal settings: books available in, 51, 211-12; funding for, 1; prisoners' access to, 1, 7, 16, 251n1, 252n5. *See also* censorship in penal settings; reading in penal settings: material dimensions of
Lion, the Witch, and the Wardrobe, The (Lewis), 146, 254n18
literacy. *See* education: prisoners' literacy levels
Lotz, Anne Graham, 56, 252n9, 252n13
Lovely Bones, The (Sebold), 76-78, 80, 252n4
Lucado, Max: *Come Thirsty*, 55, 252n10; *When God Whispers Your Name*, 187, 255n4

Machiavelli, Niccolo: *The Prince*, 213, 256n13

Maguire, Gregory: *Wicked*, 144, 254n16

Malcolm X and Alex Haley: *The Autobiography of Malcolm X*, 155, 254n2

Mama (McMillan), 157, 254n4

Mandingo (Onstott), 202, 256n6

Martin, Ann M.: *The Baby-Sitters Club* series, 139, 254n1

Master of Falconhurst (Onstott), 202, 256n6

Master of the Game (Sheldon), 40, 252n4

McMillan, Terry: *A Day Late and a Dollar Short*, 157-58, 232, 254n5; *How Stella Got Her Groove Back*, 21, 157, 251n6, 254n4; *Mama*, 157, 254n4; *Waiting to Exhale*, 21, 157, 251n6; 254n4

Me And My Big Mouth (Meyer), 186, 255n9

Melissa: abuse, sexual, 105, 107, 113-14, 126; abuse, silence about, 119-20, 126-27; addiction, 105-8, 115, 116, 126-27; addiction of family members, 105, 107, 112; on crime and punishment practices, 109-10, 115-18, 238; criminal history, 107, 108, 109, 110-11; domestic violence, 111, 112, 120; educational history, 106, 107, 110; family history, 105, 111-13; future plans, 115-16, 118, 235; on gender and victimization, 119-21; prostitution, 107, 120; reading as tool for self-education and self-reflection, 122, 123-26, 127, 128, 232; reading preferences, 118, 119, 121, 127; self-understanding, 110-11, 113-14, 126-27; on true crime books, 118-26; writing practices, 128. *See also under* true crime books

mental health: ADHD, 135; bipolar disorder, 129, 132-33, 135-36; counseling opportunities in penal settings: 13, 22, 47, 153, 166, 236, 251n2; counseling opportunities in non-penal settings, 47, 135-36; 153; depression, 150, 151, 152, 227; suicide attempts by interviewees, 13, 108, 132, 149-50, 151

Meyer, Joyce: *Battlefield of the Mind*, 56, 102, 188-89, 252n12; *Beauty for Ashes*, 56, 252n11; interviewees' enthusiasm for, 55, 186, 189; *Me And My Big Mouth*, 186, 255n9. *See also under names of individual interviewees*

Mildred: abuse, sexual, 11, 12, 13; abuse, silence about, 11, 13; on crime and punishment practices, 14, 15, 19, 20, 22, 235, 238; criminal history, 12, 13, 20; educational history, 11, 12; family history, 11, 12, 13; future plans, 13, 14; on John Grisham's novels, 16-18, 19, 21; love of the law, 20-21; mental health, 13, 22; motherhood, 11, 12, 19, 22; reading as tool for self-education and self-reflection, 16-18, 21-22; reading preferences, 16, 21

Monroe, Mary: *God Don't Like Ugly*, 102, 253n16; *God Still Don't Like Ugly*, 102, 253n17

Montgomery, Olivia and F. D. Gatlin: *Diaries of a Chocolate Cruise*, 145, 254n17

Moore, Y. Blak: *Slipping*, 100, 253n14

Morris, Ruth, 236

Morrison, Toni: *Beloved*, 83, 86, 252n13; *Bluest Eye, The*, 193-94, 233, 252n12; Denise's enthusiasm for, 4, 79; *Paradise*, 2; *Song of Solomon*, 82-84, 86, 87, 252n10; *Sula*, 83, 252n13; *Tar Baby*, 83, 252n13

motherhood, interviewees' experiences of: Audrey, 163, 166, 168, 169-70, 171, 173, 174, 229; Bobbie, 92, 94, 228, 229; Denise, 62, 63, 64, 65, 67,

70, 71; Deven, 180, 181, 182, 184, 191, 196; Jacqueline, 150, 151; Mildred, 11, 12, 19, 22; Olivia, 46, 48, 57, 58; Sissy, 28, 29, 30, 32, 38; Solo, 203-4, 208; Valhalla, 133, 145

Nason-Clark, Nancy and Catherine Clark Kroeger: *Refuge from Abuse*, 192, 255n13
Native American women: featured in interviews, 3, 241, 249n3
New Jim Crow, The (Alexander), 4, 5
North Carolina Correctional Institution for Women (NCCIW), 241
Noire: *G-Spot*, 100, 145, 253n13, 254n17
Northeast Pre-Release Center (NEPRC), 241-42

Oceans Apart (Kingsbury), 53, 252n5
Olivia: abuse, sexual, 46, 47, 56, 57, 58; abuse, silence about, 46, 47, 57-58; addiction, 45, 47-48, 49, 50; addiction of family members, 49; on crime and punishment practices, 50; criminal history, 48, 49, 52; domestic violence, 46, 49, 50, 54, 57; educational history, 45; family history, 45, 48, 49, 58, 228; future plans, 50, 235; on Joyce Meyer's books, 55-56; on Karen Kingsbury's books, 53; motherhood, 46, 48, 57, 58; reading as tool for self-education and self-reflection, 51, 53, 54-56, 231; reading preferences, 50-51, 52, 54, 56; on self-help books, 54-55; on spiritual books, 55-56; writing efforts, 57
Omartian, Stormie: *The Power of a Praying Woman*, 186, 255n11
On A Killing Day (Kennedy), 120-21
Onstott, Kyle: *Mandingo* and *Master of Falconhurst*, 202, 256n6
Orange Is the New Black: My Year in a Women's Prison (Kerman), 8, 250n15

Our Covenant God (Arthur), 186, 255n6
Outsiders, The (Hinton), 139, 254n4

Painted House, A (Grisham), 21, 251n7
Paradise (Morrison), 2
Pascal, Francine: *Sweet Valley High* series, 139, 254n2
Patterson, James: popularity of, 8, 144, 186
Payback Is A Mutha (Clark), 99, 253n10
Peck, Janice, 238
Pelican Brief, The (Grisham), 16, 251n3
Pell Grants for Prisoners. *See* education in penal settings
Pelzer, Dave J.: *A Child Called "It,"* 90, 253n18
Perry, Tyler, 88, 253n15, 253n16
Personal Responsibility and Work Opportunity Reconciliation Act, 237
Power of a Praying Woman, The (Omartian), 186, 255n11
Prince, The (Machiavelli), 213, 256n13
Prince and the Pauper, The (Twain), 200, 255n2
prison abolition movement: Critical Resistance, 7, 236; International Conference on Penal Abolition, 236
prisoners, female: advocacy organizations for, 7, 250n7, 250n13; in federal and state prisons, 4; rates of incarceration for, 4, 256n1; scholarship about, 5, 250n7. *See also* legislation and policies, penal
prisoners, male, 1, 4, 7
Purpose Driven Life, The (Warren), 186, 255n5
Puzo, Mario: *The Family*, 99, 101-2, 253n15; *The Godfather*, 101, 253n15

race: and censorship in penal history, 2; in John Grisham's novels, 18, 19;

interviewees' self-identifications of, 3, 241; sentencing trends, 2, 4, 8

rape, 6, 77, 107, 142, 193, 207, 250n12

Rawls, Wilson: *Where the Red Fern Grows*, 139, 146, 254n3

Razor Wire Women (Lawston and Lucas), 5

reading in penal settings: communal dimensions of, 10, 51-52, 55, 77, 102, 139, 140, 187; history of, 1; importance of, 8, 9, 10, 227, 230-34; material dimensions of, 1, 7, 10, 75, 185, 233, 251n18. *See also under names of individual interviewees*

Refuge from Abuse (Nason-Clark and Kroeger), 192, 255n13

rehabilitation for prisoners, critique of the concept: criminogenic nature of prisons, 117, 136, 153-54, 213, 236-37; dearth of counseling and mental health care, 47, 136, 153; dearth of drug treatment opportunities, 96-97, 117; dearth of educational programs, 117-18, 196, 211-13, 239; dearth of young offender programs, 117-18; Higher Education Act, 237; over-medicating of prisoners, 47, 118; Personal Responsibility and Work Opportunity Reconciliation Act, 237; policy recommendations, 238-39; restrictions on financial aid for drug offenders, 136, 213, 237

religion and spirituality in interviewees' reading materials: *Chicken Soup for the Prisoner's Soul* (Lagana), 88, 90, 190-92, 232, 252n14, 255n12; Christian devotional texts, 16, 251n4; Copeland, Gloria, 186, 187, 190, 255n7; *The Da Vinci Code* (Brown), 103-4; Islamic texts, 97, 215-17; Kingsbury, Karen, 53; Lotz, Anne Graham, 56; Lucado, Max, 55, 187, 252n10, 255n4; Meyer, Joyce:

55-56, 102, 186, 188-89, 255n9; Nason-Clark and Clark Kroeger, 192, 255n13; Omartian, Stormie, 186, 255n11; Rupp, Joyce, 186, 255n8; Warren, Rick, 186, 255n5; world religions, 34-37. *See also under names of individual interviewees*

research methods, 3, 5-6, 242-44, 249n2

Reynolds, Michael: *Dead Ends*, 178, 255n5

Rice, Anne, 140, 144

Robbins, Harold: *79 Park Ave. S.*, 40, 252n5

Robbins, Tom: *Jitterbug Perfume*, 143, 254n15; *Skinny Legs and All*, 143, 254n15; *Still Life with a Woodpecker*, 143, 254n15

Rodríguez, Dylan, 239

romance novels: interviewees' disdain for, 141, 211, 214; interviewees' enthusiasm for, 8, 54; Native American subgenre of, 80-81

Rowling, J.K.: *Harry Potter* series, 143, 254n14

Rule, Anne: *Dead by Sunset*, 176, 255n3; *Small Sacrifices*, 176, 255n1; *The Stranger Beside Me*, 176, 255n2

Runaway Jury, The (Grisham), 16, 17, 251n3

Rupp, Joyce: *Dear Heart, Come Home*, 186, 255n8

Sears and Roebuck catalogue as reading material, 75, 198, 199, 202, 255n1

Sears, William, and Martha Sears: *The Birth Book*, 185, 255n2

Sebold, Alice: *The Lovely Bones*, 76-78, 80, 252n4

79 Park Ave. S. (Robbins), 40, 252n5

Sharma, Suniti, 7

Sheisty (Baker), 99, 253n11

Sheisty II (Baker), 99, 253n11

Sheldon, Sidney: *If Tomorrow Comes*, 39-40, 251n3; interviewees' enthusiasm for, 39-41, 118; *Master of the Game*, 40, 252n4; resource for learning about healthy forms of sex, 40-41, 232

She's Come Undone (Lamb), 142-43, 231, 254n11

Singular, Stephen: *Charmed to Death*, 122-23, 254n5

Sissy: abuse, emotional, 29; abuse, sexual, 27-28, 40; abuse, silence about, 27, 28, 31, 32, 41, 43; addiction, 29, 43; on Black History Month, 41-42; criminal history, 29-30; domestic violence, 28, 29, 30; educational history, 23-26; family history, 23, 26-27, 31, 32-33; on friendship, 31; future plans, 43-44, 236; on crime and punishment practices, 32, 43, 44; interest in art, 33, 38, 39, 233; motherhood, 28, 29, 30, 32, 38; reading as tool for self-education and self-reflection, 34-37, 40-42, 234; reading preferences, 33, 34, 38, 39; school desegregation, 24-26; on Sidney Sheldon's novels, 39-41, 232; on V. C. Andrews's novels, 41; writing practices of, 42

Skinny Legs and All (Robbins), 143, 254n15

Slipping (Moore), 100, 253n14

Small Sacrifices (Rule), 176, 255n1

Smith, Sidonie and Julia Watson, 9

Soledad Brother (Jackson), 202, 256n5

Solinger, Rickie, et al.: *Interrupted Life*, 5

Solo: activities in prison, 204; Act Up Program, 204-6, 230; addiction of family members, 204; on Black nationalism, 201-2, 256n4; on censorship in prison libraries, 211-12; on crime and punishment practices, 203, 207-8, 210, 235, 238; criminal history, 198, 202-3, 206, 210, 224; domestic violence, 207, 222; educational history, 197, 198, 199-200, 201-2, 204, 208, 209; family history, 197, 198-99, 201, 203; on freedom, 222-25, 236; future plans, 210-11; on *Having Our Say*, 214; on Islamic texts, 215-17; on legal texts, 217-19, 233; motherhood, 203-4, 208; on prison reading group, 220-21; reading as tool for self-education and self-reflection, 215-19; reading history, 199, 200; reading preferences, 212-14, 221; on *The Wake of The Wind*, 221-22; writing practices, 219-20

Song of Solomon (Morrison), 82-84, 86, 87, 252n10

Souljah, Sister: *The Coldest Winter Ever*, 8

Steel, Danielle, 21, 52-53, 80, 211, 214

Steinbeck, John: *The Grapes of Wrath*, 141, 254n12

Still Life with a Woodpecker (Robbins); 143, 254n15

Stranger Beside Me, The (Rule), 176, 255n2

Street Lawyer (Grisham), 21, 251n7

Street lit. See urban fiction

Sula (Morrison), 83, 252n13

Summons, The (Grisham), 16, 251n3

Sweet Valley High series (Pascal), 139, 254n2

Tar Baby (Morrison), 83, 252n13

Tarter, Michelle: "Woman is the Word" program, 5, 257n5

13 Women (Faith and Near), 5

Time to Dance, A (Kingsbury), 53-54, 252n6

Time to Embrace, A (Kingsbury), 53, 252n6

true crime books: *Charmed to Death* (Singular), 122-23, 254n5; *Cruel Sacrifice* (Jones), 123-26, 127, 254n6; *Dead by Sunset* (Rule), 176, 255n3; *Dead Ends* (Reynolds), 178, 255n5; *Fatal Seduction* (Vicini), 121-22, 253n4; gendered dimensions of, 119-20, 176-78; interviewees' enthusiasm for, 4, 176, 232; *Invisible Darkness* (Williams), 118, 253n2; *On a Killing Day* (Kennedy), 120-21; *Precious Angels* (Davis), 177, 255n4; *Small Sacrifices* (Rule), 176, 255n1; *The Stranger Beside Me* (Rule), 176, 255n2; Ted Bundy, 120. *See also* Melissa, on true crime books; Audrey, on true crime books

Twain, Mark: *The Prince and the Pauper*, 200, 255n2

Up from Slavery (Washington), 155, 254n1
urban fiction: *Bad Girlz* (Holmes), 98, 253n6; *The Coldest Winter Ever* (Souljah), 8; *Diaries of a Chocolate Cruise* (Montgomery and Gatlin), 145, 254n17; *Diary of a Street Diva* (JaQuavis), 145, 254n17; interviewees' disdain for, 51, 78-79, 154-55, 186; *G-Spot* (Noire), 100, 145, 253n13, 254n17; interviewees' enthusiasm for, 1, 4, 8, 98, 99, 100, 145; *Payback Is A Mutha* (Clark), 99, 253n10; penal censorship of, 145, 231, 256n2; *Sheisty* (Baker), 99, 253n11; *Sheisty II* (Baker), 99, 253n11; *Slipping* (Moore), 100, 253n14; Triple Crown Publications, 98, 99, 186

Valhalla: activities in prison, 134-35, 137, 138; addiction, 130, 132, 133-34, 137; addiction of family members, 129, 130; bipolar disorder, 129, 132-33, 135-36; on crime and punishment practices, 135, 136, 236; criminal history, 130, 133-34; domestic violence, 130; educational history, 131-32, 134, 139; family history, 129-31; future plans, 137; motherhood, 133, 145; reading as tool for self-education and self-reflection, 145; reading preferences, 135, 139-42, 145; self-understanding, 137-38, 235; on *She's Come Undone* (Lamb), 142-43; on Tom Robbins's novels, 143-44; on urban fiction, 145; on *Wicked* (Maguire), 144

Vicini, Rena: *Fatal Seduction*, 121-22, 253n4

Waiting to Exhale (McMillan), 21, 157, 251n6; 254n4
Wake of the Wind, The (Cooper), 221, 256n19
Walker, Alice: *The Color Purple*, 209, 256n11
Walls, Jeanette: *The Glass Castle*, 140, 254n8
Warner, Kevin, 238-39
Warren, Rick: *The Purpose Driven Life*, 186, 255n5
Washington, Booker T.: *Up from Slavery*, 155, 254n1
Weber, Carl, 79, 252n6
Weil Davis, Simone, 257n5
When God Whispers Your Name (Lucado), 187, 255n4
Where the Red Fern Grows (Rawls), 139, 146, 254n3
white women: featured in interviews, 3, 241, 249n3; rates of incarceration for, 5, 250n8; in scholarship about crime, 5
Wicked (Maguire), 144, 254n16
Williams, Stephen: *Invisible Darkness*, 118, 253n2

Wilson, Mary: *Dreamgirl*, 98, 253n5
Wiltse, Ed, "Hope Across the Razor Wire," 256-57n5
Winfrey, Oprah, 140, 194, 209
Winn, Maisha: *Girl Time*, 256-57n5
"Woman is the Word" program (Tarter), 5, 257n5

women. *See* Prisoners, female
writing: conditions for, in penal settings, 42-43, 219, 220, 233; programs for female prisoners, 250n9
Wuornos, Aileen, 120-21, 178-79, 232

Yaeger, Patricia, 256-57n5

Megan Sweeney is an associate professor of
English Language & Literature and Afroamerican and
African Studies at the University of Michigan. She is the author
of *Reading is My Window: Books and the Art of Reading
in Women's Prisons.*

*The University of Illinois Press
is a founding member of the
Association of American University Presses.*

Composed in 10.25/13.25 Adobe Minion Pro
with ITC Korinna Std display
by Celia Shapland
at the University of Illinois Press
Manufactured by Sheridan Books, Inc.

University of Illinois Press
1325 South Oak Street
Champaign, IL 61820-6903
www.press.uillinois.edu